Dear Reader:

The book you are  Martin's True Crim "the leader in true account of the lates national attention. St. Martin's is the publisher of bestselling true crime author and crime journalist Kieran Crowley, who explores the dark, deadly links between a prominent Manhattan surgeon and the disappearance of his wife fifteen years earlier in THE SURGEON'S WIFE. Suzy Spencer's BREAKING POINT guides readers through the tortuous twists and turns in the case of Andrea Yates, the Houston mother who drowned her five young children in the family's bathtub. In Edgar Award-nominated DARK DREAMS, legendary FBI profiler Roy Hazelwood and bestselling crime author Stephen G. Michaud shine light on the inner workings of America's most violent and depraved murderers. In the book you now hold, MIND GAMES, acclaimed author Carlton Smith examines the troubled marriage of a psychologist and his wife—a marriage that ended in murder.

St. Martin's True Crime Library gives you the stories behind the headlines. Our authors take you right to the scene of the crime and into the minds of the most notorious murderers to show you what really makes them tick. St. Martin's True Crime Library paperbacks are better than the most terrifying thriller, because it's all true! The next time you want a crackling good read, make sure it's got the St. Martin's True Crime Library logo on the spine—you'll be up all night!

Charles E. Spicer, Jr.
Executive Editor, St. Martin's True Crime Library

MIND GAMES

The True Story
of a Psychologist, His Wife,
and a Brutal Murder

CARLTON SMITH

St. Martin's Paperbacks

MIND GAMES

Copyright © 2007 by Carlton Smith.

Cover photo of couch courtesy Petrified Collection/Getty Images.
Cover photo of house courtesy Contra Costa County Sheriff's Department.
Cover photo of Susan Polk courtesy AP Images.

ISBN: 0-312-93906-X
EAN: 9780312-93906-9

Printed in the United States of America

St. Martin's Paperbacks edition / August 2007

10 9 8 7 6 5 4 3 2 1

CONTENTS

I.
OCTOBER 14, 2002
ORINDA, CALIFORNIA

1. THE HOUSE OF
DREAMS AND NIGHTMARES

From the outside, it was a House of Dreams, a sanctuary at the top of the world.

Far above the buzz of the freeway that tied east to west in the burgeoning, oak-flocked hills of the east San Francisco Bay Area, it was a Shangri-la for a man who often said that as a child, he'd seen the face of pure evil, and had been lucky enough to survive.

He was, Frank Felix Polk said, a refugee from the Holocaust, and the wooded, peaceful compound at the top of the world was just the sort of place a terrorized child from the 1930s might only have dreamed of, back in those days of unmitigated horror. The two-million-dollar house said it all: F. Felix Polk, psychologist, had not only survived "the bad people"—he had *made* it. The house was his legacy, if not his legend.

But if it was a dream house, it was also a palace of delusion.

Capping a small knoll, surrounded with shady trees, the sprawling property was really more of a compound. There was a trilevel main house, an interior courtyard with a deck

and a pool, and an outlying "pool house." One could swim u
to the pool house and sip piña coladas while still in the wate
There was yet another outbuilding with a mini-gymnasiun
The whole place had been fashioned by a master builde
who'd produced a "Craftsman" house unique in design, exter
sively remodeled, and one that had been very appealing t
Polk and his much younger wife, Susan.

With its unusual layout, large windows, rare woods and til
floorings—surfaces and lintels carefully crafted for ever
room—and the outbuildings, the property at 728 Miner Roa
Orinda, was exactly where Felix Polk wanted to spend the res
of his life.

He just didn't think the rest of that life would be quite s
short.

Or that his wife of more than two decades, Susan Polk
would end it so suddenly, and with a very angry knife.

In October of 2002, Felix Polk was 70 years old. He had bee
married twice, and was the father of two adult children fron
his first marriage, and three teenaged boys from the second
At five feet, ten inches in height, and weighing about 17
pounds, Felix—as almost everyone called him—seemed fi
for his age. He liked to hike, and loved sports. He encourage
his younger children to be tough, hard-nosed, smart and ag
gressive; otherwise they would be overpowered by "the ba
people," Felix had advised them.

He was an intense man, given to passionate argument, i
not anger. Those who knew him readily agreed that he did no
easily make allowances for those he differed with; often, i
his view, his opponents were fools, or worse—liars. His
friends in turn willingly explained his often abrupt, abrasive
behavior: one had to understand what Felix had gone throug
as a boy to understand the way he was as a man.

Almost everyone who knew him agreed that Felix harbore

barely articulated rage that, it seemed, no one could ever as-
suage; and even when he wasn't overtly angry, he could be
imperious, demanding, accusatory, and certainly manipulative. Some thought he had a habit, or perhaps it was a ploy, of
invading the physical space of those with whom he disputed,
forcing them to back up—a form of psychological domination
that could intimidate. His personality dominated, even when it
claimed victimhood. In fact, the years had taught Felix how to
be a master at making others feel guilty.

Yet, beneath all this, even his closest friends sensed there
was something hidden about Felix, something secret, oc-
cluded by the anger or cynicism or sorrow that seemed at his
core. Whatever it was beneath his persona, it was the most
powerful part of his personality, but Felix kept this part of
himself well obscured. Nevertheless, acknowledging that Felix had a horrific past, even if one wasn't exactly sure of the
awful details, gave him professional cachet, at least when he
tried to sort out *others'* psychic woes.

After all, surviving genocide had to render a psychological
practitioner like Felix Polk absolutely unchallengeable insight
into the scale of true evil.

Didn't it?

It was, by definition, indisputable. Having been there,
having suffered that, having barely escaped it, he had to
know what evil really was. And that meant, if he said you
were wrong, you probably were. He had the suffering to
prove it.

But Dr. Polk's claimed personal history served yet another
purpose—in one way, he used this suppressed anger to drive
others away. To keep his inner, secret heart closed to almost
everyone, including his second family. It might have been a survival technique adopted very early in life by a child at risk of
abandonment, loss and death, never quite overcome—even
after the immediate threat had receded. At the bottom line, there
was little give in Frank Felix Polk, and almost no forgiveness.

As a psychologist, Frank Felix Polk was as personally indefin
tive as he was professionally dominating.

For the previous two years, Felix and his wife, Susan, ha
been locked in a vitriolic dispute over their own lives, and th
lives of their three teenaged boys. A divorce case had bee
sputtering through the courts of Contra Costa County, Califor
nia, for more than a year, with each partner in the marriag
escalating and re-escalating in a Gordian knot of mone
memory, property and power. If it hadn't yet reached the leve
of the movie *The War of the Roses*, it was getting very close

Susan Polk was five feet, four inches tall, and weighe
about 125 pounds. At 43 she was almost twenty-six year
younger than her husband. In fact, she had first met Feli
when she was a 14-year-old schoolgirl, his patient—Felix wa
her court-assigned, 40-year-old psychotherapist.

Somehow the adult–teen counseling sessions of the 1970
had mutated into an illicit man–child affair, which was one o
the proximate causes of Felix's divorce from his first wife. Fe
lix had then married Susan, there were the three sons, an
then Susan, after two decades of marriage, wanted out.

In October of 2002, just a month after telling the divorc
court that she was through with Felix forever, that she wa
moving to Montana, that she was never coming back—Susa
was back. In her view, Felix had pulled one last fast one o
her, and she wasn't about to let him get away with it. By nov
almost thirty years after their initial encounter, Susan Polk u
terly despised her husband as a manipulative, drug-dispensin
child molester. Susan believed she was his primary victim.

In several telephone calls from Montana, Susan allegedl
told Felix she would kill him if he didn't do what she wante
him to do. She told Felix, in a telephone call that the couple'
15-year-old son, Gabriel, at one point claimed to have listene
in on, that she'd just bought a shotgun in Montana and in
tended to use it—on Felix—if he didn't transfer $20 millio

m a secret bank account in the Caribbean that she believed controlled.

Felix told her she was out of her mind—the money did not ist.

Susan didn't believe him, and said that she was on her way ck to California to take care of business.

san Polk returned to the dream house on the evening of October 9, 2002. The following day, she moved her estranged sband's personal effects, including his clothes and his bed, m the trilevel main house to the pool house—a silent statent of Susan's intent to resume full occupancy of the main use, and a direct challenge to Felix's claim to control of the operty. It was yet another escalation of the War Between the lks that had been raging since early 2001.

"I told her not to do it," Gabriel said later. He knew Su-n's unilateral action could only cause trouble, of which he d seen far too much over the previous few years. Three nes in the next few days, police came to the house at Felix's quest, but each time they refused to arrest Susan, or make r leave.

While Susan seemed adamant about her rights, Felix was ermittently angry, resigned, then stubborn himself. As far Felix could see, he was once again torn between two un-latable choices, as he had been, ever since the trouble with san had started, at least in his mind, four years before—he dn't want Susan to leave, but he couldn't cope with her the y she was.

e atmosphere over the weekend of Friday, October 11, to turday, October 12, 2002, settled into a tense wariness on th sides, each marital partner doing his or her best to ignore e other. Each had court orders affecting the other—principally ving each control over the dream house—and each had

plans to get control of the three to four million dollars in
Polk family estate.

Later, when asked to reconstruct the events of the fateful d
Monday, October 14—Columbus Day—15-year-old Gabr
Polk could point to nothing that was unusual, at least at first.

He recalled that his mother Susan had driven him to scho
in Walnut Creek about eight that morning. He assumed th
his father had already left for work. Felix had told his son t
day before that he had a few patients to see, then would ta
the rest of the day off. Father and son planned to attend a S
Francisco Giants baseball game that evening. Felix was
rabid Giants fan, and the team was headed for the World S
ries that year. Felix, at 70, was diligently trying to repair I
previously unhappy relations with his youngest child.

At 12:30 that afternoon, Susan picked up Gabriel
school. Mother and son had lunch together at a restaurant
the East Bay town of Lafayette, then ran a few errands, arri
ing back at the dream house around two in the afternoo
Shortly after they arrived, Susan told Gabe that she had son
thing else to do, and left him alone in the house. Gabe la
thought that was the first sign that something was wrong:
was out of character for his mother to leave him by himse
when they could have gone together, he said.

It was only later that Gabe wondered whether his moth
actually wanted him to discover, while she was out, what s
had already done, as a way of punishing him for his suppos
disloyalty to her side in the War Between the Polks.

Gabe spent the afternoon watching television, playi
computer games and lifting weights. He did not go into t
pool house. He expected his father to come home any tim
But by 6, Felix still had not arrived. Gabe was gettin
worried—time was running short if they hoped to get to t
baseball game.

As 7 approached, Gabe became more and more certain th
something bad had happened to his father—if Felix had be
delayed for some reason, Gabe was sure, he would ha

led. Gabe began to worry that his mother had actually done
nething to his father, just as she had previously threatened.
dn't she at least twice said she'd bought a shotgun in Mon-
a, and planned to use it on Felix—"to blow his head
"—if he didn't cooperate? Or so his father had told him.

And hadn't there been various statements Susan had made
er the previous summer to Gabe, musing about the best way
get rid of Felix: maybe poisoning him, running him over
th the car, drowning him in the pool? Gabe had always be-
ved that his mother wishing her husband, his father, dead
s just her venting—she'd been waxing wroth about Felix
years, and to him, it was nothing new.

But now there was this unaccounted-for absence. Gabe had
think that maybe his mother had been serious about getting
of his father. In fact, maybe she *had* blown his head off
th a shotgun.

Just after 7, Gabe decided he had to get into the pool house
see if there was some explanation for his father's mysteri-
s nonappearance—perhaps there was a note or something.
made his way over the tiled deck to the front door of the
ol house, just outside the cool blue of the water, but found it
cked. He went back to the main house and confronted his
other.

"Where's Dad?" he asked.

"I don't know," Susan said. "Maybe he's left."

This was another gibe by Susan at Felix's parenting skills.
ver the previous two years, each parent had been disparag-
g the other as unreliable and selfish when it came to their
ee boys. But Gabe thought his mother knew more than she
s saying.

"I could tell she was lying," he said later. She always did
nething with her eyes that Gabe recognized when Susan
s not telling the truth. His mother seemed oblivious to these
spicions, though.

"Why don't you call the CHP [California Highway Pa-
l]?" Susan told him.

"Why should I call the CHP?" Gabe asked, now thinki
that his mother seemed strangely indifferent to Felix's safe

"Maybe he's had an accident," Susan said, without see
ing to care very much one way or the other if Felix had be
plastered all over the freeway. Or, on second thought, was
trying to prepare him for his father being dead?

His mother was calm—too calm, Gabe thought.

Then she said something that really alarmed him.

"Aren't you glad he's gone?"

Susan now said something about not using a shotgun,
Gabriel later recalled: either it was, "Aren't you glad I didn't u
a shotgun?" or possibly, "Aren't you glad I didn't *have*
use a shotgun?"

The difference of meaning is considerable in the vario
interpretations; but based on his mother's demeanor, Ga
feared the worst.

What was this? Was his mother telling him that she'd si
ply convinced Felix to walk away from the dream house, a
his claim of custody of their youngest child, two of the thr
main issues at the core of their long-running divorce dispu
without her having to actually *shoot him*—that Felix had
fectually surrendered, in the long-running War Between t
Polks? Or was she really saying that she'd done somethi
deadly to Felix—just *not* with a shotgun?

Susan's attitude of indifference, Gabe's perception of h
calm deceptiveness, convinced him that something bad had
fact happened to his father, and that his mother knew what
was. He had to get into the pool house to make sure. But fi
he had to think of what to do if he wasn't only imagini
things, if the worst had really happened.

About 9 in the evening on October 14, 2002, Gabe call
911, and asked for a direct, nonemergency number for t
police—just in case.

"I didn't want to look like an idiot," he said later, if
turned out nothing was wrong. The operator wouldn't give
to him, and pressed him to say what was bothering him.

"Never mind," he said. He hung up the telephone.

It was well past dark by now, so Gabe got a heavy flashlight. He went out the back door of the main house and crossed the patio to the pool house, determined to find a way inside. He went to the rear entrance of the pool house, the one that led into the kitchen from the north side, and found it unlocked. He couldn't remember which of the light switches were operable—some were not—so he turned on his large flashlight to illuminate his path. In the darkness he made his way through the kitchen, down the hallway to the living area.

There, on the other side of a banister that separated the hallway from the lowered floor of the living room, he saw his father, nearly naked, face up, arms to his side. There was blood on Felix, there was blood all over the floor, and Felix wasn't moving.

Gabe knew his father was dead.

He backed out of the pool house, closing the kitchen door behind him. He returned to the main house and picked up the telephone. Before he could dial, Susan confronted him.

"What are you doing?" she asked.

"Nothing," Gabe said, and put the telephone back in its cradle. When she wasn't looking, he palmed the cordless phone and made his way to the parking area in front of the carport, outside the main house. He punched in 911.

"Nine one one, police or fire?" the operator asked.

"Uh, murder?" Gabe responded.

"Okay, where at?"

"Seven two eight Miner Road."

"Okay, what happened?"

"Uh, I think my dad—my mom shot my dad."

"You think your mom shot your dad?"

"Yes."

The 911 operator patched in the fire department, and told the emergency people to head for Miner Road and "stage"—that is, assemble at the address, but do nothing until the police could arrive.

"What's going on there?" the dispatcher for the fire department asked.

"It's a possible shooting," the 911 operator told her.

For the next two minutes, the operator tried to keep Gabe on the line, asking him questions about his mother, especially whether she still had a gun, and where she was at that moment. Gabe identified himself and his age, and said once more that his father was dead, "in my cottage," as the Polk family called the pool house.

"What's your mom's name?"

"Susan."

"What's her last name?"

"She has a mental illness," Gabe said. "Her last name is Polk."

"How old is Susan?" But Gabe did not answer. He could hear his mother calling to him.

"Gabe!" Susan called from the darkness a few feet away. He could hear her opening and then closing the front door to the pool house. He knew that she knew that he knew.

"Where are you? Where are you, Gabe?" Susan called out.

Gabe pulled deeper into the shadows behind the trash bins by the garage, concealing himself from his mother. The 911 operator was still asking questions, but Gabe was keeping quiet.

"Do you know how old your mom is?"

Silence.

"Gabe, are you still there?" the operator asked.

More silence.

"Gabe, are you there?"

Then there was nothing—not even the dull buzz of the dial tone.

Gabe was gone.

II.
FELIX

2. THE PSYCHOLOGIST
AS A YOUNG MAN

Frank Felix Polk was born June 30, 1932, in Vienna, Austria. His death certificate, filed by the Contra Costa County coroner's office in October 2002, shows that his father was Eric Ernst Polk, born in Czechoslovakia, and that his mother was Johanna Hahn, a citizen of Austria.

In the aftermath of his death, a number of newspaper stories were published about Felix.

One, an obituary in the *San Francisco Chronicle*, characterized him as "beloved by hundreds of patients, former patients, friends and family."

Among other accomplishments, according to the obituary, Felix had taught at several institutions engaged in the training of psychologists, including Argosy University in Richmond, California. The obit also characterized Felix as serving as an officer in the U.S. Navy during the Korean War.

Felix, "was devoted to his clients and his students alike," the obituary continued. "He spent his life helping people."

Felix was described as an enthusiastic skier, hiker and runner, and a fervent fan of the Oakland Raiders and the San Francisco Giants.

"He was a voracious reader and had a special fondness for

historical espionage novels," the obituary continued. "He loved his children, Mount Tamalpais, and good food."

Felix had studied with Anna Freud, the daughter of Sigmund, in London, and this experience was vital in helping him develop a model for assessing and treating juvenile delinquency, the obituary reported.

The obituary also referred to Felix's seminal boyhood experience, dodging the Nazis: "As a child, he and his immediate family miraculously survived the Holocaust by hiding in occupied France for nearly three years."

The obituary concluded:

"There will be a Memorial Service for friends at 11 am on Saturday, November 9 at Christ The King Church . . . in Pleasant Hill. . . ."

There was no mention of the fact that Felix Polk had been murdered, possibly at the hands of the person who knew him best of all, his wife for almost twenty-one years, Susan Polk.

Based on what Felix himself first told the U.S. Navy in the fall of 1955, when he was a junior officer two years removed from college, it appears that the Polk family's escape from the Holocaust took place in 1941, when Felix would have been about 9 years old. According to Felix's statement to the Navy, the family arrived in the United States in the same year, and soon settled in Harrison, New York, a small town in Westchester County just south of the Connecticut state line.

There, according to Felix, he and his fraternal twin brother, John George Polk, his older sister Evelyn, and his father and mother, Eric and Johanna—later using the name Joan—settled into a suburban American existence. The parental Polks owned two variety stores in the Westchester community. Felix was naturalized as an American citizen in 1946—for some reason this took place in Philadelphia, rather than New York—and graduated from high school in Harrison in 1949.

That September, Felix enrolled at St. John's College in Annapolis, Maryland, where, for the next four years, he took liberal arts courses. St. John's was famed for its emphasis on the "Great Books," and on philosophy. Graduating from St. John's in June of 1953, Felix joined the Navy, and was sent to Officer Candidate School in Newport, Rhode Island.

After emerging from his OCS training in the late fall of 1953, Felix was assigned as a stores officer to a Navy cargo ship, an LST, shuttling between California and Japan until the fall of 1955. By the time of this first assignment, the Korean War was over—an armistice between the contending forces had been signed on July 27, 1953. Although Felix had in fact taken the oath as a naval officer, attendant to his enrollment in OCS, saying he was a Korean War veteran was something of a stretch, since he didn't graduate from OCS in Newport and enter active duty until the fall of 1953, well after the conclusion of the armistice.

It appears that Felix did not particularly enjoy his naval service. This emerged in the fall of 1955 when Felix was transferred from the west coast to duty in a New York naval district. A little over a month after his transfer—almost forty-eight years to the day, in fact, before his actual death on October 14, 2002—Felix tried to kill himself.

Later, the specifics of this incident would form a powerful exhibit in Susan Polk's defense: proof positive that her husband, the vaunted, celebrated psychologist, was himself mentally unstable. The records of the incident were recovered from the Navy.

Based on the files, it seems that Felix attempted to kill himself with carbon monoxide on the evening of Sunday, October 16, 1955. According to the official naval investigation, Felix, staying at his parents' house in Harrison, typed out an unsigned suicide note, and left it in the typewriter:

I have done what for a long time I know I must do. When a rock is thrown into water it sinks. It must sink as now must I. My mind is so heavy with wretchedness, with utter loneliness, with an unknown past, a frightening future and an intolerable past—present—that no choice remains.

I don't fear death at all. What is it but non-life and what is life but a continuous torture?

This final act is not sudden or impetuous. I have known that some day it would take place. The question has only been where, when and how. Until a few weeks ago there has always been some spark some hope which prevented me from the obvious. This night there is no hope. There is nothing; and tomorrow and tomorrow.

Of regrets I have few. It would be folly for anyone to assume the blame for something of which I myself and no one else is responsible.

I say goodbye to a hateful world with a smile. In life I hated pity and in death I want none.

Had I not come this far in life my loss would perhaps have been easier. I have forgotten the world and now the world much [sic] forget me.

At some point either before or after composing this farewell, Felix had telephoned an actress he'd been dating in New York City. They'd spent the weekend together in the city, attending a play on Saturday, and a performance by the mime Marcel Marceau on Sunday. After the performance, the actress had gone to her mother's house in the city, while Felix had driven back to Harrison. Around 7 that same night Felix had called the actress; she thought he sounded very depressed. Eric and Joan Polk were out of town visiting their married daughter Evelyn in Rochester, and his brother John was in the Army in Korea, so Felix was alone.

"It's too late, too late," Felix told her. "It's too late for the world." Felix advised her not to call him back.

As it happened, the woman's brother, also serving in the U.S

Army, had recently committed suicide. In fact, Felix had questioned her closely about that event. Now, with Felix saying over and over that it was "too late," the woman reached the not unreasonable conclusion that Felix meant to kill himself. She called the Harrison police and asked them to check on Felix. Around midnight, police officers went to the Polk house. The officers checked the closed garage and found Felix lying on the floor near the right front wheel of his father's car. The engine was running, and the garage was full of exhaust fumes. The two officers dragged Felix outside and gave him artificial respiration. An ambulance, a doctor and the Harrison Fire Department came, and Felix was taken to a nearby hospital in restraints. On his arrival at the hospital, Felix, while now breathing quite healthily, was irrational; it took several attendants to control him. In the struggle, Felix sustained a number of bruises.

A day or so later, Felix's commanding officer detailed Lieutenant Junior Grade Daniel R. Kaplan to investigate the circumstances of Felix's apparent attempt to kill himself. Among other things, Kaplan was told to deliver an opinion as to "misconduct and line of duty status" of Felix—in other words, to determine if the suicide attempt was real, or if it was Felix's attempt to malinger, or evade his naval service altogether.

On October 20, 1955, Kaplan and a chief petty officer interviewed Felix, who by then was confined to a naval hospital on Long Island. In a summary of this interview, Kaplan sketched in Felix's background as a refugee from the Holocaust:

LTJG Polk indicated that he has been a depressed person for a long time. He visited a civilian psychiatrist upon graduation from Officer Candidate School and again in September–October 1955 . . . He claims to have a superficially happy home life but does not know why there is a lack of real happiness for him while living with his parents. He feels very insecure about his post-navy career, but has decided he will attempt a career in medicine. He has no serious romantic engagements but has spent a considerable period of time with [the actress friend]. He remembers seeing the play *La Ronde* Saturday . . . and Marcel Marceau 16 October 1955. He remembers speaking to [the actress friend] Sunday evening . . . He does not remember any of the events preceding his attempted suicide—including writing a suicide note. He does not remember being admitted to [the] hospital. He can offer no reason or explanation for his attempted suicide. He is very vague as to the events of the week preceding the suicide attempt.

Given Felix's seeming amnesia as to possible reasons for the suicide attempt, Kaplan concluded that Felix's self-destructive intent was irrational. A medical examination, Kaplan reported, indicated that Felix was still suicidal, and that extensive hospitalization would be required.

Kaplan concluded:

Since there is no reasonable adequate motive explaining this intent to suicide, the presumption of sanity is rebutted and LTJG Polk should not be found mentally responsible for his actions on 16 October 1955. LTJG Polk's injuries were suffered in the line of duty and not as a result of his own misconduct.

For the next few weeks, Felix remained confined to the naval hospital at St. Albans, Long Island. A preliminary medical report completed on October 31, 1955, noted that Felix had been kept "on the closed ward because of his depression and hostility. It is felt that he is still suicidal. Further study has given evidence of a schizophrenic process with much philosophical, abstract preoccupation with his lack of accomplishment, his emotional distance from people and some concomitant disturbance in the psycho-sexual area."

By the end of October, the doctors at the naval hospital diagnosed Felix as suffering from "Psychotic Depressive Reaction With Suicidal Tendencies." The depression, said the doctors, actually went back to Felix's college years: "His moodiness and preoccupation with morbid subjects dated back to his time at St. John's," the navy's case summary reported. The private psychiatrist seen by Felix in New York was Dr. Kurt Goldstein, a pioneering authority on Freudian psychoanalysis, and later an originator of Gestalt therapy, who had emigrated from Germany to New York before the war.

While at St. Albans, Felix "remained depressed, talked of his confusion and was able to talk of his attachment to his sister, his concern about his sexuality, and his hostility to his father and his brother," according to the navy files.

Felix still claimed that he could not remember what had happened. A series of psychological tests was administered, which "confirmed the clinical impression of a severe disorganization of ego structure, pathological impulsiveness, severe depression and marked sexual preoccupation."

Four days after diagnosing Felix with a "Psychotic Depressive Reaction With Suicidal Tendencies," the St. Albans doctors changed their minds: Felix had suffered a "Schizophrenic Reaction."

3. DEPRESSION,
NOT SCHIZOPHRENIA

On November 18, 1955, Felix was transferred from the St. Albans naval hospital on Long Island to the U.S. Naval Hospital in Philadelphia, where he began an extended course of treatment. A report of the naval medical board found that Felix was still depressed, but no longer suicidal.

The report of January 31, 1956, recounted:

On admission to this hospital, he appeared depressed, but disclaimed suicidal wishes, and stated that he could not relate his depression "to anything." He added that he felt "passive, something like a vegetable." He spoke coherently and relevantly, but volunteered little and was brief in his replies. He expressed feelings of hopelessness and that no one could help him. No actual delusions or hallucinations could be elicited.

Other than his depression and general lassitude, Felix seemed normal, at least physiologically. He still claimed he could not remember trying to kill himself, but said he knew he was mentally ill.

Background information, obtained from the patient and considered reliable, revealed that he was born on 30 June 1932 in Vienna, Austria. The patient has an older sister and a brother who is a fraternal twin. In 1938, at the age of six, the patient and his entire family had to flee from Austria to France because of the Nazi invasion. The patient and his family spent three years in various parts of France, and as he stated, "We had to keep one step ahead of the Germans."

In August, 1941, at the age of nine, he and his family managed to get to the United States, and settled in Harrison, New York. The patient's father is fifty-five years of age at the present time and is a businessman who owns two five and ten cent stores in the community. He [Eric Polk] had been a clothing manufacturer and fairly wealthy in Austria. The patient considers his father to be "narrow-minded," weak, and doesn't get along with him. The patient's mother is fifty-one years of age, and manages one of the stores her husband owns.

According to the patient, she is the power in the family and has tended to be protective of the patient. The patient's sister, five years the patient's senior, is married and lives in Rochester, New York. The patient's fraternal twin is a second lieutenant in the Army, now serving in Korea. He is taller than the patient, a better athlete, and their relationship was competitive. The patient started school at a late date, but graduated high school in 1949 at the age of seventeen with average grades and then through a scholarship attended St. John's College in Annapolis, Maryland. He was pushed by his parents to make better grades in high school and his brother was held up as an example, which he resented.

In college, he enrolled in a liberal arts course and had much "scholastic" interest. However, he made no close friends and had fluctuating "moods of unhappiness." He became very interested in philosophy which "produced lots of self-analysis." And his letters home were filled with marked pre-occupations and esoteric discussions of philosophy. He had no definite occupational goal but was considering a medical career. Upon graduating with a

B.A. degree in 1953, he enrolled in the Navy to meet his military obligations.

After summarizing Felix's naval career up to the time of the suicide attempt, the board's report noted that Felix had been reassigned from the West Coast LST to Brooklyn on the East Coast for shore duty.

> However, his return to his home area and his parents seemed to revive his emotional difficulties . . . He explained that since his "college days" he has always felt "depressed while home, better away."

He'd first consulted Dr. Goldstein at the suggestion of his family, Felix said, after they had noticed he seemed moody and depressed after attending OCS, but before he joined the LST on the Pacific Coast. When reassigned to Brooklyn, Felix said, he began seeing Goldstein again.

> According to the records from the U.S. Naval Hospital, St. Albans . . . this psychiatrist [Goldstein] described the patient as agitated, depressed, concerned over sexual problems, lacking interest in a career, and preoccupied with philosophical and cosmic concepts during his period of treatment.

Felix did not seem to be making much progress, the doctors noted, remaining withdrawn and sullen. He had little enthusiasm or initiative.

> In interview he revealed little of himself or his feelings. When pressed he would describe his thoughts as "abstract" or mentions "dreams of glory" without further elucidation. He complained that he seemed "in a daze" and did things "mechanically." He remained amnesic for the suicidal attempt, saying it seemed "supernatural" and incomprehensible, and

adding, "I had suicidal thoughts before but never thought I'd have enough nerve to try it."

After two months in the locked ward at the Philadelphia ospital, Felix was transferred to the open ward, in the hope at having more freedom of movement might spark more en- usiasm for life. It didn't seem to help.

He spoke of feeling apart in all relationships with others and having the sensation he was "standing apart listening to an echo" when he talked. His speech was at all times coherent and relevant and no actual delusions or hallucinations were elicited. The diagnosis was retained as Schizophrenic Reaction, Chronic, Moderate, Unimproved, manifested by withdrawal, morbid preoccupation, loss of initiative, and psycho-sexual conflict; stress, minimal; predisposition, moderate (long history of emotional maladjustment); impairment, marked (requires further hospitalization).

A month later, Felix was granted a 100 percent medical ischarge, placed on the temporary retired list, and released rom active duty. The medical discharge meant that he was ligible to receive 75 percent of his monthly pay as a naval ieutenant Junior Grade for the foreseeable future. He contin- ed to reside in hospitals for the next year.

4. FELIX GOES
BACK TO SCHOOL

By late July of 1957, Felix was still in the hospital, drawing his disability pay, but now in much better shape. He had part-time job at another nearby hospital, and there was som prospect that it might be safe to release him. He was ordere to return to the naval facility at St. Albans for a new examina tion. This time the doctors found him neatly dressed, friendly and coherent. He also now had a goal: he wanted to become psychoanalyst.

> He reports that he feels generally well but occasionally still "gets his moods." He is working for Blythedale Orthopedic Home as a counselor for the summer. In the fall he plans to attend Yeshiva University to gain his M.A.

Felix was seeing a private psychiatrist three times a week and the sessions had helped considerably, the doctors noted.

> He feels now that his illness was caused by his emotional problems but that his depression and suicidal attempt seem no longer realistic.
> At the present time it is felt that this man has made great progress in recovery from his illness. He is consid-

ered competent to manage his own affairs. There has been no physical illness since his retirement from service.

Inasmuch as this man is spending $45 weekly for private psychotherapy (confirmed by his medical doctor's letter) he feels in need of his pension.

IMPRESSION: SCHIZOPHRENIC REACTION (IN REMISSION).

That fall, Felix did enroll at Yeshiva University in New York City, where he took classes necessary to obtain a master's degree in social work. A little more than a year later, he married Sharon Gail Mann in Miami, Florida. The following year, in June, Felix graduated from Yeshiva with his MSW, and soon found employment as a social worker at Cedar Knolls School in Westchester County, in Hawthorne, New York, a residential school for neglected and delinquent children operated by the state's Jewish Board of Family and Children's Services. Felix was paid a salary of $4,780 a year—approximately equivalent to $50,000 in today's dollars. He continued to attend regular psychotherapy sessions twice a week.

In July of 1960, in another periodic review by the naval medical board, Felix was found to be in "complete remission" from his mental illness, even though he continued to have recurrent

bouts of depression and anxiety . . . the patient's social adjustment has been slightly impaired due to his irritability when he feels anxious or depressed . . .

On mental examination the patient appeared quiet, passive and showed slight depression and slight blunting of affect. He was friendly, alert and cooperative, and showed no overt evidence of psychosis. He apparently had developed considerable insight into the psychological difficulty that led to his retirement from the service.

This was the final review of Felix's mental status by the Navy; it isn't clear whether the finding of "complete remission" resulted in the end of Felix's 75 percent disability pay. But the board added a final note: ". . . disclosure to him of information relative to his mental health may adversely affect his mental health." In other words, Felix wasn't to know what the Navy doctors had said was wrong with him. Somehow, though, he must have found out—that was how Susan Polk later knew that her husband had been labeled "a schizophrenic" by the Navy, which was how the records eventually came into evidence during her trial; it seems clear that Felix must have told Susan himself about his bout with mental illness.

The Navy board issued this final report on September 6, 1960. By then, Felix and Sharon Mann Polk were on their way to the West Coast, where Felix had been accepted as a student at the University of California, Berkeley. Over the next year Felix took courses to qualify him for a bachelor's degree in psychology, while also working as a therapist at the Fred Finch residential treatment center in Oakland, California, a venerable East Bay institution that provides services for children, many of them emotionally and sexually abused. There Felix encountered a man who would become one of his lifelong friends and collaborators, Dr. Marty Kirschenbaum. Kirschenbaum, the treatment center's supervising psychologist, mentored Felix as he conducted diagnostic tests on the children, led group therapy sessions, and provided individual counseling.

After earning his additional bachelor's degree in psychology from the University in June of 1961, Felix was accepted into the University's prestigious doctoral program in psychology. For the next four years, from 1961 to 1965, Felix worked on his Ph.D., while spending ten hours a week at Fred Finch, and later working as a therapist at the university's student health clinic. The experience of working with emotionally and sexually abused children—many of them teenagers—helped provide Felix with the insight and background for his dissertation, completed in July of 1965: "Toward a Typology of the Delinquent Personality."

The 132-page dissertation reflects Felix's commitment to psychoanalytic theory, in particular the Freudian concept of "superego."

In Freud's view, the mind consisted of three basic parts: the id, the ego and the superego. The "id" was comprised of basic human drives, such as rage, lust and fear, while the "superego" represented societal controls over such drives, and was therefore acquired behavior—the environment, or "nurture." The "ego" represented the self, whose task it was to "mediate" between the drives and the controls.

"The psychoanalytic concept of Superego," Felix wrote in his dissertation, "provides three ... personality variables which are relevant to the problem at hand," which Felix had defined as a need to find better methods to treat delinquent youth to prevent reoffending.

"These are: 1. Moral attitudes; 2. Ego strength (Control); 3. Affect (Guilt)."

In sorting out juvenile offenders by testing for attitudes in these three areas—that is, measuring the effectiveness of the superego in moderating delinquent behavior—Felix hoped to lay the foundation for a new methodology for dealing with juvenile delinquents, one that was less concerned with such traditional factors as race, class, neighborhood or income, which had dominated the field up until then. Felix obtained the cooperation of a San Francisco juvenile court judge, a research psychologist for the Alameda County Probation Department, and a school psychologist, in helping to obtain juvenile subjects for the extensive testing that the dissertation required.

By the time the dissertation was completed, Felix had tested hundreds of juvenile boys, sorted into various categories such as geography, race, economic class, and degree of parental and community involvement in their lives. The focus of the tests was on value formation, a measurement of superego.

How, where, and how much tested juveniles were attached

to the value structure imposed on them from their community—especially an anonymous community, in which there were no previously existing established values—were critical in the emergence of juvenile delinquency, Felix established.

In acknowledging the assistance of those who had helped him complete the study, Felix gave due credit to his wife:

> *Finally, I thank my wife, Sharon, who endured untold tortures during my graduate years, and, in spite of these, provided me with loving support and encouragement when I needed it; chastised me when I deserved it; sublimated her considerable gifts and skills for mine; and always provided me with a strong purpose and rewards for my efforts.*

That wasn't all that Sharon had provided for Felix, though. By the time the dissertation was finished, Sharon had also given birth to the first two Polk children, Andrew, born in October 1962, and Jennifer, born in March 1965.

After obtaining his doctorate from the university in September of 1965, Felix, and Sharon and the two babies, traveled to London, where for the next year he would serve an internship at the prestigious Tavistock Clinic under the supervision of none other than Anna Freud, daughter of Sigmund, and a world-famous psychoanalyst in her own right.

Felix had indeed come a long way from his comatose posture on the floor of his parents' garage in Harrison, New York.

5. GURU

Three months after the Polks returned to the Bay Area from London in the fall of 1966, Felix left Sharon and their two small children.

Although Felix and Sharon separated on December 3, 1966, a legal divorce action was not begun by Sharon until October of the following year, 1967. Alameda County files show that the divorce was uncontested by Felix.

Sharon's lawyer told the court that Felix was employed by Alameda County as a psychologist, earning $1,500 a month, equivalent to about $160,000 a year in today's money. He asked the court to award her $500 a month in child and spousal support. Among the couple's debts were $400 owing to Dr. Harold Mann, presumably Sharon's father; $900 to Felix's brother-in-law, possibly Sharon's brother; and $200 to Felix's brother John. These unpaid borrowings from family members seem to have been a habit with Felix; by the time of his death, he was locked in a dispute with his second wife Susan's mother over the fate of about $60,000 she had loaned Felix and Susan nearly two decades earlier.

On November 14, 1967, a default judgment of divorce was entered against Felix, after he failed to respond to the complaint. But that seemed to be the end of the matter—there are no further records in the file, and because Felix and Sharon were again involved in a divorce case more than a dozen years later, either they reconciled or remarried.

Thus, from this first divorce to their final separation in 1978, Felix and Sharon and their two children lived together in an attractive upper-middle-class home just off The Alameda in Berkeley, within a short distance of the University of California campus.

It's a bit difficult to get a specific grip on Felix's approach to his work as a psychologist during this ensuing decade. At one point during this era, Felix later said, he was chief psychologist for the Alameda County Department of Mental Health. It appears that he may have had some role in training probation officers, screening police candidates, and consulting with juvenile court authorities, which provided him with powerful governmental contacts. Besides this work, it appears that he also had a lucrative private practice on the side, providing individual and group therapy. Felix specialized in "family therapy," in which the dynamics of entire families were subjected to the psychoanalytic tool of transference.

In this, the analyst, by prodding the patient with pointed questions and reactions, attempted to induce the patient to "transfer" feelings he or she might have about a family member onto the therapist. The therapist then responded in such a way as to make the patient aware of how and why he had come to have those particular feelings, and how to handle them more effectively. The therapeutic technique required insight into the patient's thought processes as well as verbal agility on the part of the therapist. Most important, the therapist had to maintain an inner emotional distance from the patient, even while at times playing the role of various family members in an effort to ignite the transference. It was tricky; sometimes patients' feelings could become so fixated on the

therapist that they became difficult to unstick. Professional
boundary lines were often hard to distinguish.

In employing this type of analytic therapy, Felix—
probably influenced by his own Freudian analysis, as well
as his own early life—developed the idea that family dynamics often led one family member to become the family's
"scapegoat," a sort of repository for most of the negative dysfunction. Having selected a scapegoat, the "problem child"—
although it could also be a parent—became the focus of all the
dysfunction. Other family members worked out their own
dysfunctions by blaming the obvious target; the ensuing
transferences onto the scapegoat enabled the rest of the family
to avoid responsibility for their own part of the dysfunctional
dynamic.

Felix came to believe that a good way to restore mental
health to the family was to induce the "scapegoat" to establish
clear boundaries that apportioned responsibility where it actually belonged. That meant teaching the patient how to stand
up for himself when others were dumping on him, and to understand what the dumping really represented.

Besides individual and family sessions, it appears that Felix also organized group therapy sessions, in which unrelated
patients with different transfer dynamics would be mixed in a
sort of artificial family; in these settings, more work could be
done on the transferences, and in some cases, because of the
relative lack of pre-existing history between the patients, the
dynamic of the transferences could become more obvious to
the patient.

All of this was also transpiring in an era of significant flux
within the field of psychology. Where, fifty years earlier, the
psychoanalyst might have taken a perch out of view of the patient, who might have been lying on a couch, in part to get him
to relax, by the late 1960s and early 1970s, the therapist was
often front and center—a ringmaster of sorts.

The late 1960s and 1970s also brought with them a rather

profound change in the philosophy of psychotherapy. The era of "expanding consciousness" that had accompanied the arrival of wider illicit use of psychotropic substances was followed soon thereafter by a sort of mass individuation culture. In contrast to earlier eras' emphasis on conformity, on getting along with others, by the late 1960s and early 1970s, individuals were encouraged to discover their inner selves.

This movement peaked when another Tavistock alumnus, psychiatrist R. D. Laing, brought forth the notion that there wasn't really such a thing as psychosis, that madness was all in the eye of the definer.

"Madness need not be all breakdown," Laing asserted. "It may also be breakthrough. It is potentially liberation and renewal, as well as enslavement and existential death."

This seemed to suggest that all manner of behavior was legitimate—that it was society that was crazy. From there it was only a short hop to the notion that if a therapist's job was to liberate his patient from his hang-ups, whatever served that end could be considered acceptable. Thus, by the early 1970s, many of the old professional boundaries between patients and their therapists were beginning to erode. Some, in fact, began to have sexual relations with their patients, telling themselves that this was just one more tool to facilitate transference, and to help the patient liberate himself.

Was Felix Polk caught up in this shifting tide? There is certainly no hard evidence that this was the case, although numerous associates of Felix in the psychological community in the Bay Area certainly thought he was. By the mid-1970s, Felix had emerged, at least in anecdote, as a sort of "guru" of psychological liberation, complete with a rather intense, devoted following of patients and former patients, some of them rather prominent in the community. There were stories that Felix had occasionally had sex with some of his patients, some of them under the legal age of consent.

Since Felix was treating a fairly large number of patients for issues related to family sexual abuse, it's easy to see how such stories could gain circulation, if not credibility: after all, if a patient was sexually abused by, say, her father, Felix could play the role of the father in order to facilitate the victim's ability to "transfer," and safely confront the abuser in the form of Felix. But as noted earlier, the boundary line could be very tricky.

Yet there is no hard evidence that anything like this happened, despite the *sotto voce* whispers among area psychologists, some of whom may have merely been jealous of Felix's professional reputation. Certainly there is no record of any patient ever having complained of improper conduct by Felix to the California State Board of Psychology, which, with the rising toll of such complaints about therapists generally, had issued strong ethical warnings against the practice by the late 1970s.

Still, it wasn't until the 1990s that the state passed a law to make sexual conduct by therapists with their patients a criminal offense.

In any event, it was in this atmosphere of increasing liberality in relationships between patients and therapists that the 40-year-old Felix undertook to treat a new patient, then-14-year-old Susan Mae Bolling.

6. DREAMING

Later, there would be several accounts of how this therapeutic relationship began. In one version, Susan was referred to Felix by the school she attended for an anxiety disorder; Susan's own account suggests that there may have been more to it than that.

Susan was an extremely bright teenager, exceptionally articulate for her years, and remains so today. Dark-haired, slight of stature, she had, almost from her earliest years, an acute capacity to detect even the mildest hypocrisy, and a sharp tongue to skewer it. It's not particularly surprising that she had some difficulty fitting in with her high school peers; and in an era—1972—when questioning authority was almost a mantra, Susan quickly attracted the disapproval of school and juvenile authorities.

As she later recounted the events of 1972, she had just begun to attend Clayton Valley High School, in Concord, another East Bay white shoe suburb. The school referred her to Felix for an evaluation after she began to miss classes; it appears that some at the school believed she had some sort of anxiety disorder.

Years later, in her own timeline of the events leading up to the death of Felix, Susan wrote:

I am referred by counseling office at Clayton Valley High School to Felix for a psych evaluation for missing school.

My reason for cutting school was that I was embarrassed at not being prepared for class, and I didn't like the long walk. We lived on the edge of the school district, and the walk seemed endless to me. I had been a good student throughout grammar school, and I was recognized as very capable. When I cut school, I stayed home and read the "classics." I wasn't doing drugs or drinking or cutting with friends. I had also found school to be increasingly boring.

With the referral, Susan began counseling sessions with Felix—old enough to be her father—on a regular basis. Susan recounted in her timeline:

Appointments [with Felix] are weekly. Felix tells me my mother is crazy. After testing, Felix asks to hypnotize me. I am told not to tell my mother. The hypnosis is supposed to help me recover memories of trauma in my family. The hypnosis is supposed to be kept secret. Felix gives me tea, which I drink.

After drinking the tea, Susan claimed, she couldn't remember anything about the remainder of the sessions. But as the encounters continued into the following year, Susan began having more and more anxiety about these gaps in her memory. As far as she could recall, once she drank the tea, everything from then on was a blank—until Felix woke her up and told her it was time to go home.

But then, as the sessions progressed, Susan claimed, Felix began telling her that he was in love with her, that he "thinks of me all day." Felix told her about Sharon, their two children, and his suicide attempt in the Navy, according to Susan. He told her that they were "twins," sensitive and self-conscious, both in love with literature.

As this teatime wooing went on, Susan said, she continue
to feel strange, disconcerted—suicidal, even. Still, she contin‐
ued to see Felix on a regular basis.

"During this period, I am arrested for shoplifting," Susa
continued.

> I am confined at juvenile hall, then sentenced to the Girls'
> Center. I feel very displaced, having nothing in common with
> the other girls. I also miss my mother. I run away and go to
> stay with a friend in Oakland for three or four weeks. I call my
> mother, who arranges with Felix for me to return home and
> see Felix in "therapy."

In her timeline, Susan suggested that Felix had some sor
of pull with the juvenile court in getting her out of troubl
with the authorities. In Susan's mind—later—this gave Feli
even more power over her: she believed she had to cooperat
with Felix's demands, or Felix would call up the judge an
have her sent back to incarceration.

Susan was soon placed in a continuation school, a facilit
for students with special needs. Susan hated it, especially th
morning "group therapy" sessions.

"I felt profound contempt for the 'programme,'" Susa
wrote, using the British spelling.

> I felt that there was no escaping the structure that had
> suddenly been imposed on my life by Felix, the court, and
> now the continuation school. In a moment of frustration,
> feeling fed up with the life I was being required to lead, I
> made a suicide attempt. I took my mother's sedatives.
> She found me unconscious some hours later, and I was
> admitted to [the hospital]. When I was released, I was no
> longer required to attend the continuation school. I was
> required to see Felix twice weekly.

By the mid- to late 1970s, Susan recalled, she and Felix were having sexual relations. As she put it in her timeline, "I became aware that I was having a sexual relationship with Felix."

It was only years later, when she was 40 years old, Susan claimed, that she suddenly remembered what had been going on after the tea-drinking sessions: Felix had been having sex with her while she was in the trance.

Had this really happened? Or was it the later product of Susan's consuming hatred of her husband? If it did happen, to what extent was it a result of Susan's seduction of Felix, or Felix's seduction of Susan? Felix repeatedly said this claim by Susan was delusional on her part. This assertion by her one-time psychologist, later her husband, infuriated Susan.

In later years, both Felix and Susan were to assert that Susan's initial psychological problem stemmed from sexual abuse by a member or members of her own family. Hearing of this, Susan's family steadfastly denied that anything untoward had ever taken place. And still later, Susan was to claim this assertion about her family was untrue yet powerful evidence of Felix's decades-long attempts to manipulate her, a diabolical effort to confuse and intimidate her, to prevent her from ever exposing him as a sexually abusive psychotherapist, and possible child molester.

Of course, Felix was known for his work with sexually abused children, and particularly teenagers. As Susan's account suggests, the possibility cannot be discounted that Felix, in his reputed tea-and-hypnosis sessions, somehow "implanted" the false notion in Susan's mind that she was sexually abused by her own family in order to provide a cover for his own seduction of Susan, if indeed such took place.

Eventually, Felix would tell their three sons that Susan's "delusions" stemmed from the fact that she had, in her mind,

confused the supposed abuse by her father with abuse by him.
That was why she was so angry, Felix insisted—delusionally
angry: she had confused him with her father. As the Polks'
three sons had had almost no contact with Susan's family, this
explanation seemed entirely possible, at least to them.

One thing is quite clear from this period, however, and that is
that Susan had an extremely vivid imagination. Perhaps encouraged by Felix, Susan began recording her dreams in writing. This was a habit that would apparently continue for some
years, almost right up until the night of Felix's death, in fact.

Two of Susan's earliest recorded dreams survived the decades, and were eventually provided to one of her teams of
lawyers; both of these dreams concerned Felix, and were
given by her to him after she had written them down. They
can be dated to around 1974 or 1975, because of Susan's
reference to Carlos Castaneda's book about dreaming and
reality, *Journey to Ixtlan*, at the time a psychotropic cult favorite.

In the first dream, Susan found herself in a theater watching a movie. The movie was about a girl being held prisoner in
a room. Then Susan became the girl in the movie, the one being held prisoner. There were three doors in the room, which
was exceedingly small. Through a small window, Susan could
see a "dilapidated" garden, which she thought was "haunted."
She tried one of the doorknobs, and found that it turned, but
decided not to open the door.

"I felt that I was not good enough at making my dream
real," Susan wrote, a reference to Castaneda's thesis that one
could actually make "the other world" of the dream real by
sheer dint of the power of one's imagination.

"So I stayed in my room wondering who my captors were,"
Susan continued. "There was something attractive to me
about the room and about being a captive."

Susan felt the room, too, was "haunted," and found this com-

forting for some reason, as if the ghosts were familiar to her.
Then Susan went through one of the doors and found a man
who seemed to be spying on her.

"I imagined that my captor had fallen in love with me," Susan
wrote, "and had locked me in this room to have me all to himself. I was really enjoying something in this dream."

The next thing Susan knew, she was on a beach. She con-
gratulated herself on making this part of the dream "real,"
again a reference to Castaneda's thesis. "I had dreamed myself onto the beach, like Don Genero in 'Journey to Ixtlan.' I
was the dreamer and the dreamed."

Susan walked up the beach to get away from a crowd of
people. She began to feel that she might be trapped forever in
the dream, and might "not get back to my bed."

Susan then felt that she was being pursued by a man. Then
she wasn't sure he was really after her. She walked away, and
came to some rocks near the remnants of a wooden pier, and a
man emerged from under the pier.

"I was suspicious of him at first, and then I liked him," Susan
wrote. "There was something strange about him and he seemed
to understand the way I was and he sort of liked my strange-
ness. He was sort of like a seer or a diviner, a soothsayer. I really liked being there, on the rocks, alone with him."

At that point in the dream, Susan told the man that she was
seeing a psychologist. The man "looked askance" at her, not
certain if he wanted Susan to say anything more.

"I told him your name," Susan wrote, referring to Felix,
"and that I thought you were nice." Susan wondered if the
man was jealous. Then he seemed to be predicting something,
giving her advice, but Susan didn't remember what this was.

"I liked him," she wrote, "and then I woke up."

In a second dream, this one featuring Felix himself, Susan
dreamed that Felix had vanished. Felix had given her a bill for
his services. The bill, Susan felt, was "counterfeit," and was
Felix's way of telling her that he had been captured by the
counterfeiters. The fake bill was evidence, Felix's insurance

policy, "a clue." The counterfeiters had kidnapped Felix, Susan dreamed.

Susan went to a warehouse to look for Felix, and was captured herself.

"They shoved me into a corner where you were asleep on a bed. You sat up and I felt very sad, because your face was all burned and scarred, and I felt they had broken you, that you were a broken man," Susan wrote, referring to Felix. Felix's eyes were teary and his lip trembled in pain and fear, Susan dreamed.

"I embraced you in order to comfort you." Susan was sad that Felix had been reduced "to a broken man," that she could no longer "rely" on him.

"You seemed shorter," she said.

The counterfeiters were about to torture Susan to get Felix to tell where the counterfeit money was, but Susan offered to tell them herself, "to stall for time." She thought that Felix should really have told them what they wanted to know—"and not let them destroy you." She was disapproving of his decision to not cooperate with his tormentors.

The dream shifted, and Susan and Felix were together in an old, dirty house, apparently attempting to escape. Felix looked normal to her, but she also had the sense that he wasn't really the way he appeared to be, that there was something off about him that she couldn't identify. They found themselves in an old room in the back of the house that was littered with old clothes. The walls of the room were made of concrete, and had windows with wire screens covering them. They crossed to the windows by walking across the old clothes, and Susan and Felix realized that their feet were sinking into the clothes, that the room was actually a deep well.

Felix reached one of the windows and pulled himself up and out of the room. Susan tried to do the same but wasn't strong enough. Susan reached up for Felix's hand "shyly," expecting that Felix would help her up, but he wouldn't.

"Instead you stood around impatiently looking at me with

optimism and at the same time dissatisfaction, and an expression that clearly showed you weren't about to help me up," she wrote.

Susan's feet began sinking into the clothing, and she was afraid she was "going to disappear altogether"—to drown in the pile of old clothes.

Just when she thought she was lost, Susan remembered that Felix hadn't had any trouble getting out, "and I felt that was because you moved faster and lighter than I did."

Then Felix spoke to her for the first time in the dream.

" 'You can sink altogether and smash yourself on the bottom of the well if that's what you want to do,' " the dream-Felix told her. Susan now realized that the dream-Felix wasn't going to help her, and that, "I actually did have to do it myself, and I summoned up my determination and reserves of strength and pulled myself up and through the window."

When she emerged from the well of clothes, Felix had gone. Susan went looking for him, and encountered a friend, who told her that Felix wanted to "reward" her for her effort, and had bought her a Porsche. The friend gave her the keys to the car.

"Then I woke up," Susan concluded. Significantly, this dream was signed "Love, Susan."

There are several interesting things about these dreams. One is that in neither is there any indication of a pre-existing intimate, sexual relationship with Felix, only the apparent hope that one might occur. Thus, Susan "shyly" reaches out to Felix, hoping for his hand, but Felix reacts in a completely professional manner, suggesting that she can sink into the well or rescue herself, it was her choice.

Other aspects include the repeated theme of being "captured." If one takes Freud's approach to dream analysis and assumes that the captors are symbols for Felix—or more accurately, Susan's desire for Felix to desire *her*—the meaning of the images is clear. Susan even indicates, at least in the first dream, that the prospect of being captured and held by a man "to have me all to himself " was not unpleasant to her. And the "Love, Susan" sign-off of the second dream does seem to suggest that at least at the time, Susan was signaling her availability to her therapist.

Besides the "Love, Susan" finale, a dedicated Freudian analyst like Felix could have read a lot more into the second dream. In this dream, the valiant Susan goes to rescue the kidnapped Felix, and finds him reduced—shorter, even—bruised and bloodied at the hands of the "counterfeiters," a "broken man," with tears and a trembling lip. Susan not only succors him, but even chastises him for *not* giving in. All Felix has to do to survive is to succumb to the demands of the counterfeiters, and in case Felix still doesn't get it, Susan will do it for him.

There follows the escape through the derelict house, littered with trash, culminating in the descent into the pit . . . of old clothes. Suddenly Felix is masterful, escaping the pit, while Susan is too weak, and sinking into the used clothing, falling deeper into . . . masks, for this is what the old clothing represents. Felix has lightly trod over all the used garments, and escaped, but she can't do it. She expects Felix to rescue her, but he says it's all up to her, to take care of herself. He disappears, Susan summons all of her will, escapes the pit, and Felix rewards her with keys to a Porsche, albeit not directly, the car being a symbol of wealth, style and power.

Felix, having worked as a psychoanalyst for more than ten years by then, could hardly have failed to interpret these dreams for what they were—an expression of a desire for intimacy on the part of Susan. Given his background, he certainly must have been aware of the sexual transference that both dreams embodied. In short, he had to have known that Susan was pursuing him; yet in reality, not dreams, it appears that he still succumbed.

Which in turn begs the question: why?

Why would a professional analyst, a man by then 42 years

old, a married father of two, the well-paid chief psychologist of a major metropolitan California county, experienced with more than a decade in therapeutic sessions involving all manner of patients, allow himself to be "captured" by a 17-year-old girl? A surrender that would lead, slowly but inexorably to his own demise, at the hands of the same girl, by then a 43-year-old woman, almost thirty years later?

The answer to this would turn out to have as much to do with Felix's long-buried secrets as it would with Susan's own mental competency.

7. SECRET FELIX

The emotional, then bodily, intimate encounter of two individuals is always freighted not only with the immediacy of their physical attraction, but also with the sum of their previous lives. Each views the other through the unique prism of their own past experiences, and interprets the other accordingly, although not always accurately. The mere act of taking off one's clothes doesn't always remove the mask.

In the mid-1970s, as Susan encountered Felix, she had little real understanding of the forces that had made the 40-some-year-old man who he was. How could she? Felix, born in Austria, a refugee, a child of the 1940s, a married father of two, had experiences that Susan could not begin to comprehend. Felix, for his part, likely saw Susan not for who *she* really was—a brilliant if eccentric, unhappy person—but as, literally, a living doll, a worshipping toy who was eager to be "captured," and later, controlled. And if Susan saw Felix as an ideal, Felix's view of Susan had to have been colored by his own experience in treating abused teenagers.

As the relationship between Felix and Susan, therapeutic or otherwise, progressed in the latter half of the 1970s, the marriage between Felix and Sharon began to crumble. For some reason, around this time, Felix stopped referring to himself as "Frank," his given first name, and began to use "Felix," his middle name. In early March of 1978, he requested that the state issue a duplicate psychologist's license in the name of "F. Felix Polk, Ph.D."

By this point, Susan had stopped going to school. Instead, she enrolled in classes at a nearby community college, and studied for the Scholastic Aptitude Test, with the idea of transferring to Mills College in Oakland. By 1977, she had enrolled there. She also had begun telling people, including her mother, Helen Bolling, that she and Felix were lovers. At one point, according to Susan, she told all the others in a group therapy session led by Felix that she and their therapist were lovers, which couldn't have done much to help the group dynamic.

Eventually, according to Susan, she told the same thing to another psychotherapist, a woman who was Felix's colleague, and also a friend of Sharon's.

"Felix was enraged by these revelations," Susan claimed later. "Felix told me I could never leave him or he'd kill himself or me. He told me he had a patient who was a CIA hit man. He said his patient had his wife followed everywhere and he was totally paranoid. Felix implied he could have me followed and killed."

By October of 1978, Felix had separated from Sharon once again. Susan moved into her own apartment in Oakland. Felix, she said, "got heavily into cocaine," during this period.

For Susan, this was all very heady, being the number-one inamorata of a powerful man. She transferred to San Francisco State University and worked toward a degree in English, with an emphasis on creative writing. Sharon, meanwhile, continued to live at the house on The Alameda, and Andrew Polk prepared to go to college. Felix shuttled between San

Francisco and Berkeley, unwilling to give up Susan, or sever all ties with Sharon.

By 1980, though, Felix made his choice: he and Susan moved in together, and soon bought a house in Piedmont, a small city just outside Oakland. According to Susan, Helen Bolling, her mother, helped them buy the house with a personal loan of $20,000.

By January of 1981, Sharon had once again filed for divorce. She wanted the court to restrain Felix from selling any more community property assets, mostly stocks—Felix had controlled all the money throughout their twenty-year marriage, Sharon declared, and since the separation, he'd liquidated many of the assets, and the proceeds had vanished. An injunction was issued, and by August, Felix and Sharon had reached a property settlement agreement.

Getting this division done was necessary for the divorce to proceed, so Felix could marry Susan. Sharon agreed to sign over any interest in Felix's psychology practice, his retirement accounts, and any interest in the Piedmont house he'd bought with Susan. Sharon also agreed to give Felix $40,000 in cash from a refinancing of the Polk home on The Alameda, which Sharon continued to occupy. She got the title to the house, and $2,500 a month in spousal support, along with financial responsibility for the mortgages. Felix agreed to pay for Andrew's college expenses at Tufts University in Massachusetts, and both children's health insurance premiums.

The divorce was finalized December 8, 1981, which cleared the way for Felix to marry Susan, by then 23 years old.

Felix and Susan were married the day after Christmas. But within five months, Sharon would be back in court, suing Felix. She claimed that he had stopped making the required $2,500 monthly spousal support payments he'd agreed to, a pattern of reneging on agreed-upon commitments that would be repeated more than two decades later, when Felix and Susan were going through their *own* divorce.

Meanwhile, Susan—according to her timeline—was discovering that being Felix's young bride was no bed of perfumed blossoms.

III.
FELIX AND SUSAN

8. LIVING HIGH

f Felix was grateful for being "chastised" by Sharon—who, after all, had supported him throughout the ordeal of his doctorate—that was clearly not the case with Susan.

Based on Susan's recollections, she was the one who was "chastised" in the new marriage. And in Susan's version, this began almost as soon as the *I do*'s were done. As Susan claimed later:

> Within the first week, Felix's demeanor changes. He ridicules me, threatens me, raises his voice, calling me a slob and a pig repeatedly, and demanding that I take care of him and the house according to his precepts . . . .

Felix demanded that Susan perform certain essentials, Susan said, including "sex on demand." If she ever denied him, Susan claimed that Felix told her, he would "have to kill me."

Within a week of the vows, Susan said, she'd decided that the whole thing was an awful mistake. She told Felix she was returning to live with her mother.

Felix became furious, she said, and attacked her with his hands, then threw her on the bed and raped her. Susan later wrote:

> *I am in shock, and I retreat inward, realizing I have gotten into an intolerable situation with no escape available to me. I conclude that I must never make him angry at me again or he will kill me, and I begin walking on eggshells around him for the next 20 years. Felix is doing a lot of coke [cocaine]. He hallucinates about ants.*

This version of the first week of the marriage later became powerful evidence to one of Susan's defenders, family therapist and domestic violence expert Linda Barnard.

Dr. Barnard, an expert on "battered spouse syndrome," and post-traumatic stress disorder related to this, came to believe that Susan was a quintessential victim of unremitting spousal abuse—if not always physical, then certainly mental abuse on the part of Felix, and that this abuse reflected a pattern that took place throughout the two decades–plus of the marriage.

The fact that Susan felt trapped, and that she claimed to be held by fear that Felix would kill her or have her killed, was all too typical of most abused spouses, Barnard contended.

Whatever the level of abuse, it does not appear that Felix was physically imprisoning Susan in their Piedmont house. She continued to attend classes at San Francisco State. And Sharon Polk, in suing Felix in May of 1982 for his failure to provide the agreed-upon spousal support, claimed to the court that Felix and Susan had taken a European vacation together shortly after their marriage.

By this point, Sharon Polk had moved to Chicago to attend graduate school at Northwestern University—she wanted to resume the academic career in music she'd abandoned for the sake of helping Felix get his doctorate in the early 1960s. In April of 1982, Felix wrote to her in Chicago, telling her he wasn't going to pay the court-ordered $2,500 monthly support. By that point he'd already shorted her several thousand dollars, since marrying Susan in late December of 1981.

"Dear Sharon," Felix wrote in April of 1982, "It is hard for me to write this letter to you but there is no choice left for me." The language echoes that of the old Harrison suicide note: Felix is desperate, "there is no choice left for me."

The fact was, Felix continued, he simply couldn't afford to make the spousal support payments. At the time he'd agreed to the settlement, Felix said, it was so close to his wedding with Susan that "I signed it with great relief and without really reading the fine print." He'd never intended to agree to pay her $2,500 a month in alimony, Felix said, but only in "family support."

Now that Sharon was living by herself—Jennifer had moved in with Felix and Susan even before the marriage—she didn't need so much money, Felix contended.

He'd been borrowing money for months, Felix added, "and now I am borrowed out." He'd even bounced checks, and all he had left was a valuable cello, which he would have to sell to pay for Andrew and Jennifer's education. He and Susan would have to sell the house in Piedmont, and Susan would have to take a part-time job. That June, Felix and his lawyer went to court seeking an order to reduce his spousal support payments.

Sharon wasn't buying any of this. She responded with a declaration to the court pointing out that Felix and Susan had just purchased another house in Berkeley, one that was far larger, on Elmwood Avenue, and rented out portions of this larger dwelling to four tenants, and that Felix had moved his therapy office into the new house as well. Rather than Felix's income decreasing, it had actually increased, Sharon contended.

Felix's claim that his expenses had increased because he now had to pay more of Susan's college expenses at San Francisco State shouldn't affect her interests, Sharon said in her declaration.

Petitioner [Felix] married Susan immediately after our marriage was dissolved. He had been involved with her for some time prior and evidence exists to show he was paying her

*expenses even before our separation. His planned marriage to
her was hardly unknown. The fact that his new wife's school
expenses have purportedly increased by $200 per month . . .
does not justify Petitioner's unilateral change in my support
payments.*

Felix's attempt to reduce his payments should be rejected
by the court, Sharon argued, especially if she were to have
any chance to earn her own doctorate in music, and gain future employment.

*If Petitioner wants to live high with his new young (pregnant)
wife, he should not be permitted to do so with me as the sacri-
ficial lamb.*

The battle between Sharon and Felix would extend over
the next year, with Felix trying consistently to reduce the
spousal support payments. Eventually Felix succeeded in convincing an Alameda County judge to cut the support for
Sharon by 40 percent, to $1,500. By then, Sharon may have
had the idea that Felix's professional connections with the
courts worked to her disadvantage, a theme that Susan herself
would put forth almost twenty years later.

Sharon was right—Susan *was* pregnant. In fact, the conception had likely occurred in April of 1982, four months after
the marriage. According to Susan, Felix didn't want her to
have the baby, but she talked him into it. By then, Felix, Susan, Jennifer and Jennifer's dog "Poko" were living in the
large house on Elmwood Avenue in Berkeley. Susan and Felix
had been able to buy the larger house, which contained three
rental units, as well as Felix's office, with the assistance of another $40,000 loan from Susan's mother, Helen Bolling. That
made about $60,000 in total that Felix and Susan had bor-
rowed from Helen by early 1983.

According to Susan, Felix detested Jennifer's dog, a tiny Lhasa apso. Susan later recalled:

Felix hates Poko and talks about killing him. Jennifer is very upset by Felix's kicking her dog. Felix laughs that the dog is so afraid of him, he urinates whenever he sees Felix. I think, hopefully, that Felix is kidding.

On January 3, 1983, Susan gave birth to Adam Polk, three weeks ahead of term. The delivery was difficult, according to Susan, because the baby was a footling breech; in other words, the infant was ready to come into the world feet first. Susan had agreed to have a natural childbirth, but when she was told there was a chance that the baby could be born with brain damage because of the possible delay through the birth canal, she quickly changed her mind. She demanded a caesarian. According to her, Felix became angry at "my show of a separate will."

Just after leaving the hospital with the baby, Susan got sick with an intestinal disorder. Felix wanted her to go back to the hospital, but Susan refused—she didn't want to be separated from her baby. Her fever reached 106 degrees, though, and she agreed to the hospitalization.

When she was finally released from the hospital, Susan later claimed, Felix told her that Sharon had agreed to move back in with him and help raise the baby if Susan died. While Felix doubtless meant this to reassure Susan that her baby would survive, in Susan's mind it had the opposite effect: Felix seemed indifferent as to whether she lived or died. Then, as she recovered from her illness, Felix began complaining that Susan was too entranced with the baby, that she didn't have enough time for him. He wanted her to hire a nanny. Susan refused. According to her, Felix accused her of being over-protective of Adam. Susan felt the criticism was unfair, and belittling—she often thought that Felix enjoyed putting her into frustrating double binds to see what she would do. It was Felix's way of entertaining himself and exercising hi power to manipulate others' feelings, she thought.

It could not have been all bad for Felix and Susan, though By late 1984, Susan was pregnant again, and gave birth to El Polk in June of 1985. As Eli's birth neared, Susan finally agreed with Felix to arrange daycare for Adam with anothe family in Berkeley. The other family had a nanny. Adam, a lit tle over 2 years old, soon complained that the Swedish nann had hurt his "pee pee."

On hearing this, Felix was furious. According to Susan, he complained about the nanny to the Berkeley police and the FBI. In Susan's recollection, an investigation by the authori ties into potential child abuse by the nanny was opened.

Meanwhile, Felix began working with little Adam in an ef fort to help him recall details of the alleged abuse. According to Susan, these were hypnosis sessions, although Felix called them "guided visualizations." At the same time, Felix pre vailed on one of his patients, supposedly a federal treasur agent, to look into any connection between the nanny and rit ualistic, Satanic child abuse, then much in the news. Eventu ally the agent recommended that the Polks buy a gun. Susan said the agent helped her buy the pistol, a .38-caliber revolver then took her to a firing range to teach her how to use it. Late she put the gun away and tried to forget about it—at least un til little Eli discovered it one day a few years later. That wa when she gave the gun to Felix and told him to get rid of it.

By April of the following year, 1986, 3-year-old Adam, Fe lix and Susan all began receiving counseling from a family therapist, Dr. Hugh Clegg, an acquaintance of Felix. The se lection of Clegg to counsel Adam would turn out to be a majo mistake.

Around this time, according to Susan, Felix's use of cocain became more and more frequent, until eventually it was a sub ject of gossip at the school of graduate psychology instructio he had started with Marty Kirschenbaum and several others; later, this institution would be faulted for its on-again, off-again accreditation, and characterized by Susan, among others, as a fly-by-night hotbed of drug use and group sex. In any event, Susan claimed she told Felix that if he didn't stop using the drug, she would divorce him. This seems to be the first time that Susan actually threatened him with divorce, but hardly the last.

"I think about leaving Felix," Susan later recalled.

I am upset about his drug usage and the way he treats me as an underling. But I am too devastated by the [Swedish nanny] satanic abuse allegations to take action. Felix also suggests *I* was abused by my father. He gets angry at me for talking to my mother. When I do bring up separating, he threatens me. Felix suggests he is connected to an intelligence agency and claims to have connections with various law enforcement agencies, which he in fact seems to have through his practice.

This, it appears, was when Susan first began to believe that Felix had some sort of sinister connection to the world of cloak-and-dagger, a notion that would grow ever larger in her mind over the next decades.

But there may have been a pecuniary reason for Felix's apparent effort to separate Susan from her only sources of outside support, her mother and father. By this point, Felix and Susan became embroiled in a dispute with Helen Bolling over the money Helen had loaned them to buy, first, the Piedmont house, and then the triplex on Elmwood in Berkeley. Helen had taken out new loans on her own property to help finance the real estate acquisitions. For a supposedly abusive, "crazy" mother, Helen seemed remarkably supportive of her daughter. Although Felix had promised to pay Helen about $450 a month on the second loan on the Elmwood house, he was soon "in arrears" to Helen, as he admitted to lawyers for Sharon in September of 1982. Sharon's lawyers were then trying to stave off one of Felix's unremitting efforts to cut down on his court-ordered alimony, and Felix cited this debt to Helen Bolling to show he could no longer afford to pay what he'd already agreed to pay to his former wife.

But the record also shows that Felix soon thereafter dismissed this substantial loan from Helen Bolling as a figment of Helen's "delusional" imagination. Helen had no proof she'd loaned the money, Felix contended.

Like Sharon, Helen wasn't about to let Felix off the hook. In June of 1986, Helen sued the marital community of Felix and Susan, demanding payment of just under $70,000, including interest, while asking that the Elmwood house be placed in a constructive trust to protect her interest in the property. Helen might have been a bit wiggy, to Felix, but like him, she was hardly stupid—she knew who owed her money. She had cancelled checks and escrow documents to prove it.

Felix hired a lawyer to contest Helen's claims. The lawyer said Helen was "insane" and "crazy" for making her claims. Helen wasn't about to take this without a fight.

"Said defendants," countered Helen's lawyer, meaning the marital community of Felix and Susan, "used information concerning plaintiff's [Helen] mental condition gained through a blood and confidential professional relationship to manipulate plaintiff into loaning defendants large sums of money."

In other words, Felix had used Susan to help con her mother out of the money. In fact, Helen was two years *younger* than Felix, which also suggested that even Helen was susceptible to Felix's blandishments, as Helen later admitted.

"I made a mistake with Felix," she said, contending that Felix had a way of manipulating people to get them to do what he wanted.

But when Helen wanted her money back, or at least paperwork to secure her loans, Felix refused, and then suggested Susan's mother was delusional in claiming that any loans had ever been made.

"Specifically, the defendants suggested to plaintiff in oral communications and in letters addressed to her that plaintiff was insane, or crazy, and that said loans were figments of her imagination, or that they did not exist, and that plaintiff needed therapy rather than repayment," Helen's lawyer asserted.

Neither Helen or her lawyer seemed to be aware that four years earlier, Felix had readily admitted these "imaginary" loans under oath in his battle with his first wife Sharon, which seems to prove conclusively that Felix could and did lie when it was to his advantage.

The most interesting thing about this dispute is that Felix and Susan denied the debt by claiming that Helen was delusional, despite the fact that Helen had escrow papers and cancelled checks to prove her investment. This seems to have been a defense Felix resorted to whenever it was necessary—simple denial, supported by an accusation that the opponent was "crazy," or "delusional." He had said as much about Sharon, then Helen, and eventually Susan. This always had the effect of putting the opposition on the defensive. Of course, Felix was the psychologist—if *he* said you were delusional, you must be, because he was the authority, and had the degrees to prove it, as well as the connections to make it stick. In the vernacular of the psychobabble of the 1970s, it was a "power trip."

This pejorative use by Felix of the prejudicial terms "delusional," "crazy" and even "paranoid," in order to evade responsibility for his own conduct, or to attack his enemies, was one reason why Susan later vehemently rejected any attempt by her serial lawyers to offer a defense of "mental defect," even after she was charged with the murder of Felix. To accept a diagnosis of mental disorder was, in Susan's mind, only to validate her deceased husband's lying hypocrisy in misusing his professional authority.

While several of these attorneys hired by or assigned to Susan eventually suggested that she did, in fact, have a viable "mental defect" defense to the charge of her husband's death, she simply wouldn't hear of it. In the perceptions of these defense lawyers—almost all of them shocked by the vehemence of Susan's rejectionist posture—Susan was a client who consistently displayed signs of mental disturbance that could be used for mitigation if not outright acquittal. But if legal advisors persisted in trying to persuade her to adopt a mental defect defense, Susan would fire them. And did, seriatim.

To Susan, taking a psychologically based plea was only another form of being manipulated, and any psychological or legal expert who suggested that *she* had mental problems, not Felix, was by definition on Felix's side in the War Between the Polks. Moreover, to Susan, it meant that the shrinks, all of them, were either in on or the dupes of Felix's plot to control her, commit her or maybe even kill her, even after Felix was dead. None of them, to Susan, was to be trusted.

"Therapist," Susan later wrote, then divided the word into its syllables for a new meaning: *"The rapist."*

Linda Barnard, the expert in domestic violence, eventually concluded that Susan's steadfast repudiation of any psychological explanation for her acts, even when she was charged with Felix's murder, made sense once one considered the background of the marriage.

"If you've been controlled by somebody for your whole life, and you suddenly regain your freedom, you don't want anybody ever to control you again," Dr. Barnard observed. Any psychologist or psychiatrist, in Susan's mind, was a threat to control her, just as Felix had for most of her life. And to Susan, control only meant more abuse. She would rather spend the rest of her life in prison than put up with that.

Besides, to Susan, she wasn't the one who was mentally ill. To her, instead, Felix was the one who was crazy.

9. "THE BAD PEOPLE"

In an extraordinary public presentation in February of 1988, Felix said he knew for a fact that "Satanists" had "ritualistically" raped, beaten, killed and even eaten children, all as part of elaborate rituals caught on tape.

He had a witness, Felix insisted—his own son, Adam Polk, then just over 5 years old.

Later, this lurid exposition by Felix on the ubiquitous evil of Satanic Ritualistic Child Abusers would perplex both his friends and enemies. Felix's detractors, and there were many, contended that in espousing this child-killing Devil-worship as fact, Felix only wanted to get his name in the papers and on television—in other words, it was all about him. He just wanted to be lauded and publicly celebrated as an expert in the field.

Others said it was more cynical: Felix just wanted to cash in on fears by credulous mothers and fathers, and worked overtime to scare them to death with the notion that covert Devil-worshippers had indeed targeted their children for rape, if not ritual murder and cannibalism. Scaring people was a potential moneymaker, and Felix was quite happy to spread the paranoia around wherever he could, or so these critics said. Bread cast upon the waters meant bread eventually winding up in Felix's personal bank account in the form of therapy fees, some thought.

On the other hand, Felix's loyal supporters swore that Felix had taken up the cudgel against the fabled Satanists because he truly believed in what he was saying. These folks thought that Felix believed in evil and the Devil the way Newton believed in gravity—it was real, it was measurable, it was everywhere. The fact that Felix assembled a collection of books on the occult convinced them that Felix was serious about the ominous threat—he intended to know his enemy.

There was one other school of thought: that Felix himself was delusional. But just what Felix actually believed, and what he *said* he believed, has always been difficult to sort out. His ability to conjure up alternate "realities" in the minds of others was, after all, his forte.

By the time of his "ritualistic child abuse workshop" presentation to the Fourth Annual Two-Day Conference of the California Consortium of Child Abuse Councils, held at a hotel in Oakland, Felix had already been featured on the local evening news leading a vigil against the "Satanists," and had even organized—apparently with Susan's logistical help—a "support group" calling itself "ENOUGH!" for those who wanted to chase the Devil away from their children.

Felix made this presentation in February of 1988. He followed a very tough act: a young woman who spent twenty-five minutes claiming that "Satanists"—her own family, no less—had murdered babies she'd had out of wedlock as early as the age of 8, and for ritualistic purposes. When a Bay Area television station showed up to film the proceedings, the young woman demurred—not because she was scared of the Devil-worshippers, she insisted, but because the issue wasn't about her, *it was about the children*. Felix didn't tell her that he was the one who had alerted the television people to be there—he wanted publicity, she didn't.

As it happened, this conference took place at a propitious time. Bay Area news media had recently disseminated several accounts of supposed Devil-worshippers, not least in nearby San Francisco, where a lurid trial was about to unfold over a grisly, "Satanic sacrifice" of a homeless man. In Los Angeles, the news was being dominated by horrific accounts of the then-notorious McMartin Pre-school, in which nursery school teachers had been accused by 3- and 4-year-olds, and their hysterical parents, of devilish sodomy and murder. Another similar case of alleged sexual child abuse had just erupted at a daycare center at the Presidio, the U.S. Army installation in San Francisco. It seemed that Devil-worship was real, and it was everywhere.

"I don't do this easily," Felix started, in his presentation.

> "My wife, Susan, was to have been here with me this morning. She will be talking tomorrow on the 'hot topics.' The reason she is not here is because my son, Adam, who is a Ritualistically Abused Child, is not doing so well right now. That's one of the reasons she's not here."

Adam, Felix said, had recently written a letter to the California governor, George Deukmejian, renowned for his lock-up-all-the-criminals mentality:

Felix read from the letter purportedly written by his 5-year-old:

> " 'Dear Mr. Governor,' "
> " 'I love you with all my heart. I want you to get the bad people in jail ["We call bad people, 'bad people,' " Felix parenthetically explained to the audience], because I hate them, Mr. Governor. I want to punch them. And my Mommy and Daddy want to punch them too. Everyone in my whole family wants to punch them. And my big brother can hurt them really

*badly and my Daddy can too. And they're not going to do it,
because you get in jail for that. And mommy can bite them,
that's all she can do. And I call them bad names, and scare
them. And I send this kiss to you, and my little brother Eli
can throw a truck at them. You should put them in jail because
they're bad. Have all the bad people get in jail, dear governor.
They should get in jail because they hurt me.*

    " *'I hope I don't have any more bad dreams. Make me not
have any more bad dreams, Governor, please.'*

"That's Adam," Felix said, and paused, waiting for the impact of 5-year-old Adam's violent angst to sink in. Then Felix
went on:

    *"I grew up very Victorian, and crying was not allowed in
my family, for men. I've come a long way. I'll describe myself
very briefly. I'm a psychologist. A clinical psychologist. I used
to be chief psychologist for this county. I was taught at UC
Berkeley, among other places."*

Having established his credentials, Felix moved on to his
proof—Adam.

    *"I want to tell you about the last two mornings of my life. I
awoke this morning at three-seventeen A.M. Adam was having
another bad dream. This morning's dream . . . he was dreaming that his legs had been cut off. Yesterday, I woke up at four-
twenty-two. That's pretty good, for me. And he was choking.*

    *"I believe there's just two ways of choking, in dreams. One
is . . . choking sexually, he performed oral copulation, so
there's that kind of choking . . . the other kind of choking is
the choking he has when he dreams his head's being cut off.
Because that's what he witnessed. He's choking on his own
blood. Or so we think.*

    *"Multiple personality? My son is a multiple personality. He
has at least three clear identities. He's a girl. Why is he a girl?*

Because he was dressed as a girl. Professionally made up. Then raped, on stage. In front of an audience. So he's a girl.

"He's a killer. He has the eyes of a killer. Less so now. Much less so now. He has a wonderful therapist. And I like to think that he has Susan and I [sic], as well. He's a killer because he was looked at by people who were killers. And he has dead [eyes], because he's also seen killings.

"And he has himself. He's a wonderful little boy."

Adam had other recurrent bad dreams, Felix said, one of them about Susan being murdered. In another she was taken away.

How did 5-year-old Adam develop these nightmares? Felix explained that he and Susan had placed Adam in child care with another family in Berkeley.

"And we left him there for four months. And we checked them out. We checked out references, we did all we could. We did what people typically do. While he was there—oh, and he spent four months there, probably about twenty times. Not every day, about six hours each time. We pulled him out when there were untoward signs. Like, he bit our dog so hard, that we had to get rid of a dog we've had for years. I loved that dog, we all did. He also developed fears, we didn't understand why. And I'm a psychologist. He was in the hands of professional people. And here's what happened to him.

"He was taken from this house after my wife had dropped him off in Berkeley. . . . He was taken in what he called a school bus to other places. Other children were picked up along the way. He was taken to a number of locations. One of them, it sounds like it was a warehouse. It had cement floors. It had cages. It had a platform for performances. And it had lines, fairly large from his description. The people were dressed in red. They wore masks. Triangular masks. And there were ceremonies.

"There were professional cameras ... cameras. Like, on TV sets [sic]. There were performances. He was, and other children were, raped on stage. Raped in every form imaginable. But there were other performances, too. Children were killed. He describes—here's the one that's the hardest for me—was his description of a baby put in a plastic bag and hammered to death. He remembers the blood. There were other ceremonies. If that's what they're called.

"There were blood-drinking ceremonies ... urine, feces consumed, throw up, he says. And there was a bloody substance, which is probably flesh, from bowls, at a table. At the table there were other children as well as adults. Some of the children may have been retarded. We think they probably were. There were some signs of that. There were black children, white children. They were all young children. And apparently some of them, perhaps a lot of them, didn't survive. What were their names?"

Felix gave a very long pause.

"Uh, I have a semantic issue. What you have just heard described is, I have to read it, 'multi-perpetrator multi-victim ritualistic child abuse.' Now we have a tendency in our profession to find names that neutralize what happens. I don't like that. I know that's meaningful, and I know it's the way we can talk to one another. And I think it's helpful to think about ritualistic Satanic child abuse in terms other than that. I prefer to think of it in terms of the brutalization of children. You haven't heard the half of what happened to Adam and to the other children, with whom he was abused in Berkeley and other locations. So I want to encourage the use of other terms than that one so that you'll retain the meaning, so that [the young woman who had just spoken] doesn't have to get up and be so, as graphic as she is. Or I. And I'm being as graphic as I let myself be right now."

Felix went on.

> "He saw other things . . . He saw the burning of children, the live burial of children, the drowning of children . . . Had enough? He did. Okay. That's what happened."

No one in the audience said anything.

"I like to use more direct language," Felix said.

> "I rarely hear, if ever, rarely, that when young boy children are sodomized or raped by men, I rarely hear the term 'homosexual' applied to that. And I want to lay that out for you right now, that . . . many of these people, the 'men,' as well as the women, are homosexual. I just want to say that. It doesn't mean that I have a bias against homosexuality. I only want to spell out for you that that's the way it is. Did you hear that? That's just the way it is. I don't know why we can't be explicit about that. I am. In my own mind, I am.
>
> "Um, I'm going to tell you briefly about what happened as a result of this. We went initially to the Berkeley police. They at first were not believing. And then they did believe us. We went to the FBI, and the FBI took it on as a case, investigated it for about a year. We went to the DA's office, the state, the county. The thing that Adam had done, because he's an exceptionally bright child, I like to say that, I'm proud of him for that, is that, he identified close to a dozen of the people. So we know who they are. And they know who we are. And what happened with these investigations by the Berkeley police, by the state, somewhat, mostly by the FBI is—nothing happened.
>
> "Zero happened. So people are still living where they live, some of them are fairly eminent in the community. Nothing happened.
>
> "If you read this morning's paper about the McMartin

case, the Presidio case, the last child dropped out [did not testify]. The chance of nothing happening is very high. I doubt very much that the McMartin case will ever, that anyone will ever be convicted in the McMartin case. And spend any time in jail. By the way, the McMartin case, and the Presidio case, you may or may not know, are cases of ritualistic child abuse. Are you aware of that? It's not possible to say more than that. So, nothing happened.

"There's one way which I did not identify myself. I also— I'm an older father. This is my second marriage. I have three children with this marriage. Two by a former marriage. I'm an older father. I am a survivor of the Holocaust. I was in hiding in Europe for over a year. Most of the time unable to talk, because German soldiers were billeted in the building, the farmhouse in which we were hiding. So I have a built-in sense of survival. And I have a commitment to not letting, ever letting, anything ever happen to my children, especially my children, that happened to me. It was a horror for us, we three children, in Europe, in France. So I have no understanding at all for the acceptance of what happened to my child. I have no— I don't understand how the parents of a child to whom this sort of thing is done can do nothing. Can accept that, can become passive. McMartin parents, many of them are depressed, they're not going to act.

"See, that's not my temperament. I've alienated some people, police, FBI, politicians, on that basis. I don't give a shit about that. I don't care. I intend to see that something happens, not just in the case of my son, but also for the children."

Felix paused again for another long moment.

"My rage is omnipresent. I wake up with it every morning. Every morning. And my son Adam doesn't have to be choking for me to do that. I am enraged. My tendency, of course, is to kill them. And I'm a rather moral person. I want to kill them.

You don't hear that too often on television, either. But I won't. Not now.

"My wife and I have formed an organization called ENOUGH! Some of you I know who are here already know of that organization. I'm not enamored with organizations on child abuse. I think they're mostly masturbating, they're not acting. I'm not enamored with masturbation. In this context."

The audience, uncertain of how to react to this, gave out nervous titter.

"I'm interested in action. *So is my wife. And nothing short of that. So our group, which has had some exposure now, on the media. Some people think we're interested in fame and fortune. They couldn't be less— That couldn't be less true of us.*

"Susan and I would love nothing better than to be peaceful with our family, and just go on with life. We can't do that. And we won't do that, until something else has happened to us, we simply will not do that. We long for that, long for it."

Felix invited those in the audience to join the organization he and Susan had founded, to help push for laws to make it easier to put "ritualistic Satanic child abusers" in jail. Among other things, Felix said, he wanted to see the rules of evidence changed so that hearsay evidence passed from child to parent could be presented in court, and that evidence from very young children could be admitted. The reason no one was ever prosecuted for what Adam said he saw, Felix said, was that he was not permitted to testify as to what Adam had told him, and neither was Adam.

The law did not have the right tools to protect children, Felix said.

"My son cannot be protected. He cannot be avenged now. We refuse to go through the process, the almost inevitable failing process, that the McMartin parents and the Presidio

parents, and that zillions, a number of other parents, have gone through.

"They come to court. They can't testify, the children can't, the parents can't, in most states. Hearsay is not admissible. How can my son testify? He was a year—he was in diapers when this happened. He was in diapers! When he was raped! He can't testify. The law doesn't make room for him to testify.

"So we intend to change laws. We will not change laws. The people who should be changing laws, will change laws. What we hope for is to get so many voices shouting at people to act, legislators—people who are equipped to have influence. The clergy, police, that they cannot be ignored. And we won't stop short of that. We'll up the ante to whatever we have to until something happens. We're committed to that."

Felix apparently noticed that some in the audience were skeptical of his story about Adam.

"You will have two reactions . . . I see them now. Some of you will open your eyes and some of you will close them. I see that reaction out there now. It's about half and half. I'm used to that. I'm actually gratified that more of you [are] opening your eyes rather than closing them. That's gratifying to me. It's gratifying. And as I get more graphic, I see those two dramatic reactions.

"Opening and closing. I encourage you to hold them open long enough to see and not to do what is so tempting to do, which is to deny, or to relegate to insanity, something that in fact happens on a large scale all over the country."

The moderator of the "workshop" opened the floor to questions from the audience.

The first thing that someone wanted to know was why the police and the authorities had been stymied in investigating Felix's story about Adam's supposed experiences.

"What were the reasons they articulated, to go no further?"

"There were a number of reasons that were articulated and some which were not," Felix responded.

"The reasons which were articulated were, that in the case of the Berkeley police, they're simply not equipped or sufficiently informed to deal with this sort of a crime. With the assaults of people. The Berkeley police were extremely active for a time. There was some surveillance. They simply were not equipped or informed.

"At the federal level the FBI had to push hard to make this a federal case. The agent in charge was especially interested in the case, and involved, and pushed it through the federal attorney to get it investigated. And they had my son's testimony, it's on tape. But that's not enough. My son can't testify. He can't testify, we, my wife and I, and others, his therapist or police and FBI, are second-hand witnesses, it's called hearsay. And so there was no way to prosecute, there were no federal offenses found.

"If there were found, pictures of my son on videotape, there would have been a greater basis, or some cross-state transportation, but none of that occurred. So there was no basis for a federal prosecution. Is that enough of an answer?"

Another member of the audience, apparently a police investigator, wanted to know what he should look for in terms of physical evidence of Satanism if he happened to get a search warrant to go through someone's house.

The young woman who had claimed that her parents had eaten her babies fielded that one—she said that Satanists always consumed everything as part of their ceremonies, especially the corpses of their tiny victims. Anything permanent used in the ceremonies, such as chalices or candleholders or knives, would be concealed in plain sight, she said. In other words, no one could tell the things used for sinister purposes from ordinary household items. And, she added, even when evidence was found, it tended to vanish from the police evidence lockers, because Satanists had covert agents inside the police departments.

Felix backed her up on this point:

"While it may be hard to think about this, it's clear, although it wasn't at first to me or to a number of us, that Satanic groups are highly organized. And there are people who are well placed. In every part, the key parts of our system. I mean, that includes, some in law enforcement, some in the judiciary, some in rather high places. Some suspect, *quite* high places. And the closing down of cases, the finding of lack of evidence is, at times, I am sure, related to that. Cases are mysteriously closed down, evidence disappears. That is not a random matter. And I suppose as time goes on, it will become clearer and clearer how much involvement there is in the Satanic movement. It's been around for a long, long time.

"There are indications that it's related to Nazism. Some of you may know that. There are indications that after World War II, many Nazis, a significant number of Nazis, who were . . . [Satanists] made their way to this country, and headed up, choreographed, the Satanic movement.

"Did you know that Nazism, the rituals of Nazism, were often Satanic, were you aware of that? That's a fact. Himmler was a Satanist. For example. Avowedly so. A practicing Satanist. And he's a prime example. There were many others."

Felix was asked to describe the characteristics one might expect to see in a ritualistically abused child.

The first tip-off, he said, was when a child began showing preoccupation with ritualistic behavior. The next was when a child began trying to replicate things that had been done to him, but with other children. For instance, Felix said, Adam had once placed a plastic bag over the head of another child. This was mimicking what he had seen at the "ceremony." For another, Adam had picked as his best friend in nursery school another boy who had also been ritualistically abused.

Felix now rather casually let slip the fact that Adam did not relate his story about the Satanists until more than a year after he was removed from the day care situation; of course, that made it impossible to verify the account by obtaining contemporaneous evidence.

Then, when asked how he had managed to induce Adam to speak of the horrible events—how he'd managed to overcome his fear—Felix made another revealing remark.

> "I think with our son—let me just say a few words about that. With our son, I think you have to . . . uh . . . enter his world. The world of the child. And that means something to me, and to my wife. And to his therapist, who does that. And we even become 'the bad people,' sometimes, in order to connect with his fears. And then we do things, after he's recalled, not just in his head, but with his body and his feelings and with every possible way.
>
> "Then we parent him. We enclose him with safety. And we do that a lot, both my wife Susan, and I . . . do that a lot. We do that every day of his life. More than once. And we . . . He's very comforted by the fact that, a number of things, one that, I'm not a gun owner, that we have a burglar alarm, that we do, every hour of our lives, we do something to get 'the bad people.' That's very comforting to him."

Felix had just lied about the gun ownership—the records showed that Susan had bought the .38 revolver in 1985, over two years earlier.

But Felix went on with what Adam had supposedly required of his parents:

"'What did you do about the bad people today?'" Felix said Adam often demanded.

> "Just now, before I left home, just now, he said, 'Are you going to a meeting about the bad people?' I said yes. He said 'Good.' So those are some of the things that we do."

10. IMPLANTS

So what was going on with this?

On the surface, these claims by Felix were . . . well, bizarre. Babies being murdered and raped, eaten even, in a warehouse somewhere in Berkeley, California—by red-robed, triangular-masked adults, some of them "eminent in the community," and whose photographs were identified a year later by a 4-year-old who was "in diapers" when this supposedly happened.

It was literally unbelievable.

For one thing, where was the evidence? Where were the bodies or even remnants of the bodies? To be graphic, as Felix put it, the bones and the blood?

Why weren't there any missing persons reports—surely someone, somewhere, must have noticed the disappearances of so many children. What about grandparents? Wouldn't they have noticed the disappearances, or did Felix believe they were Satanists too? It was verging on paranoia if Felix really believed all this.

Where was this supposed "warehouse," and why hadn't someone noticed what was going on there, with so many in attendance, including "TV cameras," and even, apparently, "lines [of people], fairly large."

What about the "burning," "drowning," "live burial," of children? Where did these events take place, and why hadn't anyone noticed them?

And what about those whose photographs had been "identified" by Adam—despite the supposed masks? Wasn't it likely they all had verifiable alibis—that they couldn't have *all* been at the same place at the same time, and could prove this?

In fact, how did little Adam survive these "ceremonies," and live to tell about them, while all around him other children were being hammered, decapitated, burned, drowned or buried alive? And—where did all this violent imagery in the mind of a 4-year-old come from?

The more one tried to penetrate the mist of these assertions by Felix, the foggier it got. All was utterly vaporous, a throwback to the Salem witch trials of the late 1600s. And in fact, that was exactly what Felix was demanding, with his group ENOUGH!—a return to judicial practices that had been repudiated centuries before, in a time of trial by ordeal, in which guilt was established, not by demonstrable fact and reason, but by superstition, augmented by lies.

In short, Felix was attempting to create a sort of mass paranoia—the Satanists were everywhere, were all-powerful. They'd infiltrated not only the police, but the judiciary, the government, even "quite high places."

In the scenario advanced by Felix, no one was safe from the Devil-worshippers.

They were everywhere.

What really took place in those "guided visualizations" that, according to Susan, Felix had conducted with then 3-year-old Adam? To what extent were the lurid details actually the result of suggestive questioning—embroiderizations implanted by Felix into little Adam's imagination, then retrieved as "evidence" for Felix's own self-aggrandizement?

This would become a crucial question later, when one had to consider the origin of Susan Polk's own rather peculiar perceptions. Was Felix capable of such insidious mental manipulation? Could he really make his own 4-year-old son into a ventriloquist's dummy, or even his 20-something wife?

Was Susan's own most valid defense against the eventual accusation of cold-blooded murder a viable claim of delusion, a mind-set to validate her own countervailing "power" against Felix—that Felix was evil, and that as a "psychic," she knew him for what he truly was?

Had her husband driven her mad? Was Felix himself responsible for his wife's "delusions"? And if so, did this manipulation eventually result in Felix's own death at the hands of the golem he had created?

These questions would turn out to be the principal issues in the demise of Felix Polk. Who was fooling whom? Or did real madness rule, and if so, who was the more mentally unstable, university degrees aside?

Sometimes "we even become 'the bad people,'" Felix had told his audience. Transference role-playing was at the heart of late 20th-Century psychoanalysis. Properly done—done with honesty and distance and objectivity—it could be very helpful.

But badly done—perverted to boost the analyst's own sense of self-worth—it could be devastating to those it was inflicted upon. It was just such loaded inquiries by eager "therapists" that caused the McMartin fiasco in Los Angeles.

In that notorious case, which unfolded between 1983 and 1990, seven people, all of them affiliated with a pre-school in Manhattan Beach, California, were charged with hundreds of counts of child molestation of their 3-, 4- and 5-year-old attendees. Five of those who were charged with notorious crimes were grandmothers.

By the time the case was concluded in 1990, millions of

dollars had been spent by the Los Angeles County District Attorney's Office, the lives of scores of children and parents had been upended, if not permanently scarred, and the falsely accused had spent months, and in one case, years in jail.

So much for Felix's prediction that "no one" would spend time in jail in connection with the McMartin case; by the time of Felix's presentation in 1988, Raymond Buckey of the McMartin school had already been incarcerated—without conviction—for over 4 years, either awaiting trial, or on trial.

No judge, in the atmosphere of nationwide lynching of the so-called "Satanists," had the courage to grant him bail. This had to be one of America's most feeble exercises of jurisprudence.

By the time the case against Buckey was finally dismissed for lack of evidence in 1990, almost seven years of his life had been devoured by baseless hysteria. The whole thing had centered on the "evidence" of 3- and 4-year-old children who had essentially been told what to say by adults eager to collect government money provided to them to get the incriminating statements. And then the children had repudiated the statements.

The fantasies and fears of adults, and the cynical political posturing of a district attorney's office in Los Angeles County, had used the impressionable minds of little children to further their own selfish agendas. Eager to please their adult interlocutors, eager to join in, eager to be praised by adults, the McMartin children confirmed everything the "experts" at the government-funded clinic asked for, and even added more.

Prominent in the hundreds of videotaped interviews with children as young as 3 years old was the use by the adult interviewers of anatomically correct dolls to simulate sex acts, all part of their effort to elicit useful "testimony" from the toddlers.

Meanwhile, Governor Deukmejian's administration had provided money for the victims of crimes, and the cooperating

McMartin families were each eligible for up to $23,000 for the supposed horrors inflicted upon them.

In short, the McMartin case was a hurricane of government-financed paranoia—a form of mass madness that was very similar to Salem, Massachusetts, in the 17th Century.

But this raises the question: if one assumes that Felix, the professional therapist, the politically plugged-in guru of the New Age in Berkeley, California, knew for a fact that all this blather about Satanists was really just poppycock, why did he continue to circulate it?

Moreover, why would he use his own son Adam as a virtual prop in advancing this agenda?

Depending on how one saw it, for Felix, this might have been less insanity than it was a deliberate, cynical use of his child as a tool—an innocent victim of a nonexistent evil, that Felix wished to create for his own purposes.

That a father could use his 5-year-old child in this fashion—describe him as a "multiple," discuss him being dressed in girl's clothes, publicly assert that he had been sexually abused "in every way"—only suggests that as a father, Felix was far more interested in himself and his own public image than in little Adam's well-being.

There is objective evidence that Felix ginned all this up to boost himself. Although he told the conference attendees that he had reported all these horrors to the Berkeley Police Department, and that the department had investigated, a check in 2006 showed there was no record of such an investigation ever being undertaken, or even a report on the subject by Felix. So Felix again was playing fast with the truth when he claimed at the symposium that the police, the state, and the FBI had been stymied by the law.

Of course, the true believers in Satanism would say this only proves the Devil-worshippers have taken over the Berkeley Police Department.

The Berkeley records show only that Felix called the police department on November 21, 1987—three months before the "workshop"—to report finding a dead bird with its neck cut and "painted in unusual spots" in his backyard. Felix suggested to the responding patrol officer that "maybe" this was some sort of warning from occult forces.

The patrol officer reported that he didn't see anything unusual, according to the report. So much for Felix's stories of Adam identifying photographs of Satanists, police surveillance of possible malefactors, extended discussions with the county and state prosecutors—all of this was either prevarication or perhaps delusion on the part of Felix.

As for the FBI, it is true that one particular agent in that era had begun investigating reports of Satanic child murder, but in the absence of any evidence, the investigation was soon dropped, and the agent retired, although he continued to hold himself out as an expert in "Ritual Satanic Child Abuse"; his former colleagues in the Bureau agreed that the poor man had lost it.

In light of all the publicity Felix generated for his rather weird views about "Satanism," one has to wonder where the California Board of Psychology was hiding while all this was going on.

Felix's publicized remarks fell somewhere between sensational and reckless, and given that he was deeply involved in a private clinical practice—that is, seeing young, impressionable patients on a daily basis—the board's licensing arm should have taken the time to at least interview Felix to see if he was all there, mentally speaking, given his publicly articulated statements about the Devil and all his doings.

It does not appear, from Felix's license application, that the board was aware of his lengthy stay in the Navy's mental wards in the mid-1950s, or the diagnosis of his having suffered a "schizophrenic reaction, chronic."

But as it turned out, it wasn't Felix who had his ticket pulled—it was Hugh Clegg, Adam's "wonderful" therapist, first praised by Felix to his audience in February of 1988, then sued by him in June of 1989 . . . for, of all things, allegedly committing sex acts with his patients, including none other than little Adam Polk.

11. SECRETS

Just how Dr. Clegg metamorphosed in Felix's mind into one of "the bad people" isn't entirely clear. Susan's timeline sheds little light on the matter, besides noting that Felix had selected Clegg to conduct therapy with Adam. Clegg had first been licensed by the state of California in 1977, so it wasn't as if he was inexperienced. As Susan recalled,

> Hugh Clegg sees Adam for a while—about six months, a year. He gives Adam tea to drink. Adam does not like Hugh and he doesn't want to see him. When Adam describes what sounds like hypnosis with Hugh, I end the therapy relationship, with a plausible excuse.

But in a lawsuit Felix filed against Clegg in June of 1989, a lawyer for Felix asserted that between April of 1986, when he first began seeing Adam, and June of 1988, when he was fired,

> defendant Hugh G. Clegg engaged in a continuous course of lewd and lascivious conduct and sexual activity with the minor . . . .
> Defendant knew, or in the exercise of reasonable diligence should have known, that the minor . . . was peculiarly

susceptible to emotional distress, but nevertheless used his
position of power and trust . . . with the intent to injure the
minor . . . and inflict serious physical and mental harm.

This suit was filed by Felix two days after Clegg had been
examined by the state's Board of Behavioral Sciences.

A formal report to the board held that Clegg was: too emotionally fragile and paranoid at this time to render therapeutic
services. Such a conclusion represents a consensus of opinion
of the examining psychologist, his own treating psychologist
[Felix?] and the subject himself.

The fact that Felix sued Clegg two days after this examination was completed in June of 1989 suggests that the board's
examiner had told Felix of her preliminary findings, which
might indicate Felix's access to government pooh-bahs, a
theme that Susan would later rather more volubly assert.

The board examination of Clegg had first been ordered in
early 1989, in part because of complaints made against him
by Felix, and several other parents in the summer of 1988, after the Polks had fired him. In fact, four of Clegg's young
patients, ranging in age from 2-and-a-half to 9 years old, asserted that Clegg had acted inappropriately with them.

In the case of the 9-year-old, it was alleged that Clegg,
while playing a video game with the child, "became excited,
screamed 'Die! Die!' and wrapped a telephone cord around
the child's neck." The child's mother told officials that she'd
smelled alcohol on Clegg's breath when she came to pick the
boy up.

In the other cases, all involving children about 3 years old,
Clegg was said to have spanked their bare bottoms, used
anatomically accurate dolls to simulate sex acts, and told the
little children that they were "bad people," or that their parents
were "bad people," and that the "bad people" would die and
burn in hell.

At first, after these allegations and the Polks' lawsuit, Clegg fought back. He hired his own lawyer, who said that, at least in the case of Felix and Susan, the real problem was a lack of parenting skills.

But by early February of 1990, Clegg was in bankruptcy. Based on the examiner's report, Clegg agreed to give up his license. He moved to Washington State, where, according to Susan, Felix tried to pursue him with a new complaint to licensing authorities.

The striking thing about Clegg's demise is how it paralleled the allegations in the McMartin case, even then dribbling to its pathetic no-evidence conclusion in Los Angeles, as well as Felix's own prescription for dealing with these supposed recovered memories of small children. The use of simulated sex acts with the anatomically correct dolls was right out of the McMartin playbook, and Susan's claim that Clegg gave Adam tea to drink—not confirmed in the examiner's report, however—was classic Felix, at least in Susan's description of his therapeutic technique.

Most interesting was the role-playing—becoming "the bad people" in order to facilitate the little patients' capacity to confront. That was pure Felix.

By the time Clegg was skewered by the state's examining board, Susan had given birth again, this time to Gabriel Polk, who came into the world on January 10, 1987. Within a few years, according to Susan, Felix was providing "guided visualizations" to all three of their little boys, usually in his office at the family home.

By 1990, the marriage between Susan and Felix, always volatile, was venturing into dangerous territory. Susan, now in her early 30s, and responsible for the care of three small boys ages 7, 5 and 3, resented criticism of her parenting by Felix, who, to Susan, did almost nothing to help, but said a lot, most of it negative.

Worse, she began to suspect that Felix was having affairs with other women. Once she discovered Felix embracing a female colleague in his office in the Polk family home. But Felix was always able to reinduce her obedience, Susan said, often by telling her that she was mentally unstable, that she could not survive without him.

> Felix [again] suggests I was abused by my father, and that my mother must have known. I write a letter to my father, accusing him. I go to see Gloria Gregg, a psychologist in San Francisco. I explain that I have married a man the same age as my father, and that I feel very uncomfortable about my relationship with my husband.
>
> Dr. Gregg remarks that she sees a divorce as possible. Felix has warned me not to say anything about him having been my therapist or having sex with him while he was my therapist. He is afraid he will lose his license.

Susan told Felix what Gregg had said. Felix made her write a letter to Gregg, defending her marriage. Yet she kept fantasizing about leaving Felix. But whenever she began to talk about this aloud, Felix would warn her: he'd take the boys, and she'd wind up with nothing, probably living in an institution for people who were mentally ill.

Meanwhile, the battle between Felix and Susan's mother, Helen, escalated. Eventually, it appears, Felix conceded his debts to Helen, but in a backhanded way: the Polks bought a small apartment building in Berkeley, and Helen was granted a one-half interest in the property, representing money she had previously loaned Felix and Susan.

But almost as soon as this deal was signed, Felix pulled another fast one: he soon refinanced the apartment building, removing $164,000 in equity, and bought another apartment house in Piedmont in only his and Susan's names, without telling Helen Bolling that he'd used their joint asset for his own purposes.

According to Susan, Felix continued to discourage her from maintaining contact with her mother.

"Felix acts as if my mother is crazy and a nuisance," Susan recalled. "He complains that she makes *me* crazy when I talk to her. Therefore, I *can't* talk to her." This was a problem, Susan added, because Helen managed the four apartments in Berkeley that Felix and Susan had a half-interest in, and Felix had made Susan responsible for managing their money. It was yet another double bind: Susan had to know about the income and expenses of the building to properly manage their assets, but she couldn't communicate with the resident expert, her mother. Whatever she did, she would be "wrong," the way things had been set up.

Meanwhile, Helen was unhappy that Felix had refinanced the property without her consent. Essentially, Felix had taken Helen's equity and converted it for his own use. Eventually, the disputed ownership interests in this Berkeley apartment building would become one of the major stumbling blocks in the divorce case of Felix and Susan in 2001 and 2002.

In short, the entire domestic situation of the Polks—father, mother, sons, in-laws—was fraught with nearly continuous tension as the 1990s unfolded. That was when Susan reverted to striking out at an old, familiar, even reliable enemy: the schools.

12. CONSEQUENCES

By the mid-1990s, the Polk family had sold their house in Berkeley, and moved back to Piedmont, in part because Susan thought the schools were better there. According to her, Felix had promised that the Piedmont school officials were willing to accept the boys before the actual move, but this wasn't the case—they faulted her for illegally enrolling the boys before they actually lived in the district. Susan felt that Felix had set her up to fail, just so he could blame her. It was typical, she felt, of Felix's psychological manipulation: anything went, as long as it put those he was emotionally dependent upon in a defensive position.

As Susan later saw this period, there was a large disconnect between how she saw herself, and the way Felix treated her. To her, Felix continued to treat her as a juvenile patient, rather than the 30-something woman she had become. She felt disparaged, belittled.

Susan thought that every time she tried to discipline the boys, Felix would take their side of the dispute. He even told them to come fetch him from his office if Susan began "acting out," as if she were a rebellious teenager, not their mother. For Susan this was humiliating; for the boys, it was debilitating, as they began to lose respect for their mother. Yet Felix always seemed to blame her when the boys got into trouble.

"The boys are more and more unruly," Susan noted.

In her mind, Susan began to dream of getting away from Felix: taking the boys away from him, finding a new place away from the Bay Area, someplace quiet and clean, where life could be simple—idyllic even. More and more these images of the perfect place came into her mind—the mountains of Montana, say, or Wyoming, or even Canada, where the woods were soft and green and the streams were pure. Anywhere away from the oppression she felt from Felix.

But whenever Susan summoned the courage to confront him with the topic of divorce, Felix belittled her, saying she wouldn't be able to cope without him.

"Think of the consequences," she said Felix would tell her. And eventually, she began to believe that what he was really saying was that he would kill her if she ever left him. From there, she even began to think that, as angry as Felix would be in the event of a divorce, he might even try to kill the boys to punish her.

"I backed off, never really taking a firm position about leaving," Susan recorded in her timeline. "I was frightened."

In one confrontation, Felix again suggested that without him, Susan would never be able to take care of the boys and the family's dogs. Then he told her that one of the dogs, Max, "looked sick." A week later, according to Susan, Max died. Susan thought Max had been poisoned. Felix suggested that one of the neighbors had poisoned the dog, but Susan suspected otherwise. In her mind it was a warning from Felix.

Despite her fears, by late 1997, Susan had become more confrontational with Felix. She insisted that he move his clinical practice out of the family house. His penchant for blurring the boundaries between his personal and professional lives began to really bother Susan. In her mind, it was as if the patients were part of the family, making it almost impossible to get clarity on the issues involving only Felix, Susan and the boys, as distinguished from the problems of the patients. For example, one of the families being treated by Felix was that of a fairly prominent Alameda County lawyer. The lawyer and his wife were divorcing, and in response, the children in the family began having problems in school. Felix counseled family members together and individually, at the Polk house, and soon he was directing the Polk boys to develop friendships with the lawyer's children. Eventually the lawyer's divorcing wife concluded that Felix was part of the problem, not the solution.

It didn't help a bit that the lawyer was one of Felix's closest friends, or that Felix wrote a report to the court in support of the lawyer's argument for custody of the children, despite the lawyer having allegedly tested positive for illicit drug use. To Susan—and to the lawyer's wife—this just seemed like another example of Felix's uncanny ability to sway judges. To Susan, it was almost as if Felix and the judges were part of some secret cabal, always in cahoots no matter the facts.

That fall, Felix was required to give a deposition in the lawyer's divorce case. When presented with an earlier court-ordered evaluation of the custody issue, Felix criticized the evaluator, another psychologist, for being "a drug vigilante." And when he was made aware of that psychologist's criticism of him for blurring the boundaries between friendship and professionalism, Felix dismissed it. "Can you distinguish between professionally and not professionally?" he asked, suggesting that it was impossible to differentiate between the two.

This was at the core of Felix's philosophy—all of life was grist for the psychoanalytic process.

Then, a little over a week after giving his deposition, Felix threw a surprise party for Susan's 40th birthday.

This event would be a watershed in Susan's understanding of what had happened in her life. As she looked around the

room, filled with party guests, she observed that every singl
person there was either a patient or a professional colleagu
of Felix. Susan realized that she did not have a single frien
of her own, no one who hadn't been brought into her life b
Felix. To her, it all fit together: Felix had his cult, his circle o
patients who were his friends, who were his admirers. He ma
nipulated them and kept them dependent on him, always ther
to worship him. Although the party was ostensibly for Susan'
birthday, in her mind it was really a celebration of Felix.

This was an intense experience for Susan—similar in
way to Felix's own sense, years earlier, of standing outsid
himself, listening to his voice as if it were an echo. It was lik
suddenly seeing everyone in the room as if they were robot
artificial people, all programmed by Felix. It was scary, al
most like something out of *The Stepford Wives*.

Then, like a bolt from above, Susan realized that she, to
had no life of her own—that everything she was, that every
thing that others thought about her, was merely the construc
tion of Felix. Felix had made her, and unless she got awa
from him, he would in the end, devour her.

As she sorted through this revelation over the next few week
Susan began to recall the events that had led her to her rela
tionship with Felix so many years before. Something wa
wrong; she knew it.

But what was it? Felix insisted that Susan's problems wer
all the fault of her parents—that her father had abused he
sexually, and that she had repressed this. That her mother ha
known about it, but kept quiet. These were the real causes o
her unhappiness, Felix insisted. Felix even told her that he
parents had murdered someone, years earlier, and that the rea
son they hated him was that Felix knew the truth. In fact, Fe
lix told her, he even expected that one day Susan's fathe
would try to kill him, because of what he knew. Or so Susa
later claimed.

But Susan couldn't get this picture straight in her mind. She could never make it match up with what her feelings told her about her mother and father. She kept thinking it was *Felix* who had sexually abused her, not her father. Felix assured Susan she was wrong, that she was confusing him with her father.

And then suddenly in her mind she knew she was right—it clicked together.

"I recall all of a sudden having been hypnotized by Felix, including drinking a cup of tea, counting backwards, guided visualizations, and being forced to have sex with him in his office while under hypnosis," Susan said.

I tell Felix what I have recalled, and that I can't live with him. I ask him to leave our bed. He does not deny what I've said. Instead, he makes a very firm threat. "You'd better think of the consequences," he says, "to the children. Have you thought about that?" Then, "You'll never get custody of the kids. You aren't fit." And, "I'll kill you . . . I'll have you followed, and brought back. You'll wind up in an institution."

That was when Felix began telling the boys that Susan was delusional and "crazy," Susan claimed. Felix soon made an appointment for her to see a psychiatrist, Dr. Shane McKay.

Before making the appointment, though, Felix, Susan said, warned her to say nothing about having had sex with him when he was treating her as a teenager. Moreover, she was to say that everything was fine in their marriage. Felix sat in on her first few sessions with the psychiatrist, according to Susan.

"Felix wants me to relate the content of the guided visualizations [those describing her abuse by her family] without labeling them as such, and to simply say that I remember these things and believe them to be true about my parents," Susan recalled. She complied with Felix's instruction, but added that it seemed like a story that she'd been told, not something that she had actually remembered.

Eventually, Susan did have a one-on-one session with Dr. McKay.

"When alone, he asks me about Felix, and I am too afraid to tell him anything," Susan noted. "I am terrified of Felix, and I am sad that he hypnotized me, raped me, and that he made me marry him. But I am not allowed to tell the psychiatrist this."

According to Susan, Dr. McKay provided some samples of Risperdal, a trade name for an atypical antipsychotic medication, and told her it was for "anxiety." The drug made her feel "off . . . It flattened my affect," she recalled. Because McKay had told her to stop taking the medicine if she felt any side effects, Susan called him.

"He says, 'Stop taking it,' " Susan noted. "And I do."

Later, Gabriel would pinpoint the year 1998 as the beginning of all the trouble between his mother and his father. He recalled a family trip to Disneyland in which he realized that Susan was unhappy. He asked her what was wrong, and Susan told him that she was just beginning to recover memories of having been sexually abused as a teenager.

In Gabe's recollection, his mother told him that this abuse had been at the hands of her parents; Susan's own recollection was that Gabe and the other boys were told this particular detail by Felix, not by her. It likewise appears that Susan did not at this point tell the boys that she had begun recovering memories of abuse by Felix. However, Felix told the boys that their mother had begun confusing him in her mind with her own father. This would be pretty much all of the boys' understanding of the demon ailing their mother, right up until the fateful night of October 14, 2002—that she had been sexually abused by her own father, and had confused her father with Felix.

Susan's version of the trip to "the Happiest Place on Earth" was that Felix treated her throughout "as if I am a mental patient."

On their return to Piedmont, Susan again raised the prospect of divorce. As she later noted in her timeline:

> *After we return, I again ask for a divorce. I beg him to let me go, offering him the kids, the house, all the money. He punches me in the face. He says I can never leave him because he adores me. He also says he can't let me go because of what I might say about him.*

The strain between Susan and Felix took its toll on the lives of the boys. In April of 1998, for instance, Adam and another 15-year-old were apprehended by the Piedmont police while wandering around the neighborhood at 1:30 in the morning. While nothing came of this, it appears that up to this point neither Susan nor Felix was aware of Adam's nocturnal roamings. A few weeks later, police were called to Piedmont Middle School, where Adam had gotten into a fistfight with another student at a dance. Adam claimed that Eli had told him that the kid had been saying bad things about Adam, and threatening Eli with a knife.

Two months later, Eli became a suspect in the burglary of the house of a family on vacation, in which $150 in liquor and food was consumed. After being confronted by a detective, Eli admitted the burglary, and began his first transit through the juvenile justice system, a path with which he would eventually become very familiar.

Then, in August, Susan went missing.

13. OUT OF CONTROL

According to the report he made to the Piedmont Police Department on August 8, 1998, Felix said that he'd last seen Susan around noon, when they had lunch. When he returned home about 6:30 P.M., Susan was gone. Food was cooking on the stove. Felix learned from one of the boys that she'd left just before he got home to take the other two boys to the Piedmont swimming pool. When, by 9:30 P.M., she hadn't returned, Felix called the police.

Susan was usually very reliable, Felix told the police. She always let the family know where she was going, and when she would be back. When asked about her mental state, Felix said she'd seemed "fine" at lunch, although "a little depressed." Felix thought she was simply "overwhelmed with too many things to do." For "known associates," Felix provided the name of Inger Kirschenbaum, obviously someone related to Felix's longtime mentor and colleague, Marty Kirschenbaum. Felix said he had called all of their friends, with negative results. The police went to the swimming pool, but could find no trace of Susan or her car. Teletypes were sent to surrounding police agencies to be on the lookout for her.

A little over an hour later, Felix called the police again, this time to report that Susan had come home. She had, he said, simply gone out to dinner and gone shopping "for boots." The teletypes were cancelled.

Susan later included this incident in her timeline, apparently to demonstrate Felix's penchant for controlling her movements. While leaving food cooking on a stove is an inherently dangerous thing to do, it seems quite possible—though not recorded in the police report—that Susan had told the boy who had remained behind to keep an eye on the stove, that dinner for Felix was being kept warm. Susan's decision to have dinner by herself seems to indicate her desire to distance herself from Felix and the boys, at least for an evening, as does her failure to call Felix to let him know where she was.

One thing is clear, however, and that is that the difficulties with the boys, and their continuing run-ins with the Piedmont police, were beginning to wear Susan down. Nor does it take a psychoanalyst to posit the notion that as the troubles between Susan and Felix mounted, the boys began acting out. In some ways, this was a plea to their parents to put aside their differences and pay more attention to *them*.

Over the next three years, police would be called to deal with numerous problems with the boys, usually involving fighting with other students, and occasionally, burglary. Most of the fights erupted after one of the boys had taunted another student as "a faggot," or some such similar gay-bashing; clearly some of Felix's attitudes toward homosexuality had percolated down to his sons. Gabe would be suspended from school twice, Eli numerous times.

In virtually all of these instances, Susan defended the boys, in some cases excessively so. Police as well as school authorities began to see Susan as a paranoid parental troublemaker. Her penchant for holding authorities to strict rules—almost playing the role of a lawyer—infuriated the principals as well as the cops. In contrast, Felix was usually seen—when seen at all—as the voice of reason.

Meanwhile, according to Susan, she began to experience what she thought might be symptoms of multiple sclerosis.

This began with numbness in her hands and feet after having shared a glass or two of wine with Felix every evening. She stopped drinking wine with him, and the symptoms went away. Then, in the mornings, Felix began giving her tea and coffee. He even left the house to get coffee, Susan noted. This was unusual, since he had never liked drinking coffee before. Soon she began to notice feeling drowsy after drinking the coffee. "I start falling asleep at stoplights," she noted.

After this, she decided to consume nothing given to her to eat or drink by Felix—she believed that he was drugging her.

Susan brought up the topic of divorce again. As she recorded in her timeline:

> "Felix hits me in the face. He pinches my mouth and cheeks, scratching and bruising my face. I begin crying, begging him to let me go. He is enraged. Threatens to kill me. He calls police after I am reduced to frantic effort to get away from him, and he tries to get me 5150'd.

Under California law, people deemed incapable of being responsible for themselves or a danger to others can be involuntarily committed for psychiatric observation under Section 5150 of the Welfare and Institutions Code. The authorities declined to commit Susan.

Meanwhile, according to Susan, the threats from Felix mounted, as he warned her about "consequences" of divorce. In her version of the events, Felix became increasingly violent with her, hitting her, bumping her around the room with his chest, shaking his fist at her, or "pinning me down." Sex was also growing more violent.

As the conflict between Susan and Felix grew worse, Felix continued to describe her as "delusional" or "crazy" to the boys. She insistently denied to them that she was "delusional" or "crazy." In fact, she said, it wasn't her who was crazy—it was Felix. At that point she told the boys about his extended stay in the Navy's mental hospitals in the 1950s. Felix blew up at her for telling them this, and threatened to "destroy" her, Susan said.

The confrontations continued:

> *There are scenes all the time, with Felix backing me up, pushing, throwing things at me, food, wine from his glass, the ottoman (which breaks and is then repaired), knocking over chairs, kicking the dogs, and hitting the kids on the backs of their heads, which he pretends is playful. He punches me, sometimes, in the arm, the face, or hits me on the back of the head.*

At one point in 1999, Susan simply packed up her clothes and drove away. By the time she got to Dublin, about thirty minutes away, Felix called her and begged her to come back, saying the boys needed her.

"Felix says he loves me, and alternately, that he hates me," Susan noted. She returned to the house.

By the summer of 2000, the Polk boys were pretty well known to the Piedmont authorities, especially the school district, as troublemakers. Things had gotten so bad with the schools, in fact, that the Polks decided to move to a new district for a fresh start.

But there would be one more incident involving the Piedmont police. In October of 2000, after Susan had again insisted that he move his practice to an office outside the house, Felix demanded that she find the office for him. Susan saw this as a setup: no matter what she found, he would be sure to disapprove of it. More angry words were exchanged, and Susan decided to stay out of Felix's way for a while by spending the day at the beach. She'd never done anything like this before, Susan said later.

Before she could reach the front door, though, Felix smacked her with the back of his hand across the face. Susan

began to cry, and Eli and Adam came to see what was wrong.
Felix grabbed her by the hair and dragged her up to the bedroom, telling her she couldn't leave, that she was delusional.
He forced her into the room and told her he felt like punching
her because she was "so provocative." At that point Eli
stepped forward and punched her in the mouth.

"I fall backwards, blood spurting out of my lip," Susan
later recounted. "Felix announces triumphantly: 'Look what
you've done to your son.'"

Adam called the police. Felix told her to say that she'd injured herself in a fall—15-year-old Eli, trembling, was afraid
he'd be taken to jail. Susan was taken to the hospital and received five stitches to her lip.

Later, some would point to this incident as the most critical
of the events that led up to October 14, 2002, the day that Susan realized she had to get away from Felix, and take the boys
with her . . . that if they were to have any chance of living
happy, productive lives, they had to get away from the malign
influence of their father.

But it would take Susan another six months before she
could bring herself to hit the eject button.

In November of 2000, they closed escrow on a house in
Orinda. The purchase price was $1,850,000, about $100,000
less than the appraisal on the property by the lending bank.
The Polks obtained a first mortgage loan of $450,000, and
hired a contractor to add a third floor, eventually financing the
addition with a second mortgage, which brought the total
monthly payments to about $4,000. That meant Susan and Fe-
lix had an equity in the dream house of about $1.3 million.

As most people know, it simply isn't possible for a couple
to spend their way out of marital difficulties. If anything, the
more one spends, the worse things get. Yet it appears that this
is what Susan and Felix tried to do.

That was when they moved into the house of dreams and
nightmares.

IV.
THE WAR BETWEEN THE POLKS

14. "TAKE ME TO JAIL"

The next six months unfolded with more confrontations between Susan and Felix. On January 14, 2001, Susan again brought up the topic of divorce. She later contended that she'd once again offered to forgo any spousal support, even any share in their community property, if only Felix would let her go. In her version of the events, Felix began screaming at her, threw all her clothes on the floor, and threatened to tear up every photograph of her he could get his hands on. He threw her out of the house, calling her "ugly," "vicious," "evil," a "criminal," and a "swine." The clash upset Eli, who stormed out of the house, then returned when police arrived.

The police report for this event substantially corroborates Susan's account, except that in the report, it wasn't Susan's clothes Felix was throwing around, but "papers," apparently credit card bills. Susan was angry at Eli as well as Felix, she told the police. Eli was "uncontrollable," she said, and he had recently incurred unauthorized charges on a credit card, which may have been what had led to the paper-throwing by Felix. Eli also had a very large knife that Susan wanted the police to seize. They did, telling Felix that he could come pick it up at the police station in a week or so, after things had calmed down.

Susan told the police officer that she intended to divorce
Felix, and was looking for another place to live. She said Felix had told her, "I will do anything to stop you from divorcing
me," which Susan took as a threat. She said that both Felix
and Eli had called her "crazy," a charge she denied.

Felix admitted that he'd tossed papers around the house in
a fit of anger. Both he and Eli said that Susan *was* "crazy," despite her denials.

Because no one had been struck, the police decided to take
no one into custody.

Upset over the confrontation, Susan drove to a motel outside Yosemite National Park, checked in, and then took an
overdose of aspirin in a suicide attempt. She fell asleep, then
awoke to a ringing in her ears. She called Felix in Orinda,
who called the police at Yosemite. The police dispatched an
ambulance to the motel, and Susan was taken to a hospital.

There, she met with a psychiatrist. Susan said nothing
about her early sexual relationship with Felix. He had warned
her to keep quiet, telling her that if it came out, he could lose
his license, and then she and the boys would have nothing to
live on. Felix told the psychiatrist he thought that Susan was
delusional, and wanted her committed, but the psychiatrist
didn't think it was necessary.

Things calmed down for a bit, but by February, Susan moved
all of Felix's clothes out of their bedroom, which precipitated
another angry dispute. She told Felix that she intended to get
the divorce no matter what. If Felix threatened her, she
warned, she'd get a restraining order.

Then, on March 16, 2001, Susan composed a note to herself on her computer:

> *The purpose of this letter is to document the unethical con-*
> *duct of Felix Polk, a licensed clinical psychologist in private*
> *practice in Berkeley.*

In this document, Susan claimed that while she was his patient and still a high school student, she had been drugged and "coerced into having a sexual relationship with him." Since marrying him, she continued, he had been psychologically and physically abusive.

"He has punched me on numerous occasions, and threatened to kill me if I ever left him." The violence from Felix was growing, she said. Should she leave the marriage, she added, he had threatened to withdraw all financial support for her and the boys. She quoted Felix: " 'I will simply stop working and this family will go down the drain. You will get nothing.' "

Felix continually called her "crazy," she continued, and had told the boys she was "crazy."

"He states that I come from a crazy family and that the dynamics in our family reflect my family dynamics rather than his." Felix always blamed her for the boys' problems, she said.

During the course of our marriage, Felix has at times drugged me. Almost four years ago, when I talked of getting a divorce, Felix employed hallucinogens. Felix then hired a psychiatrist to evaluate me for anti-psychotic medication while I was experiencing flashbacks. He refers to this period of my life as a psychotic episode. He denies the use of drugs in therapy, and would most certainly deny the use of hallucinogens. I know of no other way to account for the flashbacks which I experienced during that time period. I have never willingly used LSD or hallucinogens.

Susan wrote this letter, she said later, as "insurance . . . in case he kills me or dopes me up, and gets me committed."

Nine days after writing this letter, Susan told Felix that she intended to contact an attorney and would be filing for a divorce. Felix responded, she recalled, by "bumping" her around the kitchen with his chest, chasing her outside onto the patio, grabbing her by the wrist to prevent her leaving, calling her "unfit" as a parent, and saying he would get custody of the boys if she went through with the divorce.

Two days later, yet another fight occurred; this time it was Felix who called the police. Susan's version was that Felix lunged at her as if he was going to hit her.

"I pushed him back," she said. She then went upstairs to get away from him. It was about an hour later, she contended, that Felix actually called the police.

The police report for March 27, 2001, shows that Felix called for police assistance on a "5150," that is, the legal section authorizing the confinement of a person who is a danger to himself or others. As the responding officer reported:

> **The person reporting [Felix] stated his wife is increasingly paranoid and delusional. He claimed she kicked him in the back this evening.**

Felix told police that Susan had recently tried to commit suicide, and had been briefly committed under 5150. He wanted the officers to commit her again. For some reason, he identified himself to the police as "Frank Polk." In all of Felix's subsequent encounters with the police over the next eighteen months, he would always identify himself using his first name, Frank, rather than Felix.

The officers' report went on:

> He and his wife were discussing their pending separation/divorce. Frank stated Susan became very emotional and kicked him in the back when he turned away from her. Frank said his son Eli was present in the kitchen when the incident occurred.
>
> Frank said he had just told Susan he was not leaving [the house] when she kicked him. Susan said nothing to Frank when she kicked him. Frank called the police.
>
> Frank had the odor of an alcoholic beverage upon him. Frank stated he had one glass of wine this evening. Frank and Susan have been married twenty years.

One of the officers went upstairs, where Susan was watching television, to hear what she had to say. Seeing the police, Susan got angry.

"Why are the police here?" she demanded. "Why didn't they help *me* two months ago?"

Susan meant the January 14 confrontation, the one in which no one had been arrested.

The officer wanted to know if she planned to hurt herself or anyone else. Susan said she didn't plan to hurt anyone—but if Felix attacked her, she'd defend herself.

Now Susan wanted to know why Felix had called the police. Told that Felix wanted her to be taken into custody on the 5150 provision, Susan became visibly upset. She went downstairs to confront Felix.

"Both parties met in the kitchen," the police laconically reported.

Felix told the police that they'd been arguing about the divorce when Susan had kicked him. Eli was a witness, he said. Susan was still mad that Felix had been trying to have her committed, and was angry at the police for listening to him and not her, when she'd complained about his rampage two months earlier. It wasn't fair—it was only proof that Felix had the fix in with the cops, she thought. Besides, she hadn't kicked him—Eli was fibbing to get his father's approval.

The officers explained to Felix that they couldn't 5150 Susan, since she wasn't planning to harm herself or anyone else. Felix was unhappy; he wanted Susan removed from the house that night, and held for observation. However, the police said, Felix *could* swear out an assault complaint against her for the alleged kicking, and the officers would give her a citation ordering her to appear in court.

Susan became even more upset. The police reported:

Susan began yelling she wanted Frank to leave and if he did not, she wanted to be taken to jail. Susan continued to yell, "Take me to jail," several times.

Susan then reached out and slapped Frank with an open hand in the face. Susan said, "Now take me to jail." There was no visible mark on Frank.

Susan got her wish. The police arrested her and took her to jail.

One week later, Susan formally filed for divorce. She paid the lawyer's demand for a $4,000 retainer with a Polk family credit card.

15. "ACTING OUT"

The divorce suit, filed on Susan's behalf by Walnut Creek lawyer Andrew McCall, asked that Susan be granted custody of the boys and sole occupancy of the dream house. By this point, Susan was staying in a nearby hotel after getting out of jail. She also wanted the court to grant her a protective order against Felix.

"My residence is his residence," Susan said in the application for the protective order, "so he will have to get another residence." She wanted Felix ordered to pay her hotel bill until he vacated the dream house.

Then Susan dropped the hammer: she included with her application a 3-page, single-spaced document that contained the explosive assertion that

> During the course of therapy, Felix coerced me into a sexual relationship with him. I was sixteen. This relationship continued under the guise of therapy until I was 22.

Now it was out for everyone to see: Susan was accusing F. Felix Polk, Ph.D., the well-known expert in treating sexual abuse of children and teenagers, of having been an abuser himself almost thirty years earlier. And this was the real reason,

Susan believed, that Felix kept labeling her as "delusional" or "paranoid."

Who would believe her, once Felix, the expert, had diagnosed her as "crazy"? She wasn't delusional—she wasn't paranoid—she wasn't at all "crazy," Susan insisted. It was only Felix's attempt to skate on his nefarious conduct with her when she had been his patient. And this would be Susan's posture for the next five years, even after Felix was no longer on this earth.

Within a few days of Susan's divorce filing, Felix hired his own lawyer, who filed a response to Susan's claims. Felix wanted custody of the boys, sole occupancy of the dream house, and a protective order against Susan, declaring:

> I have never physically abused, or hit in any manner, the petitioner [Susan]. I also believe that I have never emotionally abused her in any way. What I hope to make clear to the court is that for the past three years I and our sons have been living in a sort of emotional hell with petitioner becoming more and more explosive and delusional.

He'd been trying to save the marriage, Felix said, and "protect the boys at the same time. I now see that that will not be possible."

As for Susan's charge that he had drugged her and coerced her into having sex while she was his patient, Felix provided what the politicians today might call a "non-denial denial":

> While I believe it to be irrelevant I feel I must address the opening paragraphs of Susan's declaration concerning how we became involved. It is true that she comes from a very abusive home where she was the victim of her father. However, our version of history differs.

Thus Felix did not specifically deny Susan's charge of the unprofessional relationship.

The main problem in the marriage, Felix said, was that Susan was out of control, emotionally, so much so that Felix feared for his safety:

> She has been repeatedly violent toward me and struck me many times. Recently I have been sleeping in a separate bedroom with the door barricaded. Petitioner has threatened my life.

After pointing out that he was a clinical psychologist with a Ph.D. from Berkeley, Felix said, "I do not, however, want to be in a position where I am diagnosing my spouse."
But on the next page, he did exactly that:

> *It is my opinion that Susan is, for the present, unstable and very angry, and not just at me. Her relationship with the boys is difficult. All the boys are experiencing difficulties to varying degrees because of her behavior. She "goes off" on people. Last year Gabriel was expelled from Piedmont Middle School after Susan had a confrontation with the principal and told him to "go fuck himself."*

At a hearing on April 6, Family Court Commissioner Josanna Berkow declined to order Felix to vacate the house, ordered both parents to attend a mediation session with the boys, and asked that an evaluator prepare a report on the custody issue. Susan moved out of the hotel and returned to the house, the protective order that Felix had obtained against her after the slapping incident having expired. For the next ten days, each parent eyed the other warily, both having been ordered by the court to have no contact with each other, although they were living in the same house.

Then on April 17, Susan and Eli got into another argument. Eli wanted her to drive him to a friend's house, and when she said no, he lost his temper and shoved her out of the house, locking the doors behind her. Susan called the police. Shortly after they arrived, so did Felix. According to Susan, he put the blame on her. After the police left, Eli turned to Felix.

"You have to move out," Eli told his father. When Felix didn't respond, Eli confronted Susan instead, and demanded that *she* move.

"There's too much tension in this house," Eli said. "Someone has to move."

The following day, Susan rented a vacation apartment in Stinson Beach, California, a seaside community in Marin County, miles away from Orinda, where she stayed for the next month. Late in April, however, Susan drove in to the Contra Costa county seat, in Martinez, to participate in the court-ordered "mediation" session.

In this encounter, Felix again asserted that Susan was "paranoid and delusional," and told the mediator that all of Susan's problems stemmed from the supposed abuse by her parents.

In Susan's version of this meeting, Felix became "erratic," and punctuated his claims by slamming the table and glaring at the court-appointed evaluator.

"But none of this behavior finds its way into the report," Susan said later. The mediator recommended that Susan be counseled for her "medication management," although Susan wasn't taking any medications, despite Felix's assertion that she had been prescribed Risperdal. The evaluator also recommended that both sides go to "anger management."

Three days later Susan called her lawyer, Andrew McCall, to tell him she wasn't satisfied with his work, and was therefore firing him. McCall thus became the first in a long line of lawyers to be fired by Susan over the next five years. She demanded a refund of a portion of the $4,000 retainer, complaining that McCall had used "creative accounting" to pad the bill.

Not only did McCall refuse to provide a refund, he provided a new bill for another $92.13. Susan noted that McCall hadn't even attended the initial hearing on the divorce. She soon concluded that employing legal representation was a waste of time and money, and that lawyers were by nature cheats. Henceforth she would be suspicious of all legal counsel, and insist on representing herself.

Susan's absence from the house didn't seem to help the boys very much. First Eli was expelled from school for possessing marijuana, then Gabriel was suspended for other misbehavior. When Susan remonstrated with him, "Gabriel asked me what I expected from him, after I was arrested, went to jail, and all of the arguing that has been going on."

"I'm acting out, Mom," Gabriel told her. To Susan, this was the end result of Felix's continuing attempts to enlist the boys against her, which had become obvious when Eli had punched her the previous fall, and had only grown worse over the following six months—at one point, Susan said, Adam had publicly berated her as a "crazy bitch" while she and the boys were having breakfast in a restaurant.

Yet whenever the boys "acted out," to Felix it was just new evidence of Susan's unfitness as a parent, her craziness. He absolved the boys of their bad behavior, which would soon crop up even with Susan living apart.

On the night of May 5, 2001, for instance, while Susan was in Stinson Beach, the boys hosted a party at the dream house. Around 10 that night, one of the neighbors called the police: couldn't they do something to shut down the raucous party going on at the Polk house?

Soon police units from the Contra Costa County Office of the Sheriff, the Orinda Police Services Department and the Lafayette Police Department converged on the dream house. Approximately one hundred young people, most of them teenagers, were milling around, many of them holding plastic cups filled with amber-colored liquid, which the responding police rightly guessed was beer. Officer Shannon Kelly of the Orinda department was one of those who responded. He warned "Frank" that as the only adult on the premises, he was legally responsible for the underage drinking.

Meanwhile, as another police officer made his way through the crowd toward the pool house, he saw two boys slug a third boy in the face with their fists. The officer yelled at the combatants to "Break it up," and started toward the trio, but all three boys ran into the pool house. Following, the officer found one of the boys with a bloody nose. Asked what had happened, the boy said that someone had grabbed some money out of his hand, and when he'd tried to stop him, he'd gotten socked in the nose. He had no idea who the two assailants were, the boy said.

Inside the pool house, the officer encountered Eli and another boy. Both said they had no idea what had happened, although they'd been standing right next to the fracas when it began.

The police decided to break up the party and warned Felix again about allowing teenagers to consume alcohol.

By May 12, 2001, Susan had decided that just getting herself out of the marriage was enough. She wrote a letter to Felix's lawyer, Steven R. Landes, saying she would not be asking for custody of Eli and Gabriel.

"They wish to remain in Orinda, and I intend to relocate out of state," Susan wrote. The custody issue didn't include Adam, who was over the age of eighteen, and legally an adult.

All that needed to be done, Susan continued in her letter, was for both sides to agree on spousal support. This should be simple, Susan suggested, and for that reason, "I do not see the need at this time for legal representation."

Susan vacated the house in Stinson Beach on May 23. Later that day, she and Eli were on a plane to Paris, France.

Susan noted in her diary as they were flying east.

> *This is the first trip I've taken Eli on. Of course, I've had all sorts of good intentions. I'll be the perfect mom. I'll impress him with my efficiency. My ability to remain cool, calm and collected while under the stress of traveling in a foreign country. My planning skills.*

This was clearly written tongue-in-cheek, because despite Susan's resolve, the trip was a fiasco—at least as far as Susan's desire to impress her middle son. To Susan, boarding the plane was an ordeal, the flight meal was poisonous, and the flight crew was abusive; when they arrived in Paris, the hotel rooms were crummy, and the exchange rate was extortionate. Over the next two days, she tried to interest Eli in the sights of Paris, but Eli seemed a million miles away—or at least seven thousand. He wanted to be back in Orinda. Susan thought that Felix had somehow manipulated Eli into feeling guilty about

> having fun without Dad . . . Keeps saying we couldn't survive without Dad. What has Felix done to instill such intolerable feelings in son? It is so hard for Eli to have fun, let go, enjoy life.

Eli was very discouraged about himself and his prospects. He thought of himself as just another high school dropout. Susan kept trying to encourage him, but Eli couldn't shake his depression.

Susan added:

> *Felix has done such damage. Unforgivable. So sad to see [my] son suffer. I try to find a way to protect and nurture Eli, but it is so difficult. He just won't let me do very much.*

Eli's unhappiness made Susan rethink her desire to get a divorce. She realized that all the boys needed her as a counter-

weight to Felix's influence. She told Eli she was thinking
about moving back to Orinda, but this seemed to upset Eli
even more:

> *"Be nice to Dad," he says, "you have to be nice to Dad."*
> *He seems fearful of his Dad. He says "I have spent Dad's*
> *money today, and now I must be nice to him." He doesn't seem*
> *to understand that it is also my money. "Dad's worked for that*
> *money, you don't work," Eli says. "Dad works every day of his*
> *life."*
>
> *Whatever I've done is completely unacknowledged. It is*
> *sad to see Eli so intimidated by F. So cowed.*

After three days in Paris, Eli called Felix and asked him to
buy a ticket so he could come home. Susan took him to the
airport, trying not to let him see her crying. She stayed in
Paris four more days before deciding she had to go back to the
dream house to fight for her children.

16. "CRAZY"

A few weeks later, Susan took Gabe on a trip to Thailand. As with the Paris jaunt with Eli, the vacation was not a success. Susan complained about the accommodations, the food, and the tourists. After two days, mother and son decided to abandon the trip and spend the rest of the week in Hawaii. There, Gabe's spirits picked up a bit, and they were soon joined by Eli. Gabe told Susan that Felix still loved her, and wanted her to come home. But Susan's feelings for Felix were completely gone—she saw him as a hulking wreck of a man, obsessed with playing mind games with everyone around him, especially his own family. Living with Felix for so long had begun to affect her mentally, Susan thought, noting in her diary:

> *Maybe become paranoid from living with paranoid person for twenty-eight years. Paranoia by osmosis. Am convinced F. is paranoid person. Cannot trust that anyone can just love him for himself. Believes he must coerce love and loyalty. Has deep seated fear of betrayal. Winds up creating what he fears most.*

When Susan and the boys returned to Orinda, Susan moved all of Felix's clothes out of their bedroom. Felix was very unhappy about this. Susan told him that as soon as she

could, she intended to find a house to rent in Montana, and th
two younger boys wanted to go with her. With Adam about t
enroll at UCLA, this would leave Felix all alone in the drean
house.

"F. went crazy," Susan recorded.

> First said he would support them, not me. Yelled at Gabe and
> Eli that if they chose to live with me, they were not his sons.
> Threatened he wouldn't support me, and then that he wouldn't
> support them. When they said they wanted to live with me, and
> they wanted a fresh start out of this area, F. said: "I will never
> allow that" and then, "the courts will never allow that."

Felix told Susan that the courts would consider her an unfi
mother because of her "mental illness."

Felix accused Susan of "brainwashing" the boys, and sai
that he didn't believe that Gabe really wanted to go with he
She pointed out that when he'd been divorced from Sharon
Felix hadn't objected to Jennifer going with her mother to Illi
nois.

> He said that was different because I'm crazy and Sharon
> wasn't. The boys then pointed out that F. had told them that
> Sharon was crazy many times. Gabe said: "even if mom is
> crazy, which she isn't, I would still prefer to live with her (me)
> because I love her, she's a good mom, and she's fun to be
> with."

According to Susan, Felix now "blew his stack" and bega
throwing dishes of food at her and Gabe, then kicked over th
big screen television set that had cost $5,000, and went on t
turn over an antique oak chair worth $2,500. Felix came bac
to Susan and waved his hands in her face, she said, and shak
ing his finger at her, swore he would stop working and giv
them no financial support.

The following week, Susan packed a rented trailer wit

clothes and the television, put the two younger boys and the dogs in the car, and drove to Montana.

By mid-September, Susan, Eli and Gabe were in Gallatin Gateway, a small community just outside of Bozeman. Susan found a hundred-year-old cabin just outside Yellowstone National Park, not far from a sparkling stream, just as she had always idealized. The boys weren't entirely happy though—moving from a suburban to a rural environment made them uncomfortable. Still, Susan got the boys enrolled in high school, and things finally began to settle down.

That lasted until late October, when Gabe and Eli went back to Orinda to visit Felix. When they returned to Montana, Eli was again using marijuana. This led to arguments between Eli and Susan. Eventually, Eli decided he wanted to live with Felix, not Susan. He left. Gabe was unhappy without his brother, so Susan decided she'd make one more effort to live with Felix. By early December, the Polk family was together again, and as unhappy as ever.

Then, in early January of 2002, Felix finally moved out, taking one of the Berkeley apartments the Polks co-owned with Helen Bolling.

But Felix wasn't giving up the fight. In late January, his lawyer filed a new petition with the divorce court. Felix wanted the house listed for sale immediately, as well as joint legal and physical custody of the boys. Felix declared to the court:

> Susan has been using the boys as a weapon and moving them around in ridiculous ways. While at present the boys are identified with their mother, the result is that Eli, our middle boy, is suffering. He is slipping in school, he needs to be evaluated for drug use, he is not going to classes, etc.
>
> I need to have regular time with the boys, and not have it

interfered with or manipulated by the petitioner [Susan].
Since separation she has a) moved with the boys for three
months to Bozeman, Montana (where Eli drove home himself); b) taken Eli to Paris (that lasted a week, and he came
home on his own); c) took Gabriel to Thailand, Japan and
Hawaii. This is completely disruptive.

Susan, Felix said, was

healthy and well educated . . . there is absolutely no reason
she cannot work . . . therefore I think we should have a voca-
tional evaluation and a seek work order.

So much for Felix's oft-repeated claims that Susan was
"delusional." With this last request, Felix wanted the court to
order Susan to get a job. The "we" in the declaration almost
sounded as though Felix and the judge were ganging up on
Susan, only more proof, to her, of collusion between Felix
and the courts.

Felix was right about one thing, though. Eli was in trouble—
again.

On January 3, 2002, Eli and two other boys had been
picked up by the Orinda police on suspicion of trespassing.
The police officer thought "all displayed objective symptoms
of marijuana ingestion." When he looked in Eli's backpack
he found a large bag of pot, and two smaller bags, which led
him to conclude that the marijuana had been packaged for
sale. Eli and the other boys were arrested and taken to juvenile
hall, where Susan had to come to get him out. A court case
was started.

Then in mid-February, a large part of the roof caved in on
the Family Polk. Eli was involved in a serious fistfight at a
fast-food restaurant in the nearby town of Moraga.

17. JACK IN THE BOX

By now, Eli had grown into a strapping 16-year-old, slightly over six feet, and just over 200 pounds. In other words, Eli could clean almost anyone's clock. He had the body of a man, but the mind and hormones of an adolescent.

According to the subsequent Moraga Police Department report, Eli was called by a friend, who told him that another boy, who had beaten him up and stolen his marijuana stash some days before, was at the Jack in the Box parking lot in Moraga with a number of other teenagers, most of them students at a rival high school. Eli jumped in Adam's pickup truck and drove to the place, intending to even the score for his friend.

Once there, Eli walked up to the other boy, who was even bigger than he was, and who apparently had his "posse" with him in the parking lot, and told him they had "a problem." The other boy apparently didn't want any part of Eli—he said the problem wasn't with Eli, but with Eli's rather more diminutive friend.

"No, it's not," Eli said, and then slugged the bigger boy in the face, twice. The other boy hit back, then Eli swung a third time. Eli pulled the boy's jacket over his head so he couldn't see, and the boy backed up. Eli hit him again.

By now blood was pouring down the boy's face. He asked
Eli if he'd had enough to satisfy him.

"Yeah," Eli said, and the fight was over. Eli and his friend
then left in the pickup truck.

Later that night, the injured boy's father took him to the
hospital for treatment of the damage, which included a badly
broken nose and several cuts over his left eye and on his
cheek. The Moraga police came to the hospital and took a
statement from the boy, who said he didn't know Eli's last
name, or where he lived. He claimed that Eli had been holding
a small silver flashlight in his hand while hitting him, which
had the effect of increasing the power of Eli's blows, much
like brass knuckles. But he admitted knowing Eli's friend by
name, and also admitted that he'd beaten up Eli's friend and
stolen his marijuana some days earlier.

The next day, the officer did a check of the records and
found an address for Eli's friend. He went to interview him
early in the morning. The friend also said he didn't know Eli's
last name or where he lived, and said he felt sick at seeing Eli
give his tormentor such a whipping. Eli had given him a ride
home after the fight, and noticing that his shirt was covered
with the opponent's blood, observed, "I'm screwed." Even Eli
realized he'd gone too far, and that this would mean a lot of
trouble.

Later that morning, the Moraga officer met with his Orinda
counterparts, who said the description of the aggressor in the
fight sounded like Eli Polk. The officer obtained a booking
picture of Eli—apparently from the January marijuana arrest—
and put it in a photo array for the victim to look at. The victim
identified Eli.

That night, a little after 11 P.M., the Moraga officer called
the dream house and asked to speak to Eli. He wanted Eli to
come to the Moraga police station immediately to answer
questions. Eli told Susan, and Susan returned the call to the police to find out what it was all about. They explained to Susan

that Eli had been in a fight, and had committed a "brutal and vicious attack" on another boy.

When Susan said Eli was only 16, and that she didn't want him driving to Moraga that late at night, the officer agreed to meet with Eli at the Orinda house the following night to hear his side of the story.

The officer "then proceeded to lecture me on parenting," Susan said later. "When I objected that he had jumped to conclusions without completing his investigation, [the officer] said that he did not like my tone, and hung up on me."

As far as the cops were concerned, this was it: Eli had finally stepped over the line, and Susan's defense of her son only hardened them in their enthusiasm for taking Eli down. The Moraga detective failed to show up for the agreed-upon appointment at the dream house. Five days later, on the night of February 20, three Moraga police officers, accompanied by two from the Orinda department, went to the dream house with arrest and search warrants, looking for Eli and his bloody shirt.

Susan met the cops at the front door. They handed her a copy of the warrant and asked her to remove the two dogs, Tuffy and Ruffy, so they could go in the house to start the search.

Susan said she wanted to read the warrant first. She started to close the door. That was not the right thing to do. The police forced their way into the house over Susan's objections. Once inside, they explained to Susan that they were looking for a small flashlight and a bloody shirt, and told her they had an arrest warrant for Eli. They asked where his room was, and Susan told them it was the pool house, but that Eli wasn't home.

They wanted Susan to call Eli on his cell phone and persuade him to come home, so they could arrest him. Susan refused to do this. Just then the officers heard a noise upstairs, and thinking it might be Eli, started to ascend the staircase.

Susan told them she didn't want them going up there without her.

They asked her to show them the laundry room, and Susan wouldn't do this, either. She began arguing about the validity of the search warrant.

"It was evident at this point that Mrs. Polk was being uncooperative," the police later reported. "At one point they asked Mrs. Polk to walk downstairs, and she said, 'After you.'"

The police didn't want to do that—they were afraid Susan might try to attack them from behind.

"She again refused to walk downstairs and clenched her left fist and drew it back toward her body," the police reported.

"At this point the officers stepped forward and placed her left arm in a twist lock control hold. She struggled momentarily and they eventually handcuffed her and escorted her downstairs."

They explained that the arrest warrant was for Eli, not her, but Susan refused to listen to them.

"At that point she began insulting the officers," the police reported.

Eventually the police found a bloody shirt, but no flashlight. They uncuffed Susan, and left.

Susan was furious. The next day she wrote an angry letter to the Moraga police chief, roundly condemning the Moraga officers for "unprofessional" conduct, and asking how to file a formal complaint. Among other things, Susan said, the police denied her the opportunity to read the warrant before commencing their search. When she offered to show the supervising officer around the house, and they went upstairs, she found that two officers hadn't waited for an invitation, and were already busy searching Gabe's room.

Gabe, who had been doing his homework upstairs, was made to stay immobilized at his desk while the search of his own room was going on.

There were other complaints by Susan: her handcuffing was excessive, she said. And when she'd complained about this, one of the officers threatened to drag the search out, just to make her suffer in handcuffs longer.

She'd hired a lawyer to represent Eli, Susan went on to inform the Moraga police chief, and Eli and the lawyer would come in to talk to the police the next day. But the lawyer had already warned her, Susan added, that as far as the Moraga police were concerned, she had "an attitude" problem, and that, "the Moraga Police Department intends to punish my son for my attitude, by having him confined in juvenile hall tomorrow following [the] interview. . . ."

To Susan, the entire incident smacked of police-state tactics, the fascism she was convinced was sweeping the country. From this moment forward, for Susan, the police became the enemy—in fact, the tools of her archenemy, Felix.

At the interview, Eli denied holding a flashlight in his fist, and contended that he'd only been sticking up for his smaller friend. The other guy had challenged him first, he said, and had been holding a roll of quarters in his own hand. Eli's side of the story left the Moraga police unmoved. They charged Eli with two felonies: battery with serious bodily injury, and assault with a deadly weapon, the supposed flashlight. If convicted of both charges, 16-year-old Eli could conceivably be sentenced to state prison for as long as 8 years.

As the lawyer had warned, Eli was confined in juvenile hall. The only way he could get out was for Susan to agree to grant Felix custody, at least until his case was settled one way or the other. Susan wasn't happy, Eli wasn't happy, and Gabe was bewildered by the swirl of events that seemed to be poisoning their lives.

Four days after Eli turned himself in to the police, Susan wrote a long letter to the boys that said in part:

> I want to leave you with an explanation for my actions so that you do not make the mistake of blaming yourselves for what has happened . . . .
>
> In therapy, I was sexually abused by your father. I was

already given to blocking out what I couldn't bear to maintain in consciousness. I had periods of amnesia. Your dad, with a combination of drugs and hypnosis, utilized this defense mechanism in order to protect himself from being discovered . . . .

I have not been able to protect you. I have tried, but I have despaired of being able to, and I really can't stick around to find out what calamity overtakes our little family next. I have concluded that perhaps all of these events are in some way connected to me. Perhaps I am something of a magnet for trouble. A tenant who once sued me said that I have bad karma. Maybe so, and maybe by withdrawing myself from your equation, I will improve your karma a little bit. I certainly hope so . . . .

I can't live with the fear of what will happen next nor am I willing to live the life of a slave, being cowed by authority, giving in to every unreasonable order, accepting every slap in the face as my due, behaving like a prisoner . . .

Here is my advice to you, and as my life has ended so badly, you must take it with a grain of salt:

Marry wisely . . . .

Susan went on to provide other prescriptions for the boys' happiness, many of them practical suggestions for how to manage money. It was almost as if she were preparing to disappear, or worse.

I leave you all of my love. Find good homes for the dogs. You can't take them with you, and they won't want to go where I'm going.

If this was an intended suicide note, Susan seems to have had second thoughts about doing herself in. Instead, she decided to fight on, for herself, for Eli and for Gabe.

Felix was meanwhile planning his own counterattack. Eli's fistfight had given him the hook he needed. He interceded with the probation department, and had legal custody of Eli transferred to him as a condition of his release from juvenile hall. Eli had no choice: it was either live with Felix in Berkeley, or stay in the lockup for the foreseeable future. He went home with Felix.

18. CONTEMPT

By April of 2002, both of these family crises were beginning to merge into a single, huge mess. Eli's fate at the hands of the criminal justice system complicated the divorce of Susan and Felix, and the divorce complicated Eli's possible outcome with the juvenile court.

For some reason, Susan did not seek the assistance of her "tough Irishman" lawyer in dealing with these situations. She filed her own response—"in pro per"—to Felix's late January request for joint physical custody of the boys, asked the court to restrain Felix from having any contact with her or Gabe, and wanted custody of Eli returned to her in Orinda:

> The respondent is using money and the children as a means of control in a psychologically abusive dynamic which can and frequently does end in a violent outburst. This has to stop.

Both Eli and Gabe "refused to live with the respondent," she told the court. In fact they didn't want to even *see* Felix.

Susan agreed that the dream house should be put on the market "immediately." Until the place was sold, though, she wanted Felix to pay $7,000 a month in child support and another $8,000 a month in spousal support. Felix could easily afford it, she said: his monthly income from his practice and his teaching was $26,000.

She was particularly upset that Felix had used his influence with the juvenile court and the probation department to wrest custody of Eli away from her, contending that:

> Felix is sufficiently experienced and well connected, i.e., he trained Eli's probation officer, to manipulate the system to his own advantage at the expense of his children.

As a condition of his release to Felix's custody, Eli was required to wear an electronic monitoring device on his ankle, and was banned from Contra Costa County. He had to stay at Felix's "cottage" in Berkeley—by this point Felix had moved out of the apartment, and had rented a small house—where Eli slept on a fold-up couch in the living room.

> Felix, according to Eli, leaves the cottage at six or seven in the morning and usually does not return until ten or later. He is gone for most of the weekend as well. I pick up Eli in the morning, drive him to and from school, bring him food, and do homework with him in Felix's cottage. This has been completely disruptive to the stable family life that the children and I had established together.

Eli's punch-out at the Jack in the Box gave Felix the opportunity to hold him as a hostage in the contest between husband and wife; even better from Felix's point of view, it required Susan and Gabe to have at least some contact with Felix himself.

Susan was convinced that Felix had manipulated the mediator who had met with the family the previous spring when the divorce was first filed.

Felix might as well have written [the evaluator's] recommendation for him, so little relation did it bear to the reality, and so well it served Felix's interest as opposed to the boys.

Although the mediator had recommended that she be given a psychological evaluation at the previous year's session, Susan said, he failed to take into account

the sort of abuse I experienced, which began while I was a minor child in Felix's care, and continued throughout our marriage. Given the above, a psychological evaluation is not an experience that I welcome. I have a "healthy distrust" of psychiatry in general, and psychology in particular . . . .

Felix's primary concern in pursuing custody over the objections of his children is to exert control over me . . . since Eli was released to Felix's custody, Felix has called me at least once on an almost daily basis, barraging me with blame, insults and demands . . . he has managed to find a pretext to contact me almost every day, and these contacts typically end in insults and threats.

Susan contended that Felix had hidden assets:

Felix has been stashing money away and should be restrained from continuing to do so. An estimate needs to be made of the amount Felix has stashed away. Investigators may need to be retained to trace this money, and the respondent should be held responsible for payment.

Susan included declarations from Gabe and Eli.

Gabe said in his declaration:

I want to live with my mother, Susan Polk. I do not want to live part time with my dad and part time with my mom, because this would disrupt my school and my life. My dad won't give me the support that I need to succeed in life.

Eli's declaration was longer, and quite bitter. He echoed Susan's complaint that Felix had covert influence over the courts and probation department:

My father has high influence in the areas that now concern me. My dad did train my probation officer . . . at the arraignment she made it very clear that I was living with my dad . . . and she checked all the boxes that could possibly lead to my father gaining sole custody. This is not the first time he has done this type of thing to get what he wants . . . .

Now this is a sly, slick and deceiving way to gain sole custody of one's children, but I don't like being used in this way by my father, just as I have been all my life. My father knows he has lost his family, just as he lost his first family, and is not taking it lying down. It is obvious he will do whatever is necessary, right or wrong, to get control of not only his life, but the lives of his kids, and the control of his wife . . . .

My father is somebody who should be in jail himself . . . my dad is not a completely sane person . . . .

Eli said he thought his father would do anything he could to make his mother look bad in court, but

he is much worse than anything he could make up about my mother. I love my mother just as I love my father. However, he is a terrible person who has no love for us. My father will say that my mom is crazy, and delusional, and that she brainwashed the kids into thinking these things about him . . . . I hope that the court will not let my father get away with what he is trying to do.

But Felix didn't have to try to make Susan look bad in court. She did that herself.

At an April 10 hearing for Eli's criminal case for the figh
at the Jack in the Box, both mother and son lost their temper
and yelled at the judge.

Eli had a lawyer retained by Felix to represent him, wh
seemed not to have understood much of the toxic dynami
that was then roiling the Polks. The lawyer had induced th
Contra Costa County District Attorney's Office to agree t
dismiss the deadly weapon charge, in return for a guilty ple
to battery with serious bodily injury.

But the judge, William Kolin, almost immediately threw
wrench into this machinery. He suggested that Eli might no
want to plead guilty after hearing what he had to say.

Kolin had, he said, a probation report that indicated that E
was late to school, and had other problems. The other prob
lems, although Kolin did not then spell them out, were that th
probation department had accused Susan of being rude an
insulting to them.

"And so," Kolin told Eli, "stand up—put your hands behin
your back."

The judge was going to put Eli back in custody.

Eli didn't like this at all.

"You have a problem with that?" The judge challenged El
"You shake your head at the judge, you will go separately t
jail for contempt of court. You don't care? Fine. Have a sea
For the record, he's shaking his head, making gestures at th
judge, and that's unacceptable."

Susan was agitated at the way the judge was treating El
She was already upset that Felix had also shown up for th
hearing. Like Eli, she was convinced that Felix had undue in
fluence on the court. She decided to leave the courtroom.

"Mother, you can't leave," Kolin said.

"Oh, can't I?" Susan said. "Didn't this court—"

"Put her down [restrain Susan from leaving], becaus
you're going to be the next one that goes in custody in just
second," Kolin said.

Never well disposed to any authority, Susan despised tyrants. She glared at the judge.

"I am not in custody," she said. "I don't have custody of my son, and I am not going to sit around for this farce. I *am* in contempt." Susan meant it literally.

"Sit down," Kolin ordered.

"You have my complete—" Susan was cut off by the judge.

"Bring a bailiff down, and place her in handcuffs, because she is under arrest," Kolin said.

"You guys are really something," Susan said. "You decide that this man who abused me when I was fifteen years old should have custody of my son, who beat my son, who beat me, who trained the probation officer, who has told me unless I relinquished custody, my son would be in juvenile hall. You guys are disgusting."

Susan was convinced—the fix was in, and Felix was the fixer.

"You're failing to follow orders," the judge said. "The probation department indicated that you—"

"Those are lies, because you people just lie to protect yourselves. You all do," Susan shot back.

"Take her out," Kolin said to the bailiff. "Put her in the holding area. No, put her back over here, so she can hear what's going on."

"Justice," Susan said. "This is justice? This is a disgusting disgrace, and you are . . ."

"Well," Kolin said, "I find you in contempt, and I'm going to put you in jail for five days, and appoint an attorney."

Eli finally spoke.

"I don't get to say anything? Just slap on the cuffs? This is bullshit."

Kolin ordered a recess so that tempers could cool off. Susan was taken, handcuffed, to the court's prisoner holding area.

When the hearing resumed, Susan was still in the holding pen. Felix addressed Kolin at the judge's invitation.

"Thank you," Felix said. "My son Eli will have a problem with some of this. My perspective is the truth. Over the last four years we have lived in an environment of paranoia at home."

"With mother?" Kolin asked.

"Yes," Felix said, "and she in so many ways is wonderful, and that's also true. It's just the way it is."

Both of the boys were loyal to Susan, Felix said, and protective of her. Eli was "acting out," because of the stress from "the paranoid environment."

Now Eli's lawyer tried to get the court to accept Eli's no contest plea to the battery-with-serious-injury charge.

"I certainly hope, and I would expect that this court would not punish Eli for the conduct of his mother," the lawyer said. "I have been informed and believe, based on what the father said, that she suffers from mental illness which is currently not treated. I think that probably her behavior toward these proceedings would have been a little bit different if she were under the treatment of a psychiatrist and/or medicated . . . . don't really know all the details of her mental illness. I don't have a release to get those records, but it may be that the conduct is not willful or that the conduct is impaired because of that unfortunate circumstance. And again, I would not want the court to punish Eli because he has been in an environment with a parent who has not been emotionally healthy to meet his needs."

Felix wanted the case transferred to Alameda County, because he was living in Berkeley, and since he had custody of Eli, it would be easier for the Alameda County authorities to supervise Eli's probation. Of course, Felix had considerable influence with the juvenile court authorities in Alameda County, where he had worked for so many years.

Eli was by now considerably calmer. When the judge explained all this to him, he said he understood. He apologized to the judge for his behavior. The judge accepted Eli's apology, and ordered him uncuffed. It appeared that he wasn't going to put Eli in custody after all, but return him to Felix. El asked to be allowed to use the restroom, the judge granted him permission, and so he was not in the courtroom when Kolin returned to the matter of Susan's contempt.

"Now," he said, "mother had to be taken out of the courtroom because she refused to be quiet. Is she still here? Let's bring her in."

The bailiff brought Susan back in and made her sit down. Kolin asked her if she wanted to apologize. If she apologized, Kolin said, he'd be willing to listen to what she had to say about Eli's situation. Susan didn't know whether Eli had been jailed or not. All she knew was that he was no longer in the courtroom, and the judge didn't explain Eli's temporary absence to her.

"I wanted to leave the courtroom, and you told me I could not leave," Susan said.

"This is true," Kolin admitted.

"Why can't I leave the courtroom if I find the proceedings too upsetting?"

Because, Kolin said, he wanted to talk to her about the probation report, which contended that Susan had insulted the probation officer with profanities and other vulgarities.

Kolin read from two probation department reports that had Susan swearing at the officers. Somehow this put *her* in violation of Eli's probation, even though she didn't have custody of Eli.

"Excuse me," Susan said. "Why is he in this room?" She meant Felix, who was watching all this unfold.

"Okay," Kolin said, "mother, you're not listening. I'm trying to give you an opportunity to explain your conduct, to provide an excuse."

"Why is my ex-husband in this room?"

"Because he's a party," Kolin explained.

"How is he a party to this?" Susan meant the contempt charge.

"All right," Kolin said, "it's clear to me you're not listening. You don't want to apologize."

"No, I certainly don't."

"For the record, I want to give you that opportunity. Do you want me to go on?" Kolin asked.

"I'm not going to apologize," Susan said.

Okay, Kolin said, he was going to find her in contempt. He gave her two choices: she could go to jail immediately, or come back the following week with a lawyer, who could then file a writ with the court of appeal to try to vacate the contempt.

Susan chose to come back with a lawyer to file the writ.

The judge told her she couldn't leave until all the paperwork was finished.

"Excuse me. Was this a trial?"

"No," Kolin said.

"Don't I get a trial if I'm accused of contempt?"

"You can come Monday," Kolin said, obviously wishing to get the whole thing over.

"I would like a trial."

The judge said he'd already found "beyond a reasonable doubt" that Susan was in contempt. He began to cite the law for the record, but Susan interrupted him.

"Isn't beyond a reasonable doubt a judgment? I mean, you're accusing me of this. Don't I get a trial to determine whether I did it or not?"

Well, Kolin said, that was why he was giving her until Monday to file a writ on appeal. But he had the authority under the law to hold her in contempt, at least until the matter was heard by a higher court.

"So you have special powers to just rule?"

"That's true," Kolin said. "I do."

"Without giving a person an opportunity to defend themselves?"

That's why he'd agreed not to jail her until Monday—to give her a chance to hire a lawyer to defend herself, Kolin told her.

"That's up to you . . . if you don't want to come to court, or you're telling me you're not going to come to court or you don't care, which apparently you don't, because you're not going to apologize or give me an excuse——"

"Why would I apologize when I think you were wrong?"

"Fine," Kolin said, obviously weary of dealing with Susan. Susan persisted.

"You were out of line," she told the judge. The judge should have explained to her that he wanted to discuss the probation report with her. Instead he had abruptly ordered Eli handcuffed, preparatory to taking him to jail. This was upsetting, she said, and that's why she wanted to leave the courtroom.

She hadn't become physical, Susan said.

"Well, I disagree, and I'm sure the record will show that," Kolin said.

"I'm sure the record will show what you want it to show," Susan said.

Kolin told Susan she still wasn't listening to him. He said he didn't think she was going to really show up on Monday.

"It's clear that you don't care," he said.

"Probably not," Susan said, continuing her contempt of the court.

"All right," Kolin said. "I hereby sentence you to five days in jail. Bailiff, take her away. Have a good day."

19. REASONABLE

What was one to make of this performance? In many ways, it illustrates much of Susan's personality. Like a pit bull, when she got her teeth into something or someone, especially when she believed she was in the right, she could not let go. Kolin was completely wrong about one thing. It wasn't that Susan didn't care—she cared too much.

The entire proceeding can be seen in two different ways: on one hand, it shows how aggravating Susan could be; on the other hand, it can also be seen as a near-perfect example of why Susan believed that Felix had the courts rigged for his own benefit.

In fact, there are several aspects of what transpired that day that suggest why Susan might have felt the whole thing was nothing more than a charade orchestrated by Felix to enable him to get the boys back, thereby to derail the divorce, silence Susan, and maybe even get her committed—her worst nightmare.

In support of this notion, there's the rather weird opening scene. Without even hearing a single word from Eli, Kolin ordered him to stand up and be handcuffed, as if he were going to be taken to jail immediately. This is what had upset Susan—because she intuited that Felix was orchestrating the precipitous jailing for the cynical purpose of enhancing his control over Eli. In Susan's mind, Eli was going to jail because Felix wanted to punish him to get at her.

The fact that the judge later relented, and ordered Eli to stay with his father in Berkeley, only confirmed Susan's initial instinct that the whole scene was a setup by Kolin, at Felix's behest, first, to scare the bejeebers out of Eli, and second, to induce her to fulminate at the judge, and thereby make her look like a nutcase in public.

With Kolin's collaboration, as Susan saw it, Felix could manipulate the legal system to make Eli obligated to him—after all, it was only Felix's reasonableness that prevented the judge and the cops from carting Eli off to jail forthwith. This was exactly what Susan hated so much about Felix: all the Machiavellian covert maneuverings that herded his subjects toward his preferred destination, whether they wanted to go there or not.

Felix certainly knew how to get Susan going—he'd had years of practice at this. He had to have anticipated that with Eli being handcuffed at the very start of the hearing, Susan would ignite. She did, sounded unstable, and the judge held her in contempt, which served Felix's purposes in the divorce suit. But then it got even better, for Felix.

When she was returned to the courtroom and saw that Eli was gone, Susan was sure that Felix was behind everything.

"Why is he in this room?" Susan had demanded of the judge, referring to Felix.

"He's a party," Kolin had explained—innocently meaning that Felix was one of the custodial parents of Eli. He had no idea that Susan would misinterpret this. But to Susan, Kolin's explanation was just one more confirmation that Kolin and Felix were in cahoots to label her unfit as a parent—how else could Felix be "a party" to the charge of contempt against *her*?

Felix's presence as "a party" in Susan's contempt charge only convinced her that Felix controlled Kolin. In her mind, the judge and Felix had set the whole thing up—as soon as she had moved toward the door, the judge had jumped on her, without explaining why he wanted her to stay, which was another setup. They had to be plotting together against her, Susan concluded.

In retrospect, this proceeding was badly handled by Kolin. The drama of the opening scene, Eli's handcuffing, was completely unnecessary. An impartial judge should have discussed the probation report, which Susan disputed, in an evenhanded manner, and given Susan a chance to say why she disputed it—that the probation officer had been trained by Felix, and had put untruths into her report to assist Felix in the divorce case. And if all of that were true—who knows?—the probation officer should never have been permitted to handle Eli's case. The conflict of interest, with the divorce case looming, was obvious.

In fact, it appears that Kolin knew little or even nothing about the contentious divorce, or Susan's allegations against Felix. Even Eli's lawyer seemed to know nothing more than Felix's side of the story—echoing Felix's standard line that Susan was mentally ill. This too, had upset her: to Susan, even Eli's lawyer was working for Felix, who was paying the bill.

And finally, amidst all the uproar, up stepped Felix, taking the role of the rational man, and even throwing a compliment to his estranged wife: "She in so many ways is wonderful."

This event was another critical turn in the War Between the Polks, because it gave Felix substantial leverage over Susan, by gaining control of Eli.

By now, it was clear to both Susan and Felix that the Family Polk was divided two to two—Felix and Adam against Susan and Eli, with poor Gabe up for grabs.

There was still more mano-a-mano between Susan and Judge Kolin. Kolin seemed reluctant to actually put Susan in the slammer for what he referred to as her "ranting and raving." He decided to defer the 5 days in jail and give her a citation to appear on the charge. He said he'd appoint a lawyer for her if she wanted one. Susan declined; she'd rather do it herself.

The following week, Susan came before Kolin on the matter of the contempt citation.

Kolin had thought over the whole Polk problem during the intervening weekend, and had come to the not unreasonable conclusion that there were signs of serious dysfunction in the entire Polk family. He thought the best way of defusing some of the troubles was to order a professional assessment of the underlying family dynamics, and to order Susan to undergo psychological counseling. Kolin didn't know that Susan despised psychologists, or why.

"It's my understanding," Kolin told her, "based on the comments of your ex-husband, that you have been under psychological care and have taken medication. And under the circumstances, I think the best long-term interest for Eli is for you to attend counseling. Tell me your thoughts about that."

Ordinarily, the suggestion by anyone that she was mentally ill would have set Susan off. But on this particular day, she was remarkably clear and cogent, if a little angry.

"That is absolutely not true that I have been in psychological counseling recently," she said. "I was on medication maybe for a period of two weeks five years ago, so I mean, is this something I cannot respond to now?"

"No, go ahead," Kolin told her.

"I have evidence that I want to submit to the court."

"Sure, go ahead," Kolin said.

Susan then delivered a lengthy recap of the War Between the Polks, including the various restraining orders, assertions by Eli and Gabe that their father routinely hit them, Eli's unhappiness in living in the one-room Berkeley cottage with Felix, and the difficulties she'd had in shuttling between Orinda and Berkeley on a daily basis to take care of Eli. Worse, said Susan, Felix was calling her "on an almost daily basis . . . berating me with being a bad mother, with having caused all of this, with having destroyed our children.

"He calls me names. He comes to the house. He pushes me around. So that was my frame of mind when I reacted the way I did in the courtroom. I knew that I needed to leave the courtroom as soon as possible because it was— I was upset to begin with by the things that have been happening."

She was still unhappy over the way she'd been handcuffed by the police during the search, as well as the system's coming down so hard on Eli—in her mind, Eli was only defending a friend from a bully when he'd gotten into the fight.

"So I have a really, at this point, negative reaction to law enforcement. I find them really difficult to deal with."

Susan gave the judge a copy of the letter she'd sent to the Moraga police, complaining about their treatment of her. After the incident, she said, she was "kind of horrified then to see a [police] report written up in a way which kind of revealed to me the sort of teamwork that goes on in law enforcement, that people were saying that I did things I simply didn't do . . . I didn't expect to be lied about."

Susan gave copies of Eli's declaration, and her own declaration in the divorce case, to the judge.

"Well, you know, I have to say, Ms. Polk, that your demeanor today and in the manner in which you're comporting yourself is much better, obviously, than it was when we met last week," Kolin told her. "So I want to compliment you on the way you've comported yourself and the way you've explained it. And now I understand, based on what you've said, why you reacted the way you did."

Because she'd explained herself, Kolin said, he was going to dismiss the contempt finding.

But, he said, he still wanted to order Susan to undergo psychological counseling.

"I do have a comment to make about that," Susan said. "I said last week in court that I met my husband in therapy when I was fifteen, and I really don't have a positive view of therapy, and I'm not really interested in entering another therapeutic relationship. I think I was so traumatized in that

relationship, it's unreasonable to expect me to enter into another one."

She'd interviewed six therapists over the previous summer,
Susan said, "and I had such a negative experience with those
interviews. One therapist had even invited her to have "a relationship" with him.

Kolin was reasonable about this.

"Why don't we do this, then?" he suggested. "Why don't I
change it? Instead of counseling, I'm going to order a psychological assessment. In other words, you won't have to enter
counseling, but I am going to order that you and Probation determine an appropriate psychotherapist to have a psychological assessment. I'm doing this for Eli . . . so I'm going to ask
you to put aside your strong feelings about psychotherapy in
general and psychologists."

"That's fine," Susan said.

In this situation, Kolin had discovered, albeit by trial and error,
another key to Susan: by giving her credibility for her beliefs,
by complimenting her, by compromising, he substantially reduced her combativeness. The change from "psychological
counseling," in which Susan would have been placed in a subordinate position, to "psychological assessment" was deft. In
an assessment, Susan would have equality with the assessor—
she'd have an opportunity to tell her side.

Over the next month, the assessment was made by Andrew
Pojman, a Walnut Creek psychologist, and filed with the court
in late May of 2002. It was a particularly insightful evaluation
of the internal dynamics of the Polk family:

> The profile of the family . . . is a disturbing one. The par-
> ents described to [the probation officer] their home as either a
> "violent household" (mother) or a "paranoid environment
> due to the intensive conflict between mother and father and
> their impending divorce" (father). Eli is very attached to his

mother and gets caught up in parental uproar and criticalness. The intensity of his loyalty conflict and resulting desperateness is reflected in his handwritten note to [the probation officer]. In this note, Eli described his father as abusive, violent and provocative—all claims made in the service [of] going to live with his mother.

In other words, Pojman discounted Eli's assertions about his father as part of an attempt to reunite with Susan. But after being told that wasn't going to happen, Eli had then recanted—he wasn't talking about current abuse, Eli now said, but past abuse from Felix. Felix admitted having "slapped" Eli in the distant past, but not in the past decade or so.

Pojman continued:

This family is one where the parents present ["present" being a medico/psychological term for how someone might be perceived by another] in a compelling, provocative manner. Father is a mental health professional who appears depressed, ineffective, and passive. Mother is aggressive, emotionally labile [changeable], and often contradictory in her behaviors and statements.

Both parents care for Eli but have not been able to address his psychological needs. The greatest "risk" for Eli lies not with each individual parent but within the dynamics of the family. The family system is marked by conflict and turmoil. Role reversal is common, with Eli often given more power and recognition than is warranted for any child of his age. Authority issues are flagrant and pervasive for both parents. When one adult tries to be in charge even in a healthy manner, the other sabotages the process by name-calling and undermining.

While his mother's participation in this sabotage is obvious, the father also undermines the mother with his passivity and reluctance to be in charge.

Eli is very identified with his mother, who is viewed by Eli as a victim in the dynamic. Part of this identification is based

on the natural fact that his mother has been his primary care-
giver, with his father, by his own admission, over-involved at
work. Part of this identification is also a defense against ma-
ternal anger and feared abandonment. It is not surprising that,
according to Eli and police records, his involvement in the
crime was protecting and looking out for his friend, the under-
dog in this case.

Eli stuck it out with Felix in the one-room cottage in Berke-
ey until early June, although it appears that he spent considerable time at the Orinda house with Susan and Gabe, despite
he court edict banning him from Contra Costa County. Then,
on June 4, 2002, Eli severed his electronic monitoring anklet
and disappeared, at least from the control of the probation department.

As far as they were concerned, Eli was now a fugitive from
ustice.

20. GO ASK ALICE

The troubles for the Polk family continued into the summer of 2002. With Eli in hiding—with Susan's undoubted assistance—the stresses were piling up. Both she and Eli were convinced that Felix had exerted covert influence with Kolin and the probation department to force him to stay with Felix as Felix's way of keeping Susan close.

Yet Susan thought Eli had every right to refuse to live with Felix. There was substantial agreement between mother and son that Felix was using dirty tricks, and was the one who was behind all of Eli's troubles with the law enforcement system. They believed that anyone who wasn't a son of the well-connected expert on juvenile delinquency would've gotten a pass from the juvenile court, or at the very least a mere slap on the wrist.

The anger of Susan and Eli toward Felix soon affected Gabe. At one point, Gabe "acted out" by taking a sledgehammer to the windows of Felix's car. Felix sent a letter to Gabe:

> I know that you are very, very mad at me and won't talk to me on the phone.
> I want you to know that in spite of the way you have rejected me and turned on me, I am not angry at you. Frustrated, yes! Angry, no!

Both you and Eli seem to have bought into mom's horror stories about me. They are for the most part not true stories . . . I am faced with a closed system in which mom says what she says so hatefully about me and I have no chance to point out what is true and what is not. I fear you have joined mom who, at times, and certainly about me, has created a reality of her own. I have some real flaws and yet, I am not the monster she portrays me to be.

Felix said he had no plans to abandon Gabe, Eli and Adam, no matter what. He chastised Gabe for the damage to the car. But Felix indicated that he forgave his youngest son for his part in the psychodrama going on between him and Susan:

You are my kid and I love you as fully as I can love anyone.

The divorce case plodded forward through the courts. Susan's lawyer, the "tough Irishman" Dan Ryan, appeared to be making progress toward resolving some of the thorniest issues. The Polk apartment building in Piedmont was sold; Susan and Felix split the $450,000 that came from the sale. Felix agreed to pay $6,500 in monthly family support, and also to turn over his $2,500 monthly Social Security check to Susan, giving her a total income, on paper, of $9,000 a month. Of course, she had to pay the $4,000 monthly dream house mortgage out of that amount. Felix was ordered to hire an accountant to establish his net worth for the purposes of dividing all the property. Susan still insisted that Felix had salted away millions in a secret Caribbean bank account. The three-way ownership of the Berkeley apartment building continued to be a stumbling block, since Susan, her mother and Felix all disagreed on who owned how much.

A further hearing date to sort out these remaining issues was set for October 16, 2002.

But in August, Susan asked that Felix be held in contempt of court for failing to make the court-ordered family support payments. The dream house mortgage was spinning toward default because of Felix's failure to pay what he'd agreed to, Susan said. She filed a declaration in early August saying that Felix had told her he could not afford to pay the $6,500 in family support, and that he had therefore unilaterally reduced the payment to $5,000, and that he was already $5,500 behind. She wanted the court to order Felix to make up the difference immediately.

The divorce court set Susan's request for this order for an October 10, 2002, hearing. In the meantime, Susan would have to draw on her share of the sold Piedmont apartment building if she wanted to keep the dream house mortgage current. It was, in Susan's mind, just another piece of trickery by Felix, exactly as Sharon had complained of so many years earlier, when Felix had pleaded poverty in *that* divorce.

As these events unfolded, Susan began to muse aloud on ways to get rid of Felix, according to Gabe.

"She confided in me and my brother that she trusted us," Gabe said later, "and so she would . . . on a bad day say she was going to kill my dad, or kind of flop back and forth from that, if she was going to, or she wasn't . . . she just talked about it. I mean, in casual conversation, which was pretty weird, but she talked about, I guess, running him over, messing with his car, drowning him in the pool, stuff like that."

Susan's anger at Felix was becoming ever more palpable as the end of summer approached. So was her suspiciousness. According to Gabe and Adam, Susan began to make references to people who were following her. She and the boys would be out driving in the car, and Susan would point people out, and say they were using secret hand signals to keep her under surveillance. It was all because of Felix, Susan said—Felix had enlisted his allies in the intelligence community to monitor her. It seems very likely that at least some of this clear paranoia was related to Susan's anxiety about the possibility of the escaped Eli's arrest. In Susan's mind, Felix's agents were everywhere in search of Eli, so she had to be careful.

Then, on September 1, 2002, Eli was caught, and sent back to juvenile hall, for violation of the terms of his probation. This time, Felix wouldn't be able to help him. Kolin was determined to lock Eli up—if nothing else, it would get Eli out of the firing line in the War Between the Polks.

On September 6, 2002, Eli wrote to Gabe from juvenile hall.

He'd had to write instead of call, Eli said, because the juvenile authorities had put some sort of electronic block on the phone. He couldn't dial out. Eli made it clear to Gabe that he believed his predicament was Felix's fault. Gabe didn't have to come to the forthcoming court hearing on his probation revocation if he didn't want to, Eli said, "because I'm sure Dad will get a kick out of you watching me get fucked."

He'd told their dad, Eli went on, that if he was incarcerated for a long time, he'd never have anything to do with Felix again.

"I will never sell out to Dad and his group," Eli wrote. "He probably thinks that after going through all this I will take any offer from his group. I WON'T EVER. It can't get much worse than what I've been through so far . . . ."

Exactly what "group" of Felix's Eli meant was not clarified in this letter, so one can only assume that Gabe knew what Eli meant by the term. It seems likely, however, that Eli was referring to Felix's supposed influence with the juvenile court authorities—his "group"—who would do whatever Felix wanted, because of his covert power. Here, clearly, Eli had accepted Susan's perception that Felix was Mr. Big.

"Watch yourself at all times," he advised Gabe. "I wish we had stayed in Montana. Dad has just too much power in here."

Over the next week, Susan wrote two letters. One was to an Orinda real estate outfit, authorizing the listing of the dream house for sale.

"Sales price to be $2,050,000 (firm price)," Susan wrote.

The house would be ready to show to potential buyers on September 16, she indicated.

"I have moved out," Susan said. "Will be traveling across country, working on a travel log of my adventures."

In the other letter, on September 11, 2002, to Judge Kolin, Susan said that although Eli had snipped off his ankle bracelet in June, he had not "disappeared."

"He was living with me at our home in Orinda, the home where he had been living with me until he was arrested in February of 2002 and you released him to his father's custody."

When Kolin had sentenced Eli to continued home supervision with Felix in April, Susan said, he'd said that Eli could move back to Orinda if Felix did too. But that meant Susan would have to live with Felix again, and this she simply could not face. In Susan's mind, this was yet more evidence that Kolin was secretly being orchestrated by Felix—Kolin's decision only helped Felix maintain control over Susan, using Eli to force her to submit to Felix's desire to maintain the marriage in the dream house.

At first she'd offered to switch places with Felix—letting Eli and Gabe live in the dream house with him while she would take Felix's apartment in Berkeley, Susan told Kolin in her letter, but "I found it hard to follow through." She didn't say so, but it galled her that Felix always seemed to get what he wanted from the courts, while she was always described as "delusional," or "crazy." To Susan, it just wasn't fair.

Adam was back that summer from UCLA, Susan continued in her letter to Kolin, and "all of my sons wanted me to stay, and all of them wanted to live with me." Take that, Felix!

Eli was so anxious to get out of Berkeley and away from Felix, to be with Susan, Gabe and Adam in Orinda, that she "selfishly persuaded" Eli to remove the electronic anklet, "and to hide with me." She hoped that the dream house could be sold soon, and that she, Eli and Gabe could move out of the state before authorities caught up with Eli.

"I cannot find it in my heart to apologize," Susan told Kolin. "I firmly believe that your order was wrong [giving Felix responsibility for Eli's supervision]. I feel that when we are subjected to unjust laws or orders we have a moral obligation to refuse to go along. Separating me from my child was wrong . . . ."

Now that Eli had been re-arrested and was facing incarceration, Susan intended to leave the state for good.

"My suitcase is packed," she told Kolin, "and I am planning to move out of California on Wednesday."

Felix, she added, was still eager to get her back. He'd once more proposed that the whole family live in the dream house, although Felix had offered to live separately in the pool house. Eli's probation officer, Susan told Kolin, had said that the department intended "to heal this family."

Susan thought that was really Felix talking, through his influence over the probation officer. Had the probation officer not been trained by Felix, Susan said, "she would have observed that my children and I did not need to be healed. We were and remain a loving family. Felix is not part of that family. . . ."

Susan said her lawyer, Dan Ryan, had advised her not to admit that Eli had been with her during the summer, saying that Kolin could charge her with a crime, and that the "courtroom is not a place for truth."

"What? Come again?" Susan wrote Kolin. "If the court is not about truth, justice and ethics, and if your own [court] officers [e.g., Ryan] believe that it is not, then what is it about? Is it a club where the good ol' boys network glad-hand and slap backs, while the real interests of the community and the state are forgotten, ignored and sacrificed?

"You have been unjust, Judge Kolin. I do not regret my actions."

Kolin was unmoved. On September 13, he accepted Eli's guilty plea for violating his probation, and ordered him held at juvenile hall until a final recommendation on how long he should have to serve in jail was completed, expected by October 4.

Susan now drove back to Montana, looking for a condo for her and Gabe to live in. Eli was lost to her, at least for the foreseeable future, she realized.

On the very same day that Susan wrote her letter to Judge Kolin, Felix—through his lawyer Steven Landes—wrote his own missive to the divorce court's commissioner, Josanna Berkow. Felix wanted the court to grant him sole authority to dispose of the dream house, as well as custody of Gabe. Felix's declaration of September 11, 2002, reveals much about his state of mind at the time:

> Gabriel missed an entire semester of high school this past year for no other reason than that he was permitted to stay home with his mother. Eli, our middle son, "disappeared" for months when the juvenile court had issued a warrant for his arrest. He was encouraged to do so by petitioner [Susan] and sheltered by petitioner. He is only 16 [actually, Eli was 17] and it is ludicrous to pretend he was on the lam without his mother's financial help and encouragement. I am well aware that petitioner has systematically alienated the two younger children from me and I have not contested custody, on the theory that with teenage boys they should not be forced into living arrangements against their will. However, it is plain that the petitioner acts solely from self-involved motives without regard to the boys' well being.

Felix wanted the court to give him authority to sell the dream house as soon as possible. He said that in asking a "firm" price of $2 million, Susan was essentially blocking the sale.

"She knows this, her attorney knows this and the real estate firm knows this," Felix said.

Finally, he told Berkow, Susan was simply unreliable, especially regarding the welfare of the boys. First she'd told him that she was leaving Orinda on September 16, and that he should be prepared to move back into the dream house until it was sold, and to temporarily take care of Gabe, while Susan found a new place in Montana. But a day later, Felix said, Susan left a message saying she was actually leaving on September 8, and that he had to get back to the house by then to take care of Gabe.

Two days later, Felix said, he got the word that Susan was leaving for some unknown destination, and taking Gabriel with her. Then I received another message that she was leaving on the 13th and *not* taking Gabriel."

It was all too much, Felix said—Susan's abrupt changes of plans, which made it impossible for him to develop any stabilizing environment for either himself or Gabe. He wanted the court to put an end to all the dithering, and give him the power to sell the dream house for a reasonable price. Felix thought that should be $1,750,000—$100,000 less than what the Polks had paid for the house in late 2000, and fully $200,000 less than the bank's appraisal at the time of the sale—even though the Polks had substantially remodeled the place. Eventually a real estate firm said the proper listing price should be around $1.6 million.

Felix made these requests "ex parte," meaning that they came to the court without prior notice to Susan or Ryan. Moreover, on Felix's behalf, Landes filed an additional request for an order "shortening time," that is, limiting Susan's capacity to respond, to just three days. It appears possible that Landes and Felix wanted to catch Susan unaware while she was out of town—in their universe, what Susan didn't know could only help them.

The record in the divorce case, while incomplete, seems to show that Berkow quite properly declined to issue these requested court orders "ex parte," that is, without hearing Susan's side of the story, and scheduled instead a hearing for Septem-

ber 27 on Felix's requests. As Ryan had indicated to the cou
that Susan was to be out of town in Montana on that date
Berkow agreed to allow Susan to appear in court telephonically

This turned out to be the most pivotal date in the War Be
tween the Polks. For one thing, Susan made no appearance
either in person, or over the telephone. The whole thing wa
done in Commissioner Berkow's chambers. Ryan showed u
in person, while Landes chimed in by telephone. By the tim
the thing was over, Berkow had given Felix complete author
ity to sell the dream house at a price he could set—far les
than Susan's "firm" $2 million—as well as physical and lega
custody of Gabriel.

Moreover, Felix had also asked the court to reduce Susan'
monthly "family support" from $6,500 plus Felix's $2,500 i
Social Security—a total of $9,000 each month—to $1,650. Fe
lix contended that if Susan didn't have to pay the mortgage, i
she didn't have to care for jailed Eli, or Gabe, there was no rea
son she needed so much money. Commissioner Berkow agree
to take Felix's request on the family support under considera
tion, and seemed favorably disposed to his arguments.

It appears that Ryan didn't immediately tell Susan o
Berkow's decision on Gabe and the house, or the proposal t
reduce her monthly income to $1,650. Or perhaps he tried, b
Susan wasn't taking any calls.

In other words, Felix's counterattack in the War Betwee
the Polks was finally beginning to get some headway. And t
Susan, this was really the final blow—the proof positive tha
Felix and his "group" had the courts completely, corruptibly
under their control.

The day after this hearing, Susan wrote to Eli in juvenil
hall, still waiting to learn his fate for snipping off his ele
tronic monitor and hiding out in Orinda over the summer:

> *Dear Eli,*
> *I heard from Gabe what happened on Thursday. Another*
> *delay [in fixing Eli's disposition]. Well, that was to be expected.*

*They are going to drag this out as long as possible, all so that
dad can show what big balls he has. I am so sorry.*

Realizing that Kolin intended to lower the boom on him,
Eli had written to Felix, promising to live with his father and
Gabe in the Orinda house and behave, if only Felix could get
him out of the fix he was in. But either Felix did not respond
to Eli, or if he did, he had no real pull with Judge Kolin. Eli
stayed in juvenile hall, awaiting the probation department's
"assessment."

Susan said that Eli should take comfort in the fact that
"many good and fine men have been imprisoned unjustly,"
and mentioned Tupac, Gandhi and Jesus.

"Prison is just a state of mind," she advised, never dreaming she would soon have the chance to put this sentiment to
the test herself.

Two days later, Susan wrote the most extraordinary entry
in her diary yet.

By this point, around October 1, 2002, it appears that Dan
Ryan had told Susan of Felix's attempt to reduce her monthly
support to $1,650. She'd sent a letter to Ryan asking him to
secure a postponement on the hearing for this issue until she
could get back from Montana, but apparently Ryan was unable to do this.

For some reason, this portion of Susan's diary was never
recovered from the hard drive of her computer. Just how it
came to vanish from the machine later became a mystery—
with Susan and her serial defenders suggesting that subsequent police tampering with the computer had "lost" many of
the most exculpatory portions of her diary, including the one
that follows. That it came to light at all was the product of yet
another peculiar circumstance.

This extraordinary diary entry began with a fragment of
an earlier entry, in which Susan noted that the divorce court

commissioner, Josanna Berkow, was being asked to reduce
her monthly support from Felix, and wondering whether Felix's supposed power over the courts would prevail.

> . . . *plotting how to* reduce *my support, how to dominate*
> *the children to the degree that they at least act as if they don't*
> *hate him, how to heap further shame on my reputation and to*
> *prop* up *his. Tomorrow, I will make up my mind about a condo*
> *and close a deal by the end of this week. I wonder if F. can get*
> *away with giving me nothing to live on.*

The next entry in this mysterious, unrecovered portion was
for October 2, 2002.

> *That question has been answered. The judge ruled yester-*
> *day that F. only had to pay me 1,721 in spousal support. How*
> *very fortunate for him. He only had to pay 1,500 to Sharon*
> *twenty years ago. He does make almost twice as much now as*
> *he did then. The courts are generous to older professionals*
> *with influence.*

Susan said she'd learned this directly from Felix in a telephone conversation the night before.

"Brace yourself, Susan," Felix had told her. "You're in for
a shock."

> Yes, I was shocked. I shocked him a bit too, accusing him of
> misusing his position as a Mossad agent to influence the
> court. It doesn't help that the judge is Jewish. At first he tried
> the "poor S., you really do need help" routine.

But Susan went on. She told Felix that when she'd married
him, she had no idea that she was also marrying into "a
Mossad cell." The proof, Susan said, was that Felix's closest
friends were making frequent trips to Germany and Pakistan.

It was clear to her, she implied, that Felix's friends were on assignment with Mossad in various places around the world, including Germany and Pakistan.

When she'd confronted him with his secret agent status, Susan said, Felix had told her that no one would believe her. Susan responded, "The Arabs will."

"Are you going to go over to the Arabs, then, Susan?" Felix asked, according to Susan.

"No," Susan said, "I don't like them any better than the Jews."

Susan said she asked how Felix could "betray" his own country. Felix responded by warning her again of the consequences to the boys. Well, Susan shot back, she didn't see how things could get much worse—Eli was in jail, Gabe was miserable.

Afterward, Susan noted to herself that she felt trapped. She couldn't join "the Mossad," aka Felix's "group." Yet she needed Felix's financial support, for which she needed Commissioner Berkow's validation. She quickly came to perceive Berkow as yet another member of Felix's "group"—just another tool used by him to "capture" her and hold her as his "prisoner," another sign that "the Jews" had covert influence.

> *Joining is impossible. I will not become an actress like the members of F.'s disgusting family . . . shamming kindness and humanity when underneath there is nothing but betrayal, sadism, and in the best of them, a kind of robotic indifference. F. is evil, and he is a traitor.*

Susan went on to make a cosmic jump, merging her antipathy toward Felix with a far larger conspiracy. In Susan's analysis, the Israeli government had known in advance of the 9/11 attacks, but failed to pass the information on to the U.S. In Susan's mind, the supposed failure of the Israelis to provide advance warning was "a lethal message" to the American military:

"If you do not support us, we might not warn you the next time we have intelligence about a terrorist attack on American targets, and the consequences might be much worse."

Susan believed the attacks inflamed anti-Muslim sentiment in the U.S., buttressing support for the Israelis against the Palestinians, and providing public support for American intervention in the Middle East. That was why the Israelis had kept their lips zipped about the attacks, she said—to inveigle the United States into a war against Islam.

Susan went on to summarize various world events that had taken place that year, and fit them all neatly into her conspiracy theory—all showing that the Americans were just the ignorant dupes of the scheming Israelis.

Susan went on in this vein for approximately six pages, deftly "interweaving" real events with her paranoid theory. And at the end she disclosed just how she knew all this:

After the 9/11 attacks, F. bragged to the kids that one of his patients had known that it was going to happen before it did. He was talking about me. I am a medium. F. told quite a lot of people this story, it turns out, and a few of them probably have some idea that it was me and what I can do.

What they don't know is that I gave F. the date. 9/11 is such a clear number. It came through so clearly. And there was time to warn people. F.'s cousin, who has an office in one of the Twin Towers, stayed home that day. Afterwards, he sent me an e-mail. It was a sort of a chain letter about someone, unidentified, who had predicted the terrorist attacks.

I am not happy about being a medium. First of all, I am only partly conscious of what is happening when I do what I do, and sometimes, I am not conscious at all, until later when I get flashbacks. I don't know whether this is because F. hypnotized me so frequently when I saw him as a patient (it was under hypnosis that this ability was discovered by F.) and instructed me not to remember, or whether it is a function of being a medium.

I have read a little about people who have been like me in the past, and from the descriptions it is clear that some of them went into a trance-like state, out of which they performed as a medium and had little or no memory of what they had said afterwards. It is so scary to me. Aside from the fact that I am married to a man who threatens to destroy me or kill me if I leave him, it is so scary to have been in a trance and not to remember. It is like dying.

Having a gap in my memory is the most horrible feeling. And then to have F. playing a role around me as if nothing happened and then acting as if I am crazy to think that anything did: it is horrible. It is such an unalloyed state of being to find myself in. And I don't feel at all happy or blessed. On the contrary, I feel cursed. What is there to be happy about? That over 3,000 people died who didn't have to on September 11 because F. and the Mossad decided to send a warning to the Pentagon: "support us or else."

Susan said she believed that the Israeli government would use atomic weapons against the United States and find a way to blame it on terrorists if the U.S. ever threatened to stop supporting Israel.

So, I am not the only one in a box. The military leadership in the U.S. must know what is happening; they must know that they are in a box, too.

I recall telling F. over and over when in a trance, "I cannot help you," by which I meant Israel. "There is no way for you (Israel) to win. There is no solution. The Arabs will never give up. You (Israel) will never win."

This was the beginning of the end of the world, Susan wrote.

This is a war that cannot be prevented. It has already begun. In one of my dreams, Colin Powell was the anti-Christ

and we were all getting in line in the U.S., marching towards
Armageddon.

Susan wrote this in her diary under the date October 2,
2002, after having just learned that her monthly support was
being cut from $9,000 to $1,720. She was clearly under a lot
of stress after hearing about this from Felix. As Felix had put
it, "Brace yourself." The next day Susan printed these diary
pages and faxed them to Felix.

At some point over the next few days she printed more
copies of these diary pages and mailed them to all the judges
of the Contra Costa County Superior Court, after first noting:

> *Thought you might be interested in this journal excerpt*
> *about a Mossad agent's failure to provide a warning to U.S.*
> *intel. re. terrorist attack on U.S. targets as well as judicial mis-*
> *conduct on the part of one of your fellow judges.*

Susan obviously meant Commissioner Berkow.

The day after writing this diary entry, Susan faxed a letter
to her lawyer, Dan Ryan.

"Dear Dan," she wrote, and proceeded to inform him that
she would not agree to pay his fees from her share of the
house proceeds, when or if the house ever sold.

"I believe your handling of my case has been incompetent," she wrote. She fired him, the second divorce lawyer to
bite the dust, and only the third in the long line of legal counsel to fail to satisfy Susan, who was, after all, the daughter of
a lawyer.

On the same day, Eli was sentenced to serve nine months at
the Orin Allen Youth Rehabilitation Facility, also known as
the Byron Boys Ranch. Hearing about this from Gabe, Susan
mailed Eli a letter, explaining Felix's "scapegoat" theories,
and attributing them to the British psychiatrist R. D. Laing,
who had once been affiliated with the Tavistock Clinic in London, where Felix had served his internship decades before.

Laing, Susan wrote, had written a book on the subject: how "crazy-making' families do this:

> they pick one of their children to be an example for the rest of the family members, to express for the family what they are afraid of, what could happened to them. It is a way of maintaining control over the family members. The 'example nigger' also expresses for the leader of the family the flaws or characteristics in his own nature that are not tolerable: for example violence, suicide, impulsivity, feelings of failure, craziness, homosexuality, whatever it is that the leader is anxious about or driven by. These feelings are projected onto the 'example nigger' of the family. In a sense, this child is selected as a sacrifice.

Susan told Eli:

You are not the violent, dangerous, impulsive character you have been portrayed as. You know yourself as I know you. Define yourself in your own terms. Reject the labels that have been placed on you. They *do* not belong to you. Never forget who you are or why this has happened to you. Rise above it.

On the same day, Eli wrote to Gabe.

> Dear Gabe,
> Today I had court. I can't believe that dad is pulling this crap on me. You need to watch what you eat when you're living with him.

Eli had accepted his mother's assertion that Felix was using secret drugs to control people. He suggested that Felix had arranged for him to be jailed for nine months at the Boys Ranch in order to have time to "straighten you out."

Gabe should try to stick things out with Felix, Eli advised, but he should also be aware that whenever things went wrong and it wasn't Gabe's fault, it was all Felix. If worse came to worst, Eli said, Gabe should try to live with Susan in Montana.

> He will do all kinds of shit, though. He will try to make you depressed, gay, mad, confused and anything else his crazy mind can think of.

Three days later, Eli again wrote Gabe, saying that he wouldn't be surprised to have to serve the whole nine months of his sentence, because of Felix's supposed influence with the court. Gabe should suppress his feelings as much as possible, Eli again suggested, or else Felix would find some way to make him "act out." Once he did, Eli suggested, Felix would have something to hammer him with.

"Dad has demonstrated that he is willing to put us in jail to force cooperation," Eli advised.

The next day, Susan left Montana for Orinda, intent, it appears, on trying to undo what Felix had done.

On the way back, she stopped in Jackson, Wyoming, and posted the letters of her October diary entry about Commissioner Berkow to the judges. In the upper left-hand corner she wrote the name of the sender: "A. Liddell," her wry reference to herself as Alice Liddell, of Lewis Carroll's *Alice in Wonderland*.

21. THE RETURN
OF SUSAN POLK

Susan got back to the dream house on Wednesday, October 9, 2002. Gabe could see his mother was very upset at what had happened in court while she'd been away.

"She was panicking," Gabe recalled later. "She was pretty upset, because she thought she pretty much lost everything." But of course this only represents a 15-year-old boy's assessment—someone who knew next to nothing about the law. The facts were, Susan couldn't really "have lost everything," since the state's community property laws prevented that. Clearly, Susan had to be upset for other reasons— probably and most significantly, Gabe's accession to brother Eli's advice that Gabe try to make do with Felix for the foreseeable future.

For Susan, this was an abandonment of her by Gabe. And an expensive abandonment at that, what with the associated reduction in her family support. Susan's immediate objective was to retrieve her physical position vis-à-vis the dream house, and next, to recapture the loyalties of Gabe.

Having arrived when Felix was at work, Susan immediately set about transferring his newly installed possessions—his clothes—from the main house to the pool house. In this, Susan was adopting Felix's earlier offer that they all live together at the dream house, but with Felix occupying the pool house as his separate residence. On the way back to Orinda, she'd cancelled the purchase of the condo in Montana. In a way, that made sense: until she could get Berkow's recent support order modified, and get Gabe back, she wouldn't have enough money to buy the place.

That evening Felix got home from work, and he and Susan sat down together in the kitchen to have what Gabe thought, at least initially, would be a very calm, reasonable discussion. But emotions soon became heated, and the next thing Gabe knew, his mother was telling him to leave the room, that she didn't want him to hear what she was going to tell his father. But Gabe stayed put, worried. That was when Susan told Felix again, this time in a low whisper, that she was going to kill him.

Or so Gabe later said he guessed, from his father's reaction. He admitted he hadn't actually heard the words Susan whispered.

"And he got really upset and excited and walked to the phone to call the police," Gabe recalled later. It was apparent to Gabe, from his father's reaction, that Felix thought Susan was serious. Or—perhaps Felix only wanted to make more trouble for Susan by calling the authorities. None of this was very clear to Gabe, who, after all, was only 15 years old at the time, and who knew only what his two feuding parents had told him about their long, complicated, emotional history, almost all of which was directly contradictory.

As Felix was calling the police, Susan tried to leave the kitchen, but Felix and Gabe blocked her.

"We thought she might have a gun or something," Gabe said. Both were afraid that the shotgun Susan had spoken of was in the trunk of her car, and they didn't want her to get it, Gabe claimed later.

Whatever Felix had told the police seemed to do the trick, because they were there within a few minutes. Felix showed them the court order giving him possession of the house and

ustody of Gabe, and apparently asked them to arrest Susan,
ut the police wouldn't do it. The officers suggested that Felix
nd Gabe go to a hotel for the evening—maybe tempers might
ool off overnight. So Felix and Gabe left the house to Susan,
nd checked into a nearby hotel.

The following day, they returned to the house, accompa-
ied by police, and obtained a change of clothing, then went
ack to the hotel for a second night. Susan remained adamant:
elix couldn't live in the main house; she was now back in the
ain house, and the asking price was *still* $2,050,000, not a
enny less.

The day after that, Friday, Gabe returned to the house
lone, and found that his mother had moved Felix's bed from
e den of the main house into the pool house.

"I was telling her not to," Gabe said. His mother then told
im she was sure that Felix had stashed $20 million or so in a
ecret bank account in the Cayman Islands. Susan told her son
at she was going to force Felix to wire transfer the money
to her own bank account by telephone while she pointed her
otgun at him, threatening to blow "his head off " if he didn't
omply. She explained to Gabe that Felix was involved in
ome sort of conspiracy with the Mossad, and that Felix had
een hiding the money from her as well as the IRS. But, Susan
ld Gabe, she'd make sure that Felix paid what he owed.

That afternoon, Adam arrived at the house; he'd been cited
or being a minor in possession of alcohol earlier in the sum-
er, and had to attend a court-ordered counseling session the
ext day. Felix had agreed to drive Adam back to UCLA on
e following Sunday. Felix returned to the house that Friday
vening, and all three male Polks decided to steer clear of Su-
an by going to a movie, *The Ring*, in the nearby community
f Pleasant Hill. That night, Felix slept in the pool house.
here were no further confrontations between Susan and Fe-
x, as each Polk parent again tried to avoid the other.

Early Sunday morning, Felix, Gabe and Adam arose early
 begin the trip to Los Angeles. Susan was awakened by the

commotion downstairs in the main house, and got up to com
plain. That was, she said later, the last time she saw Felix.

That evening, Felix and Gabe returned from southern Cal
fornia, having made the nearly 800-mile round-trip in a litt
over twelve hours. Felix was exhausted after all the driving
and immediately retired to the pool house.

The next morning was Monday, October 14, 2002, bu
Frank Felix Polk would never see its dawn. Later that evening
Gabriel Polk discovered his father's bloody body in the poo
house, called the 911 operator, and then hid in the shadow
from his mother, fearful that she *did* have a shotgun, and wa
about to kill him, too.

V.
THE TRIALS OF SUSAN POLK

22. BLOODY MURDER

Sergeant Kenneth Hansen was a shift supervisor for the Contra Costa County sheriff's department, which provided police services to the city of Orinda under a contract arrangement. Just after 9 P.M. he was on patrol some distance away from Orinda when the police dispatcher called him on his radio to say that there was a barricaded suspect and an injured person in a house in the hills above Orinda. Hansen turned his prowl car around and headed for Orinda, arriving in front of the Miner Road house just before 9:30 P.M. By that time, four other police officers had arrived.

Gabe had run down the driveway to meet them. He gave the police a rough sketch of the compound, and said that he thought his mother might have a shotgun, although he had never seen it. The fire department's paramedics were still waiting to go in, because the protocol with a barricaded suspect possibly armed with a gun was first to establish a perimeter around the property to prevent any escape, and then to investigate—very carefully. Once the police had secured the scene, and only then, would the paramedics go in.

On his arrival, Hansen made sure that the perimeter was secure, then ascended the driveway to the main house, accompanied by none other than Orinda Officer Shannon Kelly, one of those who had so often been to the dream house on earlier occasions. Hansen knew only that there was supposed to be an injured person somewhere on the property, reportedly in the pool house. He had not talked directly with Gabe. As they approached the front door of the main house, Hansen and Kelly saw a woman through a window, approaching the door. Susan opened it and politely asked what they wanted.

She seemed calm and cooperative.

"We've had a report that your husband has been injured," Hansen told her. "We need to check to see if he's all right. Can you tell us, have you seen him tonight?"

"No," Susan said. "The last time I saw him was this afternoon."

"Well," Hansen said, "we're going to have to search for him to see if he's okay. Now, I'm going to put you under arrest for the time being until we can get this sorted out." Hansen put his handcuffs on Susan, then made her sit on a wooden bench outside the front door while he continued his search. He left Kelly, armed with a shotgun, to watch her.

Hansen crossed the deck and followed the path to the pool house. Someone had told him that the rear door of the pool house was unlocked. Hansen made his way down the hallway and soon observed Felix lying face-up, unmoving, on the floor, clad only in black bikini briefs. Hansen could see what appeared to be bloody wounds on the torso, and saw blood smears on the floor. Hansen's statements about what he did next were fairly plain. He said he'd approached "within three feet of the victim," and "I determined that he had expired . . . realizing that, I stepped carefully back out of the room as to not disturb the crime scene."

On the way back to the main house, Hansen reported back to the dispatcher that he had a homicide case; the dispatcher in turn notified the sheriff's department's homicide specialists, who would soon arrive to take over the investigation.

Back at the front door Hansen approached Susan.

"I'm sorry to tell you this, but your husband is dead,"

The pool house on the Polk property, where Felix Polk
died on the night of October 13, 2002.
(Courtesy Contra Costa County Sheriff's Department)

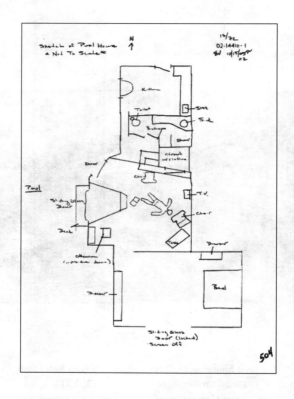

Contra Costa criminalist Song Wicks's sketch of the pool
house layout, made on the morning of October 15, 2002.
(Courtesy Contra Costa County Sheriff's Department)

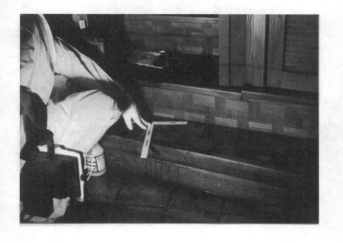

A criminalist precisely measures a drop of blood found
on the stairs in the pool house. The blood drop
showed that someone had exited the pool house by using
the back door after Felix Polk's death.
(Courtesy Contra Costa County Sheriff's Department)

An athletic shoe print found near Felix Polk's body was initially measured at 10.5 inches, but closer examination showed it was actually two prints, both the approximate size of Susan Polk's shoe. No matching shoes were ever found, however.
(Courtesy Contra Costa County Sheriff's Department)

Felix Polk was apparently reading the novel about the CIA, "The Company," when the confrontation with Susan Polk began.
(Courtesy Contra Costa County Sheriff's Department)

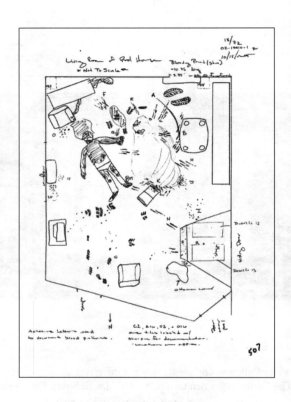

Criminalist Song Wicks's sketch of the pool house death scene. Susan contended that the sketch made the room seem larger than it actually was.

(Courtesy Contra Costa County Sheriff's Department)

Felix Polk as he appeared on his 1967 application for a psychologist's license.
(Courtesy Contra Costa County Sheriff's Department)

BELOW The house on Elmwood in Berkeley, California, where Felix conducted group therapy sessions in the family home for many years.
(Courtesy Carlton Smith)

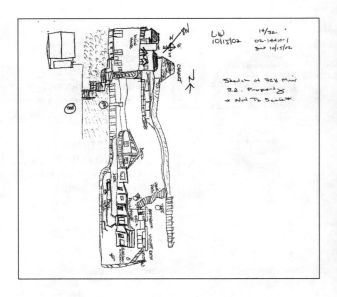

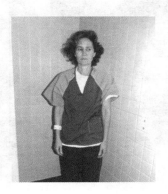

ABOVE Song Wicks's sketch of the dream house layout. The pool house is on the lower right. *(Courtesy Contra Costa County Sheriff's Department)*

Susan Polk following her arrest in the early morning hours on October 15, 2002. *(Courtesy Contra Costa County Sheriff's Department)*

Hansen told her. "It does not appear that he died from natural causes."

"Well," Susan said, "too bad."

There was a short pause.

"We were getting a divorce anyway," she said.

Or so Hansen later claimed she'd said.

23. TAG TEAM

A little after midnight, both Susan and Gabriel were in separate interview rooms of the sheriff's department's central headquarters.

Facing Susan was Mike Costa, a veteran Contra Costa detective then closing in on retirement. It was Costa who had "caught" the case, as murder detectives liked to say, simply because he was next up on the assignment list.

After finding a blanket for Susan—she said she was cold—Costa explained that while she wasn't "under arrest," she was "being detained," a meaningless distinction; once Susan was forcibly prevented from departing the sheriff's headquarters—by armed deputies—she was under arrest, no matter what Costa called it.

But Costa knew enough to read the "detained" Susan her rights under Miranda.

"You understand all that?" he asked.

"Yes," Susan said.

"Okay, do you want to talk to me about what happened?"

"I do."

"Okay."

"And I'm very, very tired," Susan said.

"Okay. So am I," Costa told her. "I haven't been to bed all day, either, but we have to do this."

"What did happen?" Susan asked.

"Well, that's what I'm hoping you can tell me. What happened?"

She hadn't heard any gunshots, Susan said. And she didn't own a gun.

"Okay. You've been occupying the main house?"

"I didn't see him all day, so I don't know."

This was almost a non sequitur.

Costa asked Susan to tell him what she'd done that day, from the time she woke up to the time he'd begun the interview. This was standard interrogation technique, designed in part to build a timeline, and in the process, lock Susan into a story that might later be probed for deception.

Susan told of taking Gabe to school, and said she'd come home immediately thereafter.

"So what has happened to my husband?" Susan persisted. "Is he dead?"

"As far as I know," Costa said. "As far as I can tell, yeah. There's a person in that house, in that guesthouse that's no longer—"

"Did my son see him?"

"I don't know. I'm not talking to your son. I haven't talked to your son."

At the same moment, down the hallway, two other detectives were talking to Gabe. As far as anyone could tell at that point, there were only two primary suspects in Felix's death—Susan and Gabe. And of the two, Susan was the more likely, since Gabe had been the one who'd reported it. But the detectives knew they had to go by the book, which required them to also advise Gabe of *his* rights.

Once that was over, Gabe having agreed to answer their

questions without a lawyer present, Detectives Jeff Moule and Jeff Hebel eased Gabe into the family background. Gabe explained that the Polks had lived first in Berkeley, then Piedmont, before moving to Orinda. Asked where he was attending school, Gabe explained that he'd been enrolled by Felix in a continuation school, and that he'd dropped out of Miramonte High School the previous year.

"How come you dropped out of Miramonte?" Moule asked. "What was going on?"

"My mom encouraged me to stay home from school."

"Why did she want you to stay home from school?"

"She didn't like Miramonte."

"Why?"

"She is crazy, and so she thought all the teachers at Miramonte were against me or something, and so I missed a month-and-a-half at the end of the year."

This, of course, was when Eli was going through his travails with the juvenile justice system. Susan had been worried that Eli's enemies from the battle of the Jack in the Box might retaliate against Gabe. That was one reason why Susan had tried to convince him to be "homeschooled" by her over the final month.

"You said your mom is crazy," Moule said. "Tell me about your growing up, things that she has done that justify you saying that she is crazy."

"My mom was fine up until about five years ago, when— I don't really— I am not clear on what happened, but she had memories of her childhood," Gabe told Moule and Hebel. "And her parents were real scumbags. Her father raped her, and just abused her and stuff. And she became delusional, apparently, at that time, and was put on medication for a few months. And after that— I don't know the name of that medication, but it was for— to stop her from being so delusional and paranoid. I think her and my dad went to a bunch of psychologists, and she eventually stopped taking the medication

And then in a few years she, like, directed all of her, I guess, just delusions and paranoia, towards my dad.

"And what my dad said is, that she got him confused for her—with her father. So, she had all this anger towards my dad, which was actually the anger that she had towards her father, which was probably pretty scary for my dad. And so this, the last four years have been really just hell— They have been arguing, just at each other's throats."

Back in the other interview room, Costa was taking Susan through the rest of the day. He seemed interested in Gabriel's movements, and picked up on Susan having left Gabe home alone to rent a video in Lafayette. The only other time she'd left the house, Susan told Costa, was in the morning, between 10 and 12, when she'd gone walking to look for one of the dogs who had gotten loose. Otherwise, she'd spent the day cleaning and cooking.

"I was pretty much there for most of the day," Susan said. 'I didn't hear anything. And I didn't see his car. I didn't see his car this morning."

Costa now established from Susan for the first time that Felix's car seemed to be missing.

"Okay. Okay," Costa said, jotting notes. "How long have you guys been married?"

"It would be twenty-one years in December."

"Okay, how long has the marriage not been going well?"

"Well there were times off and on throughout the marriage when I brought up getting a divorce."

"Uh-huh," Costa nodded.

"And particularly five years ago, I said that I couldn't see living with him any longer, and asked him to move out."

"Uh-huh. Okay. That was five years ago, but you're still living in the same property?"

"Well, he said, you know, that he would never let me go

and that kind of thing . . . and he was really, it was just very difficult. I don't have a job and, you know, he is my source of income."

But it was more than that, Susan admitted.

"But I just, you know, I couldn't—and I was very attached to him, too. So I mean, it was like, yeah, you know, I wanted a divorce. But then he would say things and then it would be hard to go through with it."

Costa wanted to know where the divorce case stood right then. Who was her lawyer?

"I fired my attorney," Susan said. "I don't have an attorney right now."

Susan explained about Eli and Kolin, Felix's obtaining custody of Eli, Eli's sentence to the boys' ranch for nine months, and her decision to move with Gabe back to Montana. Gabe had wanted to come with her on the last trip, she said, but she'd told him to stay with Felix until she found a place. That was when she'd heard that Felix had convinced the court to give him the house and Gabe.

"And then while I was away, Felix got into court, really, really quickly, and got custody of Gabe . . . and had my spousal support reduced from like seven thousand five hundred dollars—it was actually at that point seven thousand five hundred dollars—to one thousand seven hundred dollars, based in part on income statements that he submitted while I was away, which weren't really accurate."

Susan explained that Felix, in asking the court to reduce the spousal support payments, had counted his taxes twice to make his expenses seem larger, and that her lawyer, Dan Ryan, should have noticed this. That was why she'd fired Ryan, she said.

"So while I'm in Montana, I get this phone call, *Guess what*, you know, *you just lost custody of your son, your husband has exclusive use of the house, and you get one thousand seven hundred dollars a month to live on*. I'm like, *You've got to be kidding* . . .

"So I come back very quickly, and try and get things resolved. Fired my attorney. Felix was like, 'Well, you're just gonna have to, you know, hang around now, and handle this in court.' And I'm like, 'That's very clear that I'll have to do that and I'll need a place to stay.'

"And he says, 'Well, you can't stay in the house, *I* have the house now.' And I'm like, *Oh my God*. Then he said I could stay in the cottage [the pool house]. And I found that just really insulting."

That was when the police had come to the house, Susan said. She said the order that Felix had from the court was only rubber-stamped with the commissioner's signature, not personally signed. She considered that her order was more valid than Felix's—for all she knew, Felix or his lawyer had a fake copy of Berkow's rubber stamp, and were trying to pull yet another trick on her.

"This was this last weekend?"

"Yeah. And he—he had actually threatened to kill me right before the police officers came. . . ."

"Uh-huh."

"And he didn't deny it. He said that I had a shotgun. And I said, 'No, I don't have a shotgun.' And at any rate, I was in the house with Gabe—actually, Gabe and his dad left for a few days and they went to a hotel, because while I was away, Gabe kind of, you know, turned loyal to his dad. And, you know, he changed from being 'I love my mom and I want to live with my mom,' to 'I love my dad and I want to live with my dad.' "

"Uh-huh."

"And went from 'My dad is crazy' to 'My mom is crazy.' "

"So," Moule was saying to Gabe at the same time in the other interview room, "over the last five years she's been acting out at the house and—"

"Yes."

"Would you tell me, what kind of stuff does she do?"

"It's just crazy shit, like— Do you want to know stuff that she says about her father, or stuff that she says—"

"Sure. What does she say about her father?"

"Well, my dad is like— I don't know— I don't really know a lot of stuff. I don't know too much about her family and everything. But I know that she makes some stuff up, and some stuff is true. Like she made some stuff up about her dad and her whole family that—she just imagined it or something."

"So, what time— Has she acted violent around the house?"

"Violent? Let me try and think," Gabe said. "Not— She is really provocative. She is completely delusional. Like she says stuff like that my dad is in the Mossad. She thinks he is a Mossad agent, working for the CIA or something, and she called a bunch of embassies and stuff and told them all that. And she thinks people follow her. She thinks my dad pays people to follow her. She thinks people standing on the street are giving her hand signals or something."

"Have you actually seen her and heard her say these things?"

"Yeah."

"You mean, driving down the street, and she will say, 'That guy is trying to signal me,' or something like that?"

"Yeah."

"Really?" Moule said, apparently impressed.

"Yeah."

"And is that a regular thing?"

"Yup, pretty much. She thinks people— She thinks my dad has like a bank account in the Cayman Islands with like twenty, or like forty or fifty million dollars."

"What does your dad do for a living?"

"He is a psychologist."

"Now, what does your husband do for employment?" Costa asked Susan.

"He's a psychologist."

"Psychologist. So he worked out of his house, or did he have an office somewhere?"

"He used to. He used to work out of our house for many years. He has an office in Berkeley now."

"Berkeley. Do you know the name? What does he call the business?"

"F. Felix Polk, Ph.D., a Psychological Corporation."

Susan explained to Costa that the family had been having financial trouble over the previous few months, what with the high mortgage payments and unpaid taxes. She said that although they had a lot of assets, they needed to reorganize to pay the taxes and eliminate more of their debt. Susan herself owed about $100,000 in taxes from her share of the sale of the Piedmont property. That was one reason she decided to cancel her purchase of property in Montana.

"So then I thought, *I can't do that*, and just spent a lot of time thinking about our finances on the way home and how to get things, you know, handled. 'Cause we owe a lot of— We have like about seventy thousand dollars in [credit card] debt. So I came back, I paid my taxes, paid off some of my debt."

She and Felix had been having discussions about what to do about the Orinda house—sell it or refinance it, Susan said. She said that Felix wanted to refinance it. Felix had finally agreed to stay in the pool house until the spousal support issue was resolved, she added. Felix had even agreed that the reduction was too much, and that they would try to get things straightened out the following week at the scheduled October 16 court hearing.

Costa wanted to get back to what Susan knew, and when she had known it.

"Well, okay, let me ask you this. When is the last time you saw your husband?"

"Sunday morning around five, five-thirty, when I came downstairs and chewed him out for just roaming around the house." Susan had chided Felix with her previous court order—the one she considered still to be in force—which held that Felix had to stay away from the main house. This was in contradiction to what Susan had supposedly told Sergeant Hansen, that she'd seen Felix some time Monday.

"So you're saying Sunday, they drove back down to UCLA, right?"

"Yeah. Right, they left around five-thirty."

"And then Gabe and your husband came back that night, Sunday night."

That was right, Susan said. They'd arrived about ten P.M. but she never saw Felix.

Costa moved on to another issue.

"Okay. So what's all this about a shotgun that I heard about, that you supposedly said you were gonna get a shotgun?"

"No."

"You've never had a shotgun?"

"No," Susan said. She didn't believe in guns. Gabe wanted a gun, she said, but she said he couldn't have one, because he was a minor. Besides, she said, "When people get guns, they're tempted to use them, it's just a little bit easier. I mean it's like a gun has a purpose."

"Uh-huh."

"So I said, 'If you want a gun, go into the military and then you can, you know, get into all of that. But no, you know, I don't think you should."

"Did he indicate that he already had one?"

"Oh, God, no."

"No?"

"No, he's a good boy," Susan said.

"Did you ever see your mom hit your dad?" Moule asked Gabriel.

"I have seen— No, I haven't, but she got arrested for it.

have seen my dad, like, slap my mom, but it is as much as he did, you know. I mean, and I can—you know, I personally can see a reason for it. She is totally out of her mind. I mean, she can act perfectly normal. I am sure in the next room over there she is acting perfectly normal. And she does for the most part, but she just has a distorted reality. . . ."

Moule was impressed with Gabe's vocabulary. He wanted to know if Gabe had discussed his mother's mental state with his father.

"I have discussed it with my father, I have discussed it with my brothers, and I have discussed it with a psychologist." But he didn't like the psychologist, Gabe added, so he'd quit going.

Gabe told the detectives of Susan's suicide attempt at Yosemite.

"How did she try to kill herself?"

"Overdosed on pills."

"And then she called home and told you guys what she did?"

"She called home and wanted to talk to my dad, and this is like supposedly what she told my dad. And she says that she loves him, that she is really sorry that she tried to kill herself, and that she is like dying, or whatever."

"So, then what happened?"

"My dad called the police, and they picked her up, and she was put in a—she was at the hospital, and they were interviewing her for a, just a mental examination. And they felt like she was perfectly sensible. Like I said, she can act perfectly sane most of the time."

"Have the police ever been out to your house?"

"Many times," Gabriel said.

The most recent visit from the police had come the previous week, Gabe explained, when Felix had tried to have Susan arrested. If only they'd done what Felix wanted, Gabe suggested, maybe none of this would've happened.

"I don't know the details on it, but the police came out. He showed them the court— My mom came back to handle stuff with the courts, supposedly. I think she actually just came back to murder my dad, is what she did. She says she was coming back to take care of business."

Susan was telling Costa about her conversation earlier that night with Gabe.

"And I said, 'Well, why don't we just call highway patrol and see if there's been a problem?' Like an unreported accident or something."

"Uh-huh."

"And he said, 'No, I'm gonna handle this.' And he gets a flashlight and leaves the house."

Susan said she'd been taking a bath just before this, but when Gabe left the house with the flashlight, she got dressed and went outside and called after him.

"Who?" Costa asked. "Gabe?"

"Yeah. He didn't answer. And then I went down in the driveway and I saw flashing lights and I didn't know what was going on."

"So Gabe left the house after that first phone call? Where was he going?"

"He came back in again, and then he went back out. And he said, he accused me of having done something to his dad."

"What did he accuse you of?"

"Of having killed his dad. And I'm like—"

"Where were you at that time?"

"I was in bed reading a book."

"But that was after the phone call, where he wanted to talk to an officer?"

"Yeah, I think so."

"Okay," Costa said. "So let me see if I got this right, because it's very important that we—"

"I might be getting a little mixed up on this," Susan admitted

Susan said she'd followed Gabe outside, and then had seen the flashing red lights of the emergency vehicles, "and then I thought, *What is going on?*"

Susan told Costa she'd thought about walking down the driveway to join Gabe to see what was happening.

"And then I thought, *Well, I don't want to be a gawker.* So I went in the house. I was waiting for Gabe to come back."

"Okay," Costa said. "But you said at one point he accused you of hurting his father."

"Yeah."

Costa asked when that accusation had been made—before or after Gabe had left the house with the flashlight.

"I think it was after," Susan said.

"Where were you at, when he accused you of hurting his dad?"

"I was in my room. I got up and I came to talk to him. Our rooms are right next to each other."

"Uh-huh. And what did he say?"

"I think he said, 'You killed him.'"

"Uh-huh. And what did you say?"

"'What?' I don't remember exactly. I was like, 'Gabriel . . .'"

"Gabriel—what?" Costa prodded.

"I don't want to say exactly what I said, because I don't remember exactly."

"Uh-huh."

"I was just shocked."

Gabe was sketching in the events of the preceding two weeks—the court decision that had granted Felix custody of Gabriel and the house, along with the reduction in spousal support.

"She knew through the courts," Gabe said. "There was a court hearing while she was gone, and her lawyer called her from court and told her about everything else going on, so she knew that my dad had physical custody of Miner and physical custody of me."

"So, is that when she became angry?"

"Yeah, she got infuriated about that. She was already mad, and she already talked about killing my dad."

"She talked to you about killing?"

"Countless numbers of times, she did."

"What did she say to you?"

"Just the different ways she would do it, or whatever . . . It's just been escalating. She has become more and more delusional."

"Did she say how she would kill him?"

"Drugging him and drowning him, maybe run him over, tampering with his car."

"Why was she telling you all this?"

"She thought I, like, would— I don't know . . . I don't know. She thought that I, like, agreed with her or whatever, when I was going along with what she was saying, or that— I don't really know why she told me. She just trusted me, trusted me."

"When was the last time she spoke about killing your dad?"

"Yesterday."

"You don't know what happened to your husband?" Costa asked.

"No."

"Okay, something happened, obviously. That's why we're all here. That's why you're here. You've had ongoing marital problems for some time now, living in different places, money difficulties. So something happened, Susan."

"That doesn't mean that I killed him."

"Well, somebody did. What do you think happened?"

"I don't have enough information to speculate about what happened. I don't even know—"

"Was he seeing any other ladies?"

"I don't even know that he's dead."

"Was he seeing any other women?"

"I mean, do I *know* that he's dead? I mean—who has identified him? Did my son find his body?"

"Yes," Costa said.

"Oh, my God," said Susan.

"Oh, you know what?" Gabe said, in the other room. "When she was coming back from Montana, she actually called my dad and told him what she planned to do, that she would—she threatened to shoot him with a shotgun."

"Your dad told you this?"

"I was there. I was on the phone . . . She just said that she— Oh, yeah. That if he didn't let her stay in the house with me, that— She wanted him to be out in the cottage, and if he didn't let that happen, let her in the house, she would kill him."

"Did she say how she would kill him?"

"She would shoot him with a shotgun."

"Does she own a shotgun?"

"How did he die?" Gabe asked, surprised.

"I am not sure."

"You don't know yet?" For the first time, Gabe seemed to be entertaining a doubt that his mother had killed his father.

"We are figuring that out right now," Moule said.

"Okay. I've got to tell you, Susan, you know, right now we have to look at you as possibly doing this, having done this. You have the motive, you know, the marital problems going on. I'm sure tempers are not good between you, you know, as in any divorce."

"He's my sole source of income . . . There is no life insurance . . . He makes . . . He grosses about eighteen thousand dollars a month from his practice and his teaching."

"Uh-huh."

"I would not kill my husband. I can't pay the bills."

"Well, you know, right now I have to focus on you because you're the only one that had the opportunity."

"That's pretty clear, yeah," Susan seemed to agree with Costa.

"That had opportunity to do it," Costa reiterated.

"Well, I don't know that," Susan was now disagreeing.

"I think the best thing you can do for yourself is tell us what happened. You know, maybe there's some—"

"I've told you."

"Maybe there's some self-defense issues here."

"But it's clear, it's clear that I'm a suspect."

"If it was you laying there, you know, deceased, we'd be looking at *him*. *He'd* be sitting here. There's no signs of forced entry that we could see. It's not like this was a robbery or a burglary that went bad."

"He was not a good husband in many ways for the last few years . . . but I was very fond of him before. And I wasn't angry enough to kill him."

"It only takes a split moment to get angry enough to do something like that. It happens all the time. It happens all the time."

"That's why I don't own firearms."

"I think you need to tell us what really happened today."

"I have told you."

"This is your turn. This is your time to get it out, what happened. Maybe, you know, like I said, maybe there's a self-defense issue here. We're not gonna know about it—" Costa was about to say that if self-defense was involved, they'd have to hear it first from Susan.

"I didn't do it. I did not kill my husband."

"Did you put somebody up to it?"

"Of course not."

"You need to tell the truth [about] what happened, you really do."

"I told the truth."

"It's the only thing that's really gonna help you."

"That is the truth. I've told you the truth."

"You're gonna have us believe that just some stranger came in there and did this to him?"

"I'm not going to speculate about what happened. My husband did not lead an impeccable life. He's had his life threatened before."

"By who?"

"Well, you know, I wish I could give you the name."

"Uh-huh," Costa said, disbelieving. "Okay. I've got to tell you, you know, something happened between you and Felix today that got out of hand."

"No way."

"Well, that's my feeling."

"Did not."

"And you're sitting over there, and you're probably just dying to spill it out what happened. And you can't, for whatever reason. I don't know, afraid of going to jail or—"

"No."

Costa now told Susan that he would check to see if the detectives still at the house had found anything new.

"Be right back with you," he said, and left the room.

When he returned, he was accompanied by Moule, who had briefed him on the questioning of Gabriel.

"What's this about you believed your husband was with the Mossad, he had like millions stashed in a Cayman Islands account somewhere? Why would your son think that?"

"Well," Susan said, "you want to take those separately or together?"

"However you want to tell me."

"When we got married about twenty-one years ago, he had me sign a pre-nuptial agreement, but I didn't have an attorney present . . . and usually— I mean, I was really, really young and I was very naïve. And usually when people sign a pre-nup it's because there's something to protect, right? And over the years, I mean, he sort of had a way of talking about things that was kind of like not straight out, but it was kind of like hinting

around, and under the surface and, you know, a lot of just kind
of— You know, it was double-talk . . . He sort of would talk
about having assets, it seemed like to me that I would always
be provided for, and the kids would.

"But now . . . that we're getting divorced, I've asked him,
you know, about that, he's like, *No*. And so, yeah, I did, I did
believe that he had offshore accounts. Because it doesn't seem
reasonable to me that a man from his background would turn
over all of his assets to his . . . twenty-four-year-old wife. And
that's ostensibly what he did. I managed everything."

"So how about this Mossad thing?"

"That is more speculative," Susan said. "I kind of, keep a
diary. It's part fiction and it's part— You know, it goes between fantasy and reality. And he has a friend who I think
probably is a Mossad agent because of statements that his
friend has made that sort of imply that he is."

"Uh-huh."

"And you know, that his wife, his ex-wife married a
Mossad agent, ha ha. And he said, 'We like to keep it in the
family,' and offered when Eli grew up to put him in the Israeli
Air Force and things like that. And so I just sort of speculated
that he probably was."

"Did you ever see anything that indicates these offshore
accounts?"

"No."

"No books or anything?"

"No," Susan said.

Costa having failed to induce Susan to confess, Moule now
tried his hand.

"Mrs. Polk, I truly believe that the best thing for you to do
is to tell us why it happened," he said. He said she needed to
think about the boys, who knew she had done it, but deserved
to know why. He told Susan that evidence technicians would
find out what happened, and be able to prove she did it. What
they wanted to know was—why?

"I did not kill my husband."

"Okay. How did it happen, then?"

"I don't know. I mean, that's what Officer Costa was asking me. I don't know. I'm not an expert. And I didn't see what happened, so I don't know."

"Well, if you're adamant that you didn't do it, Susan, then the only other explanation is you had somebody do it for you."

"Why would I kill my source of income? That would be stupid."

"So you could have it all," Costa told her.

"Have all of what? We're separated. We are legally separated . . . I will get a lot less now that he's dead than I would otherwise."

Moule left the room, apparently to get Susan's formal arrest started.

"You really need to get something working for yourself here, Susan. I mean, you're living—"

"I mean, what is my—"

"Let me finish," Costa said. "You're living in some sort of dreamworld right now, where you think this is all gonna go away if you just deny it."

"Well, I think that— I think it's been so, I've been living in a dreamworld for many years."

It was time to get out of the dreamworld, Costa told her. The first step out was to tell the truth about what had happened.

"I'm very, very tired," Susan said. "If you're gonna put me in jail, put me in jail, so I can go to sleep, okay?"

"We're taking care of that," Costa assured her.

After his questioning was over, the detectives allowed Gabe to call Adam. Apparently one of the detectives told Adam what had happened, then put Gabe on the phone.

"Mom fucking shot dad with a shotgun," Gabe told Adam.

"Yeah. Fucking crazy bitch." There was a pause as Adam apparently asked Gabe something.

"We still have an apartment house," Gabe said. "We still have the apartment. We get income. . . . Dad left us a pile of . . . That's for sure. . . ."

"What the hell is wrong with her? I hope they give her the fucking death penalty."

24. THE MURDER EXPRESS

Early the next morning, back at the dream house, two evidence technicians began scouring the palatial estate for evidence to explain Felix's demise. They began in the main house, looking for any bloodstained clothing, towels or weapons, but found only a knife that had been taken from the running dishwasher by Costa the night before. They soon moved on to the pool house.

It seemed pretty clear that the pool house had been a structure that had evolved over time. It sort of spilled down over different levels, linear in construction as well as architecturally impromptu, add-on upon add-on. At the north end of the line of rooms was a kitchen, with its own door to the outside, the one Gabe said he had gone through the night before [see the police diagram of "the pool house" sketched by criminalist Song Wicks, employed by the Contra Costa County sheriff's department,].

Then there was a bathroom, followed by a small landing about two steps higher than the red-brick-tiled living room floor, separated from the living room by a wooden banister. According to Gabe, he had come only this far the night before.

The living room itself was oddly shaped, beginning with the front door, which was set at an angle to the rest of the room. The north "wall" of the living room, consisting of the banister, two steps up between the end of the banister and a floor-to-ceiling closet on the east half of the room, was also angled, so that the living room was not square. The most unusual feature of the living room was a sort of stagelike projection jutting out from the west wall, which itself had a sliding glass door that gave access to the swimming pool. It was almost as if a resident of the pool house could mount the stage from the tiled living room, open the glass door, give a Tarzan-like yell, and dive into the water. The bizarre, protruding obstruction of the stage added to the overall weirdness of the scene.

South of the living room, up two steps, was a bedroom, which had a sliding glass door on the south wall that gave onto yet another deck.

Entering through the kitchen door on the north, the criminalists—Wicks and Alex Taflya—were almost immediately confronted by the ugly reality of Felix's dead body on the tiled floor. Faceup, his hands thrust outward, clad only in black bikini briefs, it was almost as if Felix in his death had assumed a cruciform pose. Blood seemed to be everywhere.

But it was also apparent that he had been rolled over at some point—the blood pooling on the adjacent red tiles to his left, the immediate west, suggested that he had first lain facedown for some time, bleeding, before someone had come along to flip him over onto his back. A stream of blood appeared to flow from the back of his head from this supine position southeast underneath a heavy leather chair, toward the lowest part of the tile floor.

This suggested that a comatose Felix had bled in two different positions, first on his stomach and later on his back, and that therefore there might have been an initial frontal attack, the prone bleeding, followed by a somewhat later assault resulting in the head wound to the rear of the skull, then the flipping over, resulting in the supine bloodstream to the lowered southeast corner of the pool house.

The head wound was a particularly ugly injury, a large

gash, apparently caused by a heavy, blunt object. Yet, when inspected, it seemed to show little or no blood—it was a peculiar wound, given the bloodstream that seemed to be associated with it.

The wounds to the rest of the body were clearly *not* gunshot wounds, but stab wounds. No shotgun here, that was for sure.

Nevertheless, someone, in an apparent frenzy of violent anger, had taken a knife to Frank Felix Polk, and had repeatedly stabbed and sliced him. The cuts were all over his body—even what appeared to be cuts on the bottoms of his feet. And minutes later, possibly, he had been whacked hard across the top of his skull, maybe, just to make sure.

The overall picture of the living room of the pool house showed that a violent encounter had taken place over a span of only a few minutes, at least initially. The blood spatters all around the room indicated that whatever had happened, it began and ended fairly quickly. This was not a slowly developing encounter. That was potential evidence that the combatants were familiar with one another before the battle had begun.

In one corner of the room, a leather ottoman had been overturned, spattered with blood on its underside, which indicated that it had been flipped before the blood began to flow. Its cover lay about a dozen feet away, near the oddly angled front door.

The wide distribution of blood spatters at different points around the room, including the various smears, suggested a large number of wounds, as well as the frenzy of the attack. The "velocity" of blood drips on the walls and floor, even some on the east wall, suggested someone wielding the killing knife with great rapidity—the deposit of the blood in these places indicated repeated, fast, intense movement of the killing blade. As a general rule, psychological profilers had long previously postulated that the greater the number of knife wounds, and the wider the distribution of surrounding cast-off blood spatters, the more emotional was the attack—in

the profilers' view, this "frenzy" of stabbing almost always indicated that the perpetrator was someone emotionally involved with the victim.

People who didn't *really* care, emotionally—say, a professional killer, like the Butcher of Barcelona in *The Guns of
Navarone*—didn't repeatedly stab. For them, once or twice
was usually enough. That left far fewer blood spatters, and for
the "hit man," much less evidence. So the cast-off blood pattern indicated that the person using the knife had been an
emotional amateur, someone well-known to Felix.

It seemed evident, from the blood-spatter patterns, that the
struggle had begun in the center of the room. A book—Robert
Littell's historical CIA novel, *The Company*—lay on the floor
at Felix's feet, opened to Chapter Three, its pages bent and
bloodied, as if the book had at one point been squashed under
his bleeding body.

He had seemingly just finished reading the part of Littell's
book where one of the main characters is ordered to undergo
ritual circumcision to facilitate his cover as a gentile posing as
a Jewish spy, and where the same character, actually a dedicated Communist, has just begun to muse between the moral
differences among Communism, Judaism, and Christianity.

Or perhaps the killer had opened the book to that page as a
message—"staging," as the police liked to refer to it, using a
murder victim as the pivotal prop in the ultimate sort of "performance art."

In that case, one had to look at Felix's bloody body—face-
up, arms akimbo cruciformly, barely dressed in black bikini
briefs, a book about Jews and Christians, Nazis and Commu-
nists open at his feet to a pertinent page, and spattered with his
blood. . . . Was the killer making some sort of statement about
his or her beliefs, or those of Felix?

The most interesting aspect of the murder scene was the number of bloody shoeprints found around the body, and leading

out of the living room into the kitchen, growing fainter as they
went away from the body. The two most distinct prints were in
the southwest corner of the room, near the overturned, partly
bloodied ottoman. These prints on the tiled floor had been
made by a pair of rubber-soled athletic shoes. Wicks measured them: at first viewing they seemed to be ten and three-
quarters of an inch long, and three and three-quarters of an
inch wide. Each print represented a right foot, and they were
pointed in opposite directions [see Song Wicks' crime scene
diagram].

The trail of shoeprints approached the head of the bloody
patch where Felix had been facedown, circled around the head
area past the adjacent left side where he subsequently lay on
his back, then led to the steps to the landing, the bathroom and
the kitchen. More faint traces of the shoeprints were found in
the kitchen.

Since Felix was both nearly nude and barefoot, these
rubber-soled shoeprints had to have been left by someone
who'd stepped in Felix's blood at some point after he had
been killed, or at least while he was dying on the tile floor.
The track between the prone and supine blood patterns suggested that the person who'd left the shoeprints had inspected
the body while it was still lying on its stomach—maybe, even,
had used that opportunity to bash Felix in the back of the head
from the right with the blunt object before departing.

It wasn't very likely that the same person had flipped Felix
over onto his back at that time—the blood pattern and the
track of the shoeprints indicated that any such "body flipper"
would have to have turned Felix's body over onto his or her
own feet, and the blood pattern seemed to show that hadn't
happened. There were no shoeprints to show that the person
who had moved the body had stepped back to the west to
have leverage to roll Felix's body over onto his back. The
shoeprints seemed to circle both blood patches, but none
were left in a place to effectively leverage the body from
the prone to the supine position.

Yet, the logic of the two separate blood patches was compelling: there had been a violent encounter, and then, someone had sometime later entered the pool house, and, finding Felix dead and facedown, had flipped him over to lie on his back, arms akimbo, without leaving shoeprints. With the blood stream that had apparently, subsequently, run from the head wound to the southeast corner of the room, it seemed possible that Felix might well have still been alive, if comatose, when his body was turned over to repose in its supine, cruciform position. Perhaps this was when the book was opened to its bloody if pregnant passage.

By the time Wicks and Taflya arrived, many hours after the discovery of the body, to say nothing of the time of the actual killing, the blood on the floor was mostly dried. Based on accounts of those who had been in the room, the blood had been "tacky"—that is, sticky—the night before, at the time of the discovery of Felix's body by Sergeant Hansen. That suggested that the bleeding had occurred twelve hours, or slightly less, before the discovery—in other words, around 9 A.M. Air dries blood fairly quickly.

Gabe had said he didn't go into the living room, so if he was telling the truth, the shoeprints couldn't be his. That left Susan, as well as a possible Mr. X—perhaps an angry patient, or someone else, maybe someone bent on getting Felix's supposed money in the Cayman Islands, or even someone involved with Felix and his supposed intelligence connections with the Mossad or the CIA.

There was one other significant discovery in the living room of the pool house, and it was uncovered in Felix's bloody right fist. There, clutched in mute accusation, were several strands of long, dark hair. These were carefully collected for future comparison to Susan's head hair. Hopefully, some of the roots

f these hairs could be tested for DNA. If the DNA from the
air in Felix's hand was the same as Susan's, that would be
owerful evidence that she and Felix had been in a violent
truggle at the time he was stabbed.

While Wicks and Taflya were documenting the crime
cene, Detective Costa was searching the main house. He
vanted to find Susan's Apple laptop computer. Gabe had said
hat Susan kept a diary on her computer, and Costa wanted to
heck it out to see if there was any indication of possible pre-
neditation of murder in the diary. After all, Costa had already
dvanced his theory of the motive—Susan "wanted it all."

On October 15, 2002, someone had turned Susan's Mac-
ntosh laptop computer on just before 6:40 A.M., according to
he internal clock, and begun trolling through her files, in-
luding one called "diary," and another titled "my eyes only."
This troller obviously wasn't Susan, since Costa had jailed
er by then.

Whoever was using the computer apparently was not suffi-
iently skilled in computer legerdemain, as it later appeared
hat a significant number of the files were corrupted, to the
oint that they were later judged to be unrecoverable. This
vould eventually create a significant dispute between Susan
nd her prosecutors—Susan contending that the police had
purposefully?] damaged the computer and in so doing, evis-
erated substantial portions of her diary, which had docu-
nented her allegations of Felix's years of abuse. Eventually,
n outside computer analyst confirmed that Susan's files had
een damaged, probably by this police access on the morning
f October 15.

By this point, someone in the Contra Costa sheriff's de-
artment had pulled the records on Eli's various scrapes with
he law over the previous few years. That there was bad blood
etween Eli and his father was evident. Although Eli could not
lave committed the crime, having been confined at the boys'
ranch since October 9, the detectives thought it would be use-
ul to see what he thought. It was always possible that Eli had

made arrangements for the killing with some other inmate o
either juvenile hall or the ranch. Two detectives drove out t
the boy's ranch on the morning of October 15, and asked El
to come to an administrative office for a chat.

The detectives told Eli that his father had been murdered
This also appeared to be the first time anyone told him, a 17
year-old boy locked in intense conflict with his father, that hi
mother was thought to be a potential killer.

"Eli appeared appropriately shocked and upset at learnin₁
of his father's death," the detectives reported later. "We at
tempted to interview Eli, and although he answered several o
our questions, he stated that he no longer wanted to talk witl
us. Eli left the room for about five minutes, and then returned.'

After composing himself, Eli told the detectives that Susar
had come to visit him on Sunday, October 13, the day before
the murder.

"Eli was emphatic that his mother did not kill his father. El
described his mother as a 'mellow' person."

It was true, Eli went on, that the divorce had been stressful
There had been a few incidents of domestic violence, but he
had never seen any personally, and as far as he knew, these
were examples of "mutual combat," as the detectives put it ir
their report.

"I asked Eli another question," one of the detectives re
ported, "and he immediately stated, 'I don't feel right answer
ing any more of these questions. I would never do anything to
put my mom in jail, and that's where this is leading.' Eli endec
the interview, got up and returned to his dorm."

That afternoon Eli was removed from the boys' ranch and
booked back into juvenile hall, "for his protection and an as
sessment of his well-being," the probation department late.
reported.

Costa, meanwhile, was at Felix's Berkeley office, near Alta
Bates hospital, where he found the door locked. He talked to

Dr. Justin Simon, a psychiatrist who owned the office building. Simon was busy with a patient, but had enough time to tell Costa that he barely knew Felix, had certainly never counseled him, but had prescribed some medicine to help him sleep. Costa realized he would probably need a search warrant to get into Felix's locked office—there were likely to be confidential files in there. On the other hand, there might also be information that could shed light on the murder; one never knew.

That evening, Detectives Moule and Hebel had a second interview with Susan.

Once again, the detectives advised her of her legal rights, and once again Susan agreed to speak with them.

Susan sketched in the most salient events of the War Between the Polks, including her decision to return from Montana to contest Commissioner Berkow's decision reducing her support. Susan insisted that the last time she'd seen Felix was on Sunday morning.

Moule by now had talked to Adam over the telephone. Combined with the statements Gabe had already given late the night before, he was beginning to get the boys' picture: Susan was mentally ill, and she and Felix had had a mutually abusive relationship. He apparently believed that if he could get Susan to talk about the marriage, he could ease her into a confession, and maybe even help her to defend herself with a claim to justifiable homicide—in other words, self-defense.

He suggested that things had been rough for both Felix and Susan, and that they'd finally boiled over.

Susan said she'd been trying to divorce Felix for the previous five years, but that he would try to convince her to stay in the marriage, Susan said, and had threatened to kill her if she ever left him.

"And so he has always seemed to me like he wanted a sort of reconciliation," Susan said. "He would say to me that, 'I put twenty-five years of my life into this. You're not going anywhere,' like I was some sort of a project."

Moule wanted to get Susan's version of the threats Gabe

had said she'd made to kill Felix. Threats to kill were made on both sides, Susan admitted.

But, she said, "I did not kill my husband and I didn't make any real threats to my husband."

"Adam is saying that you have—and I need to tell you this, and I feel bad, but Adam is saying that there's some psychological issues with you, okay?" Moule told her.

"Well, that's Felix's cover story all through the years," Susan said.

"Adam seems like a smart kid," Moule told her. "He's not like . . . a little kid, that would just go along with this kind of thing. Adam doesn't seem like a follower, like the kind of guy that would [be] like, 'Okay, Dad, I'm gonna say that.' You know what I mean? Explain that to me, would you?"

"My husband is an expert," Susan told him. "He was a hypnotist, he's certified, that was his, you know, training. He knows how to do that. He knew how to build a scene in a family to lay a framework for a certain kind of thinking."

"Uh-huh."

"And thinking all along, the family was, like I was like one of the children, I was not the wife, from the time they were really, really young. If I tried to do any sort of discipline in the house, he'd come running out of his office. The kids would just yell, run to his office or knock on his door, 'Mommy says we can't do such and such,' or they'd just yell. He'd come running out of his office and he'd say, 'What's going on here?' "

The detectives seemed to disbelieve that Adam and Gabe could be manipulated by Felix so easily. Moule decided to increase the pressure a bit. He told Susan that the criminalists had been working over the crime scene since that morning, "like *CSI*," as he put it.

They'd collected all of her shoes, Moule said, "and there's a shoe[print] present. It's not the same shoe, I'm not gonna say it's the same shoe because I'm not so sure it is the same shoe. But it's the same size shoe, okay, it's your size in the blood, okay?"

"There is no way that I went in there," Susan said.

"Did you go—"

"No, I did not."

"You didn't go in afterwards?"

"No, I did not."

"Okay," Moule said. "There is biological evidence from your body. I'm not gonna go into what it is, 'cause that's just not appropriate right now. But I'm not playing around, Susan. I'm serious. We came straight over here when we got this information, 'cause I wanted to give you a chance. I'm not trying to be tricky or manipulative or anything like that. You're a smart lady and you're smart enough to think this through and know what's best for you. There's biological evidence that demonstrates that you had an altercation with him. And there's evidence on your body right now that Detective Hebel and I are aware of and have discussed, that is evidence of a struggle with that gentleman. It's done."

"You were in that room," Hebel accused, playing the bad cop.

"And it's consistent with his injuries," Moule added, "and you were in that room. And there is part— Your DNA is in his hand right now."

"I did not go in there."

"You were involved in a struggle."

"Tell us how that— Tell us how your DNA, then, got in his hand?" Hebel challenged.

"I don't know what you're talking about."

Hebel switched gears, trying to give Susan an inducement to tell her side of the fight that both detectives were certain had occurred between the Polks.

"Susan, you are a smart lady. I know that," Hebel said. "I've sat here and watched you this whole time, trying to observe how you behave. And I see an intelligent woman. You know what DNA testing is all about. You know the capabilities that we have."

"I don't."

"Yes, you do. You've heard about it, you've seen it. It's all in the newspapers, everybody knows it. It's one hundred percent reliable."

"I was not there."

"You had a struggle with him. There's DNA in his hand. You have injuries on your face consistent with injuries on his body. You were in a struggle with him in that room."

"No, I was not."

"It's about what happened and about your future right now," Hebel said.

"It's in your best interest, Susan, to be honest," Moule told her.

"Be honest," Hebel said.

"I was not in there."

By the end, the two detectives were practically begging Susan to think of her future, but the more they cajoled her, the more stubborn she got. It was almost as if they had taken on the role of Felix: "Think of the consequences, Susan," they might as well have been saying.

Which, to Susan, had always been fighting words, although the two detectives had no way of knowing that.

Just after 8 the next morning, October 16, 2002, Dr. Brian Peterson, a forensic pathologist whose private-sector medical group had contracted for such services with several central California counties, began an autopsy on the remains of Frank Felix Polk.

Peterson reported

The partially clad, cool, unembalmed body is that of a well-nourished, well-developed, white male . . . . In general, large amounts of dried and drying blood are on the body . . . the external genitalia are those of an uncircumcised adult male. . . ."

Three and a half hours later, Peterson had finished. He had found twenty-seven wounds to the body, including five major stab wounds, two "blunt force" injuries, and a variety of smaller cuts or lacerations to various other parts of the anatomy. But Peterson had found more than that.

Listed as his second "anatomic diagnoses," Peterson said he found "severe atherosclerotic coronary vascular disease," and third, "cardiomegaly with left ventricular hypertrophy."

In other words, Felix had had a bad heart, and might well have died of a heart attack.

But what about the twenty-seven wounds, including the severe whacking to the back of the head?

As Peterson later testified to the grand jury, none of these injuries, while serious, were individually fatal. That meant that while the wounds might have precipitated a fatal heart attack, Felix had not bled to death, or died of head trauma. And in fact, the living room of the pool house demonstrated that: there simply wasn't enough blood on the tile floor for Felix to have lost his life from the knife wounds. But the shock of the attack—the terror of it—might well have killed him.

That same day, a preliminary examination of the hair clutched in Felix's hand found that it was consistent with Susan's own head hair. With this, Susan was on the express lane to a murder trial. Only a little later, Costa met with a Contra Costa County deputy district attorney, and steps were taken to charge Susan with the crime of murder.

25. DADDY DEAREST

The next day the local newspaper, the *Contra Costa Times*, headlined the story on its third page: **Wife of Psychologist to Face Murder Charges**.

"A Berkeley psychologist was stabbed and beaten to death in the pool room [sic] of his sumptuous house, police said Wednesday," the paper reported, identifying the victim as Felix Polk.

"Authorities say Susan Polk is the only suspect in the slaying," the story continued, adding that according to police, "she has not made any statements to police about her husband's death."

That wasn't quite true—in fact, Susan had repeatedly denied killing Felix in her conversations with Detective Costa, and later, Detectives Moule and Hebel.

The newspaper report and the omission of her denial only fed Susan's paranoia about the authorities—she was sure they would try to "frame" her for murder out of a corrupt sense of loyalty to Felix.

The next day, Susan was taken to court for arraignment on the murder charge. Contra Costa County Deputy District Attorney Hal Jewett, who supervised the office's major case staff, decided it might be a good idea to get a grip on the state of Susan's mental health before proceeding. He asked Paul Berg, a psychologist well known in Contra Costa and Alameda County courts, to see if he could make some sort of determination as to Susan's sanity before the hearing.

Berg approached Susan in a court holding cell about 2 P.M.

At first, Berg later recalled, he asked Susan if she was willing to talk with him. She seemed agreeable, but after she asked Berg several questions—he described them as "relevant questions"—she refused to converse with him any longer, though not before lashing out at him with what Berg recalled was an anti-Semitic rant. He subsequently filed a report with the district attorney:

> My observations, based on the brief period of meeting with her, were that she was calm, composed, mildly withdrawn, and quite serious-minded. She did not show any obvious signs of mental disturbance, particularly none of any loss of contact with reality or other signs of a thought disorder.
>
> Furthermore, she was clearly aware of her rights and chose to exercise them appropriately.

This was the only time the state attempted to directly delve into Susan's mental condition.

After Susan was formally charged, the judge, Bruce Mills, asked Susan if she had legal representation. Susan said she did not. Mills asked if she wanted him to appoint a public defender, and Susan said yes.

At that moment, as the *Contra Costa Times* reported the following day, "a man stepped forward from the audience and identified himself as her father."

Susan's father, the attorney, had come from Sacramento in his daughter's hour of need.

Susan now began to weep.

Susan's father told the judge that he had retained a San

Francisco lawyer, William Osterhoudt, to represent Susan, and asked that the arraignment be postponed so that Osterhoudt could meet with her.

The judge agreed to the postponement, as well as a deferment on a request by the prosecutor's office to increase Susan's bail from $1.5 million to $5 million. The higher bail was necessary, said Deputy District Attorney Tom O'Connor, because with the Polks' assets, Susan was a flight risk. The "gruesome" quality of the death made Susan a danger to the community, and especially to Gabe, who would have to be a principal witness against her, O'Connor told the judge.

With that, Susan was taken from court and jailed once more, while a probation department official began to prepare a report to the judge on whether bail should be granted.

Susan would remain in jail for more than two years, denied bail. William Osterhoudt soon departed the case, but not before suggesting to Susan that she plead to some sort of mental disease or defect defense. He was replaced by Berkeley attorney Elizabeth Grossman, who suggested that Susan negotiate a plea to involuntary manslaughter. Susan fired Grossman, and asked that the Contra Costa County public defender be appointed to represent her.

Meanwhile, Adam, rushing back from UCLA, tried to figure out what to do with his 15-year-old brother, now deprived of any parent. He made arrangements with Dan and Marjorie Briner, parents of one of his friends from the high school football team, to take Gabe in. At first Susan was grateful to the Briners for their assistance, but as the winter of 2003 turned to spring, Susan turned on the Briners, particularly Marjorie—she believed that they were conspiring with her brother-in-law, John Polk, to loot the estate, and that they had poisoned Gabe's mind against her.

Much of this had to do with representations made to Susan

by Budd MacKenzie, a Lafayette lawyer hired by John Polk to handle the probate of the Polk estate. In a series of conversations, according to Susan, MacKenzie told her that if she were to be convicted of murder or manslaughter in Felix's death, the law required that she be prohibited from enjoying any of the estate's assets. Legally, Susan says MacKenzie told her, it would be as if she had died before Felix. She said MacKenzie convinced her to resign as trustee of the Polk Family Trust, which owned at least a 50 percent share of the Arch Street apartments valued by Susan at $1.2 million, and as trustee of the F. Felix Polk, a Psychological Corporation, Pension Plan, with assets of around $500,000. Susan soon regretted resigning, when MacKenzie and John Polk moved to sell the Arch Street apartments. The income from the sale, she complained, was necessary to keep up the payments on the dream house mortgages. Susan then came to believe that the Briners—Dan Briner was in real estate—had taken advantage of her situation to profit from the apartment sale, an accusation strenuously denied by Dan and Marjorie Briner.

In the spring of 2003, Eli was released from juvenile custody on probation. He stayed with the Briners for a while, but by then Susan's suspicions of the family had been accepted as fact by Eli. He tried to convince Gabe to return with him to the dream house, but Gabe didn't want to go near the place. Relations between Eli and Gabe, once the closest of brothers, rapidly deteriorated, with each sending the other vitriolic emails.

In August of 2003, Susan was indicted on murder charges by a Contra Costa County Grand Jury. Again she was denied bail, and she remained in jail until the fall of 2004, while the public defender's office worked to get the indictment dismissed on a variety of grounds.

Finally, in September of 2004, Susan was at last granted bail, but having no control over any assets, was unable to pay the premium. After negotiation with her, John Polk and Budd

MacKenzie agreed to split half of the Pension Plan money with Susan. She therefore finally posted bail and was released pending trial. She returned to the dream house and Eli. She was ordered to have no contact with Gabe. At about the same time, though, Adam and Gabe filed a wrongful death lawsuit against their mother, and asked a court to order Susan and Eli to vacate the dream house. Susan responded by filing a counterclaim accusing John and MacKenzie of fraud, and demanding that John be removed as trustee of the Pension Plan and Polk Family Trust.

Susan now fired her public defender and hired a fourth lawyer, Peter Coleridge of Martinez. Coleridge took a look at the thousands of pages that all the court cases—divorce, criminal, probate and wrongful death—had spawned, and soon asked for a continuance in the murder case. He needed more time to prepare. Lawyers for Gabe and Adam objected to the delay, and the brothers filed declarations alleging that it was Susan, not John Polk, who was depleting the estate through the delays in the criminal case. Resolving the charges as soon as possible was vital to clearing the legal questions of who was entitled to what.

Susan's criminal trial was scheduled to begin on May 5, 2005. But before it could start, her bail was abruptly revoked, and she was arrested again—this time for violating the no-contact order with Gabe. Coleridge thought that the charges were frivolous—all Susan had done was copy emails she had sent to Adam to Gabe.

That was still enough to require the bail revocation, Judge Mary Ann O'Malley told her, so she would have to go back to jail. At that point Susan fired Coleridge, and told O'Malley she wanted to act as her own attorney. Granted that right, Susan asked the judge to reconsider her decision to revoke the bail. When this was denied, Susan filed motions demanding that Judge O'Malley recuse herself from the criminal case because of prejudice against Susan. Although O'Malley denied any prejudice, the case was reassigned to a new judge, David Flinn.

A few days later, Susan made her next appearance as counsel of record in *People* vs. *Polk*, and at that point Judge Flinn declared that he had a "doubt" as to Susan's mental competence.

This was no idle observation by Judge Flinn. Under California law, once a judge states on the record that he has such a "doubt," the legal proceedings are suspended until a hearing can be held to determine if a defendant is mentally competent to assist in his defense.

Competence and insanity are two different issues. A person may be found to be incompetent under the law, but still sane, in that, while they may be viewed as incapable of understanding the proceedings against them, or assisting their defense counsel, they may be also be considered "sane," because they are said to be able to appreciate the nature and quality of their act, and its rightfulness or wrongfulness—the McNaughten rule.

Having officially expressed his "doubt," Judge Flinn now legally required Susan's lawyer, under the statute, to confer with her to "form an opinion as to the mental competence at that point in time." The problem was, at that point in time, *Susan* was Susan's lawyer, and she had no doubts that she was competent to assist herself. She objected to any psychological examination to determine her competence, and more specifically, refused to waive the requirement that she be tried within sixty days of the date trial was supposed to begin, which had been May 5, 2005.

Flinn eventually tried to resolve the question of Susan's competence by appointing two psychologists to evaluate her. As she had with Dr. Berg, more than two years earlier, Susan refused to cooperate with either. But one, Dr. Paul Good of San Francisco, based his report to the court on the probation officer's report—one that Susan had long contended represented the probation department's bias against her. Susan did write to him, Dr. Good said—apparently to explain again why she didn't trust psychologists. Good concluded that, based on the extent of Felix's injuries, Susan was probably "in an altered mental state of rage and persecution." Good also reported to the judge that Susan might be suffering from "delusional disorder," as he identified it.

Susan was furious at Good's assessment of her. She wasn't "delusional," she insisted. She'd only been defending herself against an enraged Felix that night, and there was nothing crazy about it.

Flinn ordered the trial to finally begin in August of 2005. Susan now made another attempt to have the case dismissed for the delay in prosecution, filing another lengthy handwritten argument that the speedy trial rules had been violated. This motion was still pending when Susan gave another press interview to the *Times*' Bruce Gerstman.

ORINDA WOMAN ACCUSED OF KILLING EXPLAINS STRATEGY, the paper headlined on August 21, 2005.

In this story, Susan apparently told Gerstman that she expected to be convicted, if for no other reason than that she'd decided to act as her own attorney. But, she said, it was worth it—"because I wasn't going to get the defense I wanted . . . if I'm going to lose when represented by counsel, I might as well represent myself. At least I'll give them a fight."

Gerstman asked her how she would cross-examine Gabe, who was expected to be the main witness against her.

"I don't think of it as cross-examining," Susan said. "I see it as an opportunity to talk to him."

This story appeared on a Sunday. Unbeknownst to Gerstman, though, it was out of date before it had even been printed.

Susan had decided to hire a lawyer after all—two of them. in fact.

26. THE BEST DEFENSE

For some weeks, lawyers Daniel Horowitz of Lafayette and Ivan Golde of Oakland had been casually following the news reports about Susan's case. According to Golde, he'd had a passing acquaintance with both Felix and Susan when the Polk family had lived in Piedmont.

Horowitz and Golde both felt the case, at least as described in the public prints, was eminently defensible. To the two lawyers, Susan's intended self-representation seemed a recipe for disaster. The main problem was, if she hoped to convince a jury that she'd killed Felix to stop him from killing her, she would have to make Felix the real culprit. But trying to establish this representing herself, she'd almost certainly wind up being seen as the more aggressive of the two. Once she started cross-examining witnesses, the preferable image of meek and vulnerable, put-upon Susan would evaporate. Especially when she went up against her own children.

For this reason, both Horowitz and Golde believed—along with almost every other attorney in town—that it would be far better for a lawyer, not Susan, to portray Felix as the aggressor and for Susan to sit meekly by as the innocent victim who had been lucky to escape with her life. Let the lawyer take the rap for being mean, not the defendant. But Susan seemed oblivious to this essential aspect of human nature.

"Initially," Golde said later, "we felt compassion for Susan Polk. I knew something about the family, from Berkeley, from Piedmont."

As it happened, both Horowitz and Golde had highly visible public profiles, at least among the talking legal heads on television. Both had appeared frequently as commentators/explainers on MSNBC, Court TV, *Dateline*, and other such shows that focused on high-profile criminal cases. Each had provided commentary in the Scott and Laci Peterson case a few years earlier.

Horowitz and Golde called Eli and asked him whether he thought Susan would be amenable to meeting with them. Eli said he didn't know, but he'd ask. A day or so later, the word came back: Susan would talk to them.

Over the weekend of August 20–21—the day before jury selection had been scheduled to start—Horowitz and Golde met individually and later together with Susan, for about twenty hours of discussions. Susan told them her version of the events, and her suspicions of the court system. The following Monday, Horowitz and Golde filed a notice of appearance in Judge Laurel Brady's court. They would represent Susan Polk.

POLK TAKES NEW TACK, NOW WANTS ATTORNEYS, the *Times* headlined on Tuesday morning, August 23, 2005.

Gerstman reported that a major factor in Susan's decision to switch to representative counsel was the prospect of having to cross-examine Gabe.

"I said, 'This is how I'd question him,' and she said, 'Will you represent me?'" Horowitz told Gerstman.

Horowitz and Golde now had just a few weeks to digest the

thousands of pages of reports and photographs the case had spawned, and to devise ways of attacking the charges.

"It was fifteen hours a day, seven days a week," Golde recalled afterward. He and Horowitz retained the services of Valerie Harris, with whom both had worked before, as a case manager. A professional software engineer from Mountain View, Harris would eventually become perhaps Susan's most intimate friend, and a true believer in her cause. Horowitz's wife, Pamela Vitale, a former computer executive, organized the thousands of pages of discovery into a computerized, searchable form. Three professional investigators were hired, and expert witnesses were contacted. It was clear that the case might well turn on medical evidence, combined with the crime scene reconstruction.

More important—could the wounds be consistent with what might have occurred during a fight, as Susan insisted, or would they be more consistent with an unprovoked attack? If a case could be made for a fight, that was potential reasonable doubt, certainly as to murder.

Golde, for one, was confident that the case was at worst manslaughter—that the crime scene and wounds, taken together, did not prove that Susan ever intended to kill Felix. And, Golde thought, it was possible that the scene could establish that Susan had indeed been attacked by Felix. That would put self-defense clearly in play.

At one point during their first week, Horowitz and Golde inspected the pool house. They realized that if they had any chance of selling self-defense to a jury, the panel would have to view the unusual room, with its narrow width, angled walls and stagelike projection. They filed a motion asking that the jury hear Susan's testimony in the actual death room, a rather unusual procedure, almost straight out of *Perry Mason*. They thought that if they could show how the much taller and heavier Felix had rushed at Susan within the narrow confines, it would be obvious to anyone that Susan had defended herself.

Soon Horowitz and Golde filed a number of motions with the court. In one, they again demanded that Judge Brady disqualify herself for bias; in another, they asked for the internal disciplinary records of the police investigators; and in a third, they requested that the statements made by Gabe to the police on the night of the killing be suppressed as "coerced." They filed a motion requesting that Gabe be assessed by an independent mental expert—to see whether he'd been the subject of pressure to testify before the grand jury by outside influences. They also wanted Brady to dismiss the charges based on the damage to Susan's computer, along with a motion to suppress Susan's own statements to the police on the night of October 14–15, and the following day, alleging that the police had failed to adequately advise her of her legal rights when they'd first questioned her.

There were several salient points raised in this flurry of defense motions. As to the computer, for instance, Horowitz and Golde demonstrated that someone from the police had turned the computer on early on the morning of October 15, 2002, and had accessed some of the files—three days before a warrant specifically authorizing them to search the computer had been approved by a judge. So far, no one from the sheriff's department had owned up to jumping the gun with the computer, or for allegedly destroying its files. The lawyers argued:

> The police seized and destroyed the defendant's computer hard drive, and in doing so, destroyed absolute proof that the defendant had no intention of harming Felix Polk, but instead was in great fear of him due to his lengthy history of physical and emotional abuse.
>
> It would have established that Susan Polk had a positive, nurturing nature and that her concern was for her children and for getting away from Felix Polk. It was Felix Polk who was brutal, controlling and threatening. This record is destroyed forever . . . .

This destruction of critical evidence was grossly negligent at best, cynically deliberate at worst, and in any case constitutes bad faith destruction of exculpatory evidence.

As for the motion to take testimony in the living room of the pool house, Horowitz asserted that not only would Susan testify, but that she would answer every question. After he and Golde had reviewed the crime-scene reports and inspected the room, Horowitz said, it became obvious that the police theory of what happened was flawed:

The layout and size of the rooms are critical to proving actual innocence in this case. This is because actual innocence depends, in part, upon a showing that Susan Polk could not have surprised Felix Polk and hit him from behind, as has been alleged . . . when combined with the description of objects, blood spatter, and several other matters reported by the police, the chance of a surprise attack becomes minuscule . . . the location of the chair is such that Felix Polk would have had his back to a wall and would have seen all three entrances to the room. Susan Polk's position [in the room] is completely boxed in . . . it is this restriction of space that is so palpable in that room.

This was coming right at the heart of the prosecution's case. By this point, the police and prosecutors had theorized that the deadly encounter had begun while Felix was asleep in the chair. In their theory, Susan had approached a sleeping Felix from behind and clobbered him on top of the rear of his head. Then, in their conception, Felix had somehow fallen forward, perhaps rolled over onto his back, and had, in the course of the fight, grabbed Susan's hair while she was stabbing him in the front, and then the back.

The problem with this theory was that Felix's head had been pointed toward the chair he'd supposedly been sleeping in, and there was a large bloody patch next to his left hand, indicating that he'd lain on his belly for some time, before later being flipped over to lie on his back. More significantly, and also damaging to the prosecution's theory, was the fact that the chair was backed up against a wall—there was no way that Susan could have gotten behind him initially, if indeed Felix had been in the chair when the attack began. Felix had to be out of the chair, standing up, at the onset of the fight.

Susan's story to Horowitz and Golde was more consistent with the crime scene. She'd told them that Felix had asked her to come down to the pool house to talk that night. When she got there, the conversation had escalated. In her version, Felix had rushed her with the ottoman, and used it to push her into the west wall. She'd hit him with a blast of pepper spray. Somehow, Felix got a knife, she said. She had been knocked to the floor, and Felix was kneeling over her, grabbing her hair and stabbing at her with the knife. She somehow got the knife away, and then had stabbed Felix several times in the front. He'd begun kicking her, possibly sustaining the cuts on the bottoms of his feet, when suddenly he'd fallen over backward, slamming his head on the tile floor. He told her, she said, that he was dying, and then did. She believed that Felix had actually died of a heart attack.

This explained how Felix's head had come to be pointing toward the chair, not away from it, as it would have been if Susan had really attacked him from behind.

A close examination of the room and the blood patterns, in conjunction with Susan's testimony, Horowitz contended, would demonstrate just how and where Susan had come to be on the floor—for one thing, she'd had to avoid the projecting stage.

One can see why she would have had almost no ability to stop Felix Polk from grabbing her by the hair and throwing her down. There was no escape route, no way to back out of the

way. She had to go to the ground. . . . If the jury hears Susan
Polk describe what happened they will see that the physical
evidence supports her and, most of all they will see why she
could not defend herself standing up. It is simply a room
where the larger and rageful person is going to have too much
of an advantage. This is the very crux of guilt or innocence in
this case.

After Horowitz filed this motion, several legal experts
marveled at it—none could recall a case in which actual testimony from a crucial witness had been taken at the scene of
the crime. It posed large logistical problems—for one, the
room was so small it would be impossible to fit everyone into
it, if the bailiff, the clerk, the court reporter, the news media
and the public, not to mention the judge, the lawyers and Susan were included. It was reasonable to take the jury to the
scene, but not to hear testimony while they were there, most
experts thought.

Meanwhile O'Connor filed motions of his own. He wanted
the court to limit testimony on "battered wife syndrome" and
"post traumatic stress syndrome." There had to be evidence
that any of this had actually taken place, before any expert
could testify more than generally about such possibilities, he
said—in other words, the jury should be told that the experts'
testimony proved nothing as to whether "battered wife" con-
ditions really existed with regard to Susan Polk. Without such
hard evidence, it was all ethereal, he argued.

As for the computer, O'Connor said that the defense claims
that the police had damaged the hard drive and lost significant
amounts of exculpatory material was "without factual support . . . the defendant's hard drive was not erased . . . if any
of the alleged documents are missing, it occurred prior to the
seizure of the computer." The import of this assertion was that
it had been Susan who had erased or damaged the hard drive,
not the police. But given the computer clock's recording of

when the computer had last been turned on, that was hardly credible, especially since a computer expert hired by the defense suggested that at least some of the files had been deleted or corrupted *after* Susan had been arrested. Horowitz and Golde decided to force the prosecution to track down and disclose the identity of the malefactor who had purposefully or inadvertently damaged Susan's best defense witness, the Mac.

By September 13, Horowitz and Golde had filed a motion to put on evidence regarding the respective mental states, and mental histories, of both Felix and Susan. This began with a statement of facts written by Horowitz which essentially asserted that it was Felix who was mentally ill, not Susan:

> When the full story is told, people will finally be able to understand Susan Polk's dogged insistence in her attorneys' getting the facts correct, and her resistance to giving into a system which she correctly perceives as being skeptical of the innocence of defendants, and of often fitting defendants into categories or standard roles.
>
> Susan Polk is completely innocent. She is a loving mother who was brutally attacked by a schizophrenic with a history of sexual and physical violence . . . .

Ever since the discovery of the killing, Horowitz said, there had been repeated allegations by Gabe and Adam that Susan was "delusional." He suggested these allegations had been made by Susan's two sons for pecuniary motives. Helping the district attorney to convict their mother was in their own financial interest, Horowitz observed.

> What could be more convenient for the prosecution than a person crazy enough to kill, but knowing right from wrong and the nature and quality of her acts? Combined with a claimed financial motive and a claimed twenty-seven stab wounds (when there were only five!), the prosecution had an excellent

theory. But it had one problem. Susan Polk was desperately
sane and desperately fighting to be heard by attorneys, the
prosecution, by police, by anyone who would listen. But no
one would.

Well, that was going a little overboard—after all, police
had pleaded, almost begged Susan to tell them that she had
been defending herself, but she had adamantly denied it.

Horowitz moved on to Felix. The prosecution, he said,
wanted to paint the picture that

> the delusional wife killed the long-suffering, sane, won-
> derful husband . . . it now turns out, the opposite is true.
> Felix Polk was a schizophrenic who suffered from audi-
> tory hallucinations, bizarre delusions, which he mixed
> with rage and violence. However, using his Ph.D. and his
> considerable intelligence, he hid his illness under a ve-
> neer of civility and professionalism. At home, however, it
> was a different story. He was rageful, violent, manipula-
> tive, controlling and dangerous . . . .

Felix had taken sexual advantage of Susan when she was a
teenager, and she had responded by forming defense mecha-
nisms "which were standard and specific to those that arise
from the psychological and sexual exploitation of teenaged
girls by their therapists. . . ."

The defense had identified "at least two other teenage victims" of Felix, Horowitz asserted.

"Felix Polk pathologically exploited teenaged women to
fulfill his own sexual lust and he then controlled them by various means. . . ."

Felix's relationship with Susan only began when he was
able to use the courts to facilitate his control of her, Horowitz
said. In later years, he said, Felix had written a rambling trea-
tise on his therapeutic techniques, including some passages on

the power of cultish mind-control techniques, and titled it "Thoughts of Chairman Felix."

"Chairman Felix created a world of damaged people, who surrounded him and treated him like a god," Horowitz said. It was no wonder that Susan had finally rebelled against this sinister manipulation; and when physically attacked by Felix, Susan had reacted by ending his life.

27. SUSAN AGONISTES

By mid-September of 2005, with all these motions pending, Brady began clearing the underbrush by hearing arguments. This pre-trial phase is where a judge really earns her money. Her responsibility is to weed out the irrelevant, the extraneous and the unjust, for the purpose of insuring that both sides get a fair trial, while at the same time making sure the jury gets enough information to decide the facts.

On paper, things seemed to be swinging in Susan's direction. For the first time, her side of the story was being told, and told articulately, if not entirely dispassionately, by competent lawyers who were raising viable, even constitutional, issues. So Susan should have been happy.

She wasn't.

On September 13, she told Brady she wanted to fire Horowitz and Golde and take over her defense by herself once more. She told Judge Brady that she wanted the right to speak for herself. Brady held a closed-door hearing outside the presence of the prosecutor to hear Susan's grievances. Brady said she'd take this request under submission, but in the meantime wanted to go ahead with a hearing concerning Susan's description of the events on the night of the murder. Horowitz and Golde had contended that these October 14–15 statements were coerced—they said police had given her the impression, at least at the start, that they had arrested Gabe for Felix's death. That was emotional manipulation to get Susan to talk, they said, and why she hadn't invoked her right to speak to a lawyer.

Susan took the witness stand to tell her side, and when O'Connor began cross-examining her, she began objecting to his questions and arguing with him.

Brady formally admonished Susan for her behavior as a witness. A witness was only supposed to answer questions, not advocate, but Susan refused to abide by the distinction. It was Judge Kolin all over again, and if Horowitz and Golde didn't understand what they'd gotten into with Susan before this, they certainly did now. How in the world were they going to be able to convince a jury that she was meek and unaggressive when she argued with everyone? Susan simply couldn't help being "provocative," as Felix might have put it.

The following day, Brady toured the pool house, so that she could see it for herself. That afternoon, she denied the defense request to take Susan's trial testimony at the pool house, but suggested that she would agree to let the jurors see the scene in person.

She then denied most of the other defense motions as well.

By the following week, both sides were examining potential jurors. A panel of 105 Contra Costans was brought in; Horowitz and Golde almost immediately asked that the entire panel be dismissed and a new one empanelled, because some of the jurors had inadvertently seen Susan in handcuffs and belly shackles. Brady rejected this.

After three days of jury selection, Susan reiterated her request that Horowitz and Golde be dismissed so she could take over her own defense. Brady said she'd hear from Susan about this the following day. Susan objected to that, too, and demanded that Brady recuse herself from the case. Brady refused.

Three days later, on Monday, September 26, Susan once more asked that she be allowed to represent herself. Brady now gave several legal citations to Susan, and suggested that she read them before Brady considered the matter. That afternoon, after another wrangle, Brady once more denied Susan's demand to act as her own attorney.

Two days later, Brady made one of her most crucial rulings: she would allow the jury to hear evidence of Felix and Susan's propensity for violence against each other, and against the boys. She would also permit evidence to be heard of Felix and Susan's mental health histories, going back to Felix's days in the Navy's mental wards.

With all this done, Brady recessed the trial for the next ten days.

When the trial resumed again on October 11, each side gave their opening statement. Almost three years to the day from the time the killing had been discovered, Susan Polk was at last face-to-face with a jury.

By this point, the éclat that Horowitz, Golde and Harris had with the national television people had begun to take effect. *Dateline*, for one, was hard at work at assembling a broadcast piece on the woman accused of killing her psychotherapist husband, the Holocaust survivor, a woman who, as his patient, had allegedly been seduced by him when she was still a teenager, and who had then become estranged from two of her three sons. As an added fillip, the psychic Ms. Polk claimed to have predicted the 9/11 attacks, and had asserted that her husband was head of a secret Mossad cell in northern California—could it get any more tabloidish than this? The case of *People* vs. *Polk* leapfrogged into the front ranks of television fodder, much as the once-missing Chandra Levy, or the murdered Laci Peterson, had previously been all-news, all-the-time.

Golde, for one, later concluded that this thrusting of Susan into the national limelight had deleterious effects on her.

"Susan changed," he said later. "All the publicity, all the

notoriety, made her different." In one sense, he said, she became much more full of herself, and far less willing to listen to her legal counsel. It was all part and parcel of being a political prisoner, as Susan increasingly saw herself—in short, Susan, in her own mind, had become a martyr, as well as a media "star," the Tupac of the East Oakland Hills.

28. DOUBLE IMAGE

TWO PICTURES PAINTED OF POLK AS TRIAL BE-GINS, the *Contra Costa Times* reported on October 12, 2005, the day after the trial's start. There were two subheads:

Prosecutor calls her alleged crime "Cold and Calcu-ated"

Followed by:

Defense says she killed "Monster" husband in self-defense

That pretty much summed up the situation—either Susan was a pecuniary predator, or she had been preyed upon. This would be up to the jury to decide.

Deputy District Attorney O'Connor sketched in the events leading up to the discovery of Felix's body, making much of the fact that Gabriel had discovered his father's corpse.

"Immediately he knew who was responsible," O'Connor said. "That woman right there," and pointed at Susan. Susan glared at him.

Susan had killed Felix to prevent him from having the dream house and custody of Gabe, and for succeeding in re-ducing her spousal support, O'Connor told the jury. Like Mike Costa had surmised three years earlier, in this assessment, Su-san's motive was simple: being greedy, she wanted it all.

That simply wasn't the case, said Horowitz, when it was his turn.

"Susan Polk defended her life against a vengeful, aggressive man who was also her husband."

Horowitz summarized the two decades of the marriage, drawing mostly on Susan's timeline, which Harris had pressed her to write in the days before the trial. Felix, Horowitz said, had a "chronic mental illness" that precipitated outbursts of rage. He played a portion of the tape of Felix's old Satanist rant—"My rage is omnipresent," Felix's voice came from the grave. "I wake up with it every morning."

Felix had become almost like a cult leader, Horowitz contended. He had complete control of his wife, and used his children "to keep their mother in line." At one point, he said, Eli had even punched her in the mouth to get his father's approval. Significantly, Felix had prescriptions for anti-anxiety drugs from a local doctor. None of them had been found in his system at the autopsy, which seemed to show that Felix had been off his medications at the time of the confrontation.

That afternoon, the court adjourned to the pool house so jurors could see the peculiar layout of the death room for themselves.

Over the next four days, O'Connor assembled his case against Susan methodically, calling Officer Shannon Kelly, then Sergeant Hansen, to set the scene of the killing as they had found it. While Hansen testified that Susan had made her remark "We were getting a divorce anyway," Kelly could not confirm this. However, both Kelly and Hansen agreed—Susan seemed remarkably unemotional when they told her that Felix was dead. A number of grisly photographs from the crime scene were entered into evidence.

After skipping a day, the trial resumed on Friday, October 14. O'Connor called Detective Mike Costa as a witness. Costa told of his encounter with Susan at the interview in the early morning of October 15, 2002, and how he had then begun his investigation.

Brady then adjourned the trial for the rest of the day, and both sides prepared to return the following week for more testimony.

By this point, the defense felt good about what had been accomplished so far. They'd at least gotten the notion that there had been a violent encounter in the pool house before the jury, along with suggestions that Felix had been given to moments of rage and bullying, if not madness. That was a good start to the necessary strategy of casting Felix as the villain, and if the jury kept an open mind, it meant there was a chance for acquittal on grounds of self-defense.

That Friday night, the defense got another boost when *Dateline NBC* broadcast a detailed report on the War Between the Polks. Susan was interviewed extensively, telling her side of the story, and so was Eli, who backed her up. Helen Bolling also supported Susan. Gabe and Adam declined to be interviewed, and Felix's side of the story was presented by his lawyer friend in Oakland, who claimed there was no way "on God's green earth" that the killing had been in self-defense, but who also admitted that he didn't know everything that had taken place behind closed doors at the Polk domicile.

In one segment of the broadcast, Susan told of going down to the pool house on the night of October 13 to talk with Felix.

"At a certain point in the conversation," she told the *Dateline* correspondent, Keith Morrison, "I think that I said some things that triggered rage in him. And at one point, he just said, 'I can never let you leave with what you might say about me.' He just went after me."

Susan said Felix had rushed at her with the ottoman, trying to back her up against the wall. She'd squirted him in the face with pepper spray, she told Morrison.

"And it was supposed to stop a grizzly bear, but it didn't

stop him," Susan continued. "He dragged me by the hair, threw me on the ground, punched me in the face and he pulled a knife . . . he smeared the pepper spray into my face. What I saw, through the blur and the burning, was him stabbing at me. And I saw the knife go through my pants and so I thought, 'He—he stabbed me.'

"I thought, *He's gonna kill me. I'm gonna die here unless I do something right now.* And I just kicked him as hard as I could with the heel of my foot in his groin, and at the same time I went for his hand. And his hand loosened just as I kicked him, and I just grabbed the knife out of his hand and I said, 'Stop, I have the knife.'

"And he didn't stop. He just came over me, grabbing at the knife, punched me in the face and I stabbed him in the side. And he was trying to grab it out of my hand."

She kept her grip on the knife, Susan went on. "And I stabbed him again. And— I think I stabbed him five times. At one point I waved it back and forth . . . and I said, 'Get off, get off, get off, get off.' And he stood up and it was over . . . He said, 'Oh my God, I think I'm dead.'"

Felix fell backward, Susan indicated, and appeared to be dead.

Afterward, Susan said, she sat down on the stage and thought about the years together with Felix. She thought about calling 911, but decided that once she made the call, her life would essentially be over. So she put it off, thinking that she'd somehow work up to it, but first she would tell Gabe, to prepare him, as she put it. But then she put that off, too—knowing that as soon as she told him, their lives would never be the same.

The defense was very pleased with the broadcast, and even Susan thought the presentation came off well. She certainly didn't act or sound delusional, and the self-defense claim seemed plausible enough, at least on the surface. After all, there was evidence of redness in Susan's eyes the night of the discovery, and some slight bruising. That was what had first made the police think she'd been in a fight—why they'd implored her to tell them the truth of what happened.

So Horowitz and Golde, and their team, were optimistic as the weekend began. But then, Saturday evening, everything came apart, when Horowitz discovered the murdered body of his wife, Pamela Vitale.

29. SUSPICIONS

Afterward, Valerie Harris recalled that Saturday evening, October 15, 2005, "as the most surreal day of my life."

She'd been at the Safeway, grocery shopping, when one of the team's investigators called her on her cell phone to tell her that Pamela Vitale had been killed—murdered, no less. Harris had just come from a defense team meeting at the Horowitz office. At the meeting, everyone had been upbeat.

"Dan was in a really good place," Harris recalled. "The *Dateline* piece had just aired the night before. Susan was ebullient."

At about six P.M., Horowitz had returned to the modular home he shared with Pamela in the hills of Lafayette, a temporary residence while a larger, permanent house on the property was under construction. He found Pamela Vitale's body lying in the entryway to the modular house. It appeared that she had been battered to death by many frenetic blows to the head, inflicted by a heavy, blunt object. The killer had then carved a gothic symbol into her back.

In a state of shock, Horowitz called the police, and many of the same detectives who had worked on the killing of Felix Polk arrived at the property. Soon, the same pathologist, Dr. Peterson—who had performed the autopsy on Felix—would

e asked to do the same on the body of Pamela Vitale. And
since Horowitz had been planning to rake Dr. Peterson over
the hot coals for insufficiencies in his autopsy on Felix in Susan's case, that created a very awkward situation.

The murder of Pamela Vitale threw the Polk case into a state
of intense confusion. It certainly didn't help Susan's state of
mind. To her, such an event could only be the sign of larger,
sinister forces at work.

And on the other side, if there is anyone paid to be professionally paranoid besides lawyers, homicide investigators certainly qualify: while the attack on Pamela Vitale might appear
to be a random event—a spur-of-the-moment confrontation
with parties unknown—the fact that the Polk case had finally
come to trial demanded examination of other possibilities.

For one thing, there was seemingly no attempt to rob the
house, or even Pamela's body; moreover, there were signs that
the killer had actually taken a shower at the modular house,
and that he or she had removed some of Horowitz's own
clothing and taken it when leaving. That certainly was one indication that the killer could have been known to the victim—
or maybe someone who was trying to cast suspicion on
Horowitz himself. Since it was clear that Horowitz had been
elsewhere at the time the crime had been committed, he was
quickly dismissed as a suspect.

Who could have done this thing, and why?

One possibility, at least for the Contra Costa homicide investigators, had to be that someone on Susan's side of the War
Between the Polks had murdered Pamela to deliberately gen-
erate a mistrial in Susan's case.

That almost immediately promoted Eli as a possible suspect. On Sunday, detectives interviewed him, with Ivan Golde
present as his lawyer. Eli was asked to remove his shirt—
detectives believed that Pamela had injured her assailant during the confrontation. Eli was cooperative, and had an alibi—he

was not guilty. But he, too, had something unusual to report: the previous night it appeared that someone had tried to break into the dream house while he was out. He'd found a screen door pried open. Was this connected to the murder of Pamela Vitale? No one could say.

And in Susan's fertile imagination, these events might have suggested all sorts of ominous possibilities—was it the Mossad? Someone retained by her archenemies, John Polk and Budd MacKenzie, or even the Briners? Someone who wanted to make sure Susan was convicted of Felix's murder, and had killed her lawyer's wife to force him off the case? Did it have anything to do with offshore bank accounts? She couldn't help but feel, instinctively, that the death of her lawyer's wife *had* to be related to what was happening to Susan herself.

The very next day, back in court, the consequences of Pamela Vitale's murder became evident.

In a conference in Judge Brady's chambers, she invited both sides in the Polk case to consider their options.

Brady said she wanted to hash out what to do, at least at first, in private.

"I'm just doing this, frankly, because this is such a, I don't know what other word to use, but a bizarre situation. . . ." the judge said.

Horowitz, of course, was not present. But Golde had already indicated to Brady that there was no choice: Brady *had* to declare a mistrial.

"Mr. Golde indicated to me," Brady told Susan, "that for a variety of reasons, including the fact that Mr. Horowitz's computer, which he had been working with, has been seized as part of the new homicide investigation, and the fact that your attorney [Golde] and investigator . . . are personal friends of Mr. Horowitz's wife—they have some issues about going forward."

Golde, Brady continued, had asked for a mistrial. But in order for Brady to declare a mistrial, she had to have a formal request from Susan—"otherwise it's double jeopardy."

If Susan didn't want to ask for a mistrial, Brady said, an alternative might be to postpone resumption of the proceedings for an extended period—at least until Horowitz felt able to resume.

But Golde was against this.

"There are so many conflicts involved with this case," he said. "It's the same pathologist doing Ms. Vitale's autopsy as did Felix Polk's autopsy. The criminalist who went to the scene of the Polk home is the same criminalist who went to the scene at Mr. Horowitz's home. The Contra Costa County sheriff's department, who has done most of the investigation in the Polk home, is doing most, if not all, the investigation with Mr. Horowitz, with the tragic death of his wife."

The very fact that the investigators had seized Horowitz's computer was a major conflict, Golde said, since it had all of the Polk defense team's work product on it—defense strategies, memos, investigative reports—in other words, the works.

"So they're accessing that as we speak," Golde told Brady.

"I'm sure there will be appropriate measures taken in handling that information, with a special master," Judge Brady told him.

"I hope so. I hope so," Golde said, sounding unconvinced. Of course, after the fiasco with Susan's own computer, he had reason to be skeptical.

Brady again asked Susan what she wanted to do.

"I trust my attorneys' judgment," Susan said. "And I think personally that the primary objective at this time should be the safety of the people involved in this case—my children, my attorneys, their families, Ms. Harris, and her family."

"And your constitutional rights," Golde added.

Susan said her main concern was Gabriel's safety. She wanted him given some measure of police protection. "A lot of threats were made to me by my husband, and I just think Gabriel needs . . . to take precautions as well."

Brady clearly favored going ahead with the trial after a postponement, but she had to admit that Golde had raised some problems. One was the fact that the same pathologist had been selected to handle both cases; apparently Golde had attempted to short-circuit that decision by asking that someone else be selected, but had been rebuffed.

Brady agreed that the selection of Dr. Peterson "would put the defense in a somewhat untenable position, because it's been obvious on the record that it's the defense intention to attack Dr. Peterson's work."

With that, Brady seemed to agree that there was no alternative to declaring a mistrial. She asked Susan if she was willing to waive the sixty-day requirement, which would allow the court to set the new trial for the next year, and Susan apparently said she was, or at least that's what the court reporter recorded.

A few minutes later, once again in open court, Brady told the jurors that they could hardly have missed the news accounts of the murder of Horowitz's wife.

"I have reached the conclusion that at this juncture it is not possible to continue the trial," Brady told the jurors, thanking and excusing them.

The case of *People* vs. *Polk* was back to its starting point.

The possible connections of Pamela Vitale's murder to the Polk case largely evaporated the following week, and with them the potential conflicts, when Contra Costa County sheriff's deputies arrested Scott Dyleski, a 16-year-old neighbor of Horowitz and his wife, for the crime. It appeared that Pamela had surprised him while he was waiting at the modular home to collect mail-order marijuana growing equipment purchased through a credit-card fraud, which was to be sent to the Horowitz address as a blind drop. Caught, the five-foot-five 110-pound Dyleski beat Pamela over the head nearly one hundred times with a piece of moulding, then carved the gothic symbol into her back. Having wrapped up the Pamela Vitale murder so quickly, it was apparent to almost everyone—except

Susan—that the killing of Pamela was a tragic coincidence, not part of some hidden plot against Susan Polk.

A month later, Horowitz told Brady he was ready to take Susan's case to trial. The judge set a new trial date of January 31, 2006.

Susan was not happy. She wanted the trial to begin before January 1. The judge pointed out that she'd already agreed to a waiver of the sixty-day rule. Susan denied that she'd waived the time, and insisted that if the transcript said she did, then it was in error.

"I frankly don't trust the court reporter," Susan said. Brady told Susan that she'd insulted the reporter, and that if she'd been a member of the bar, she'd have reported Susan for disciplinary action. Susan didn't care—she was only expressing what she really thought, as usual.

But by this point, Susan was losing her trust in Horowitz, too, although it would take almost another month for this to become clear in her mind.

On December 31, 2005, Susan wrote a 7-page letter to Horowitz and Golde, saying she had once again decided to represent herself. She wanted them to withdraw. She wasn't happy with the work they had done on the case, she said.

> My compassion for you, Dan, cannot supersede my common sense opinions about how my defense should proceed, nor can I let go of the expectations I had when I agreed to your representation. Those expectations included that I would be represented as having defended myself as not guilty of manslaughter or murder, as not having acted with malice or in the heat of passion . . . that the prosecutor and Sheriff's Department would be discredited for having tampered with the evidence, that my husband would be discredited as the sick, malicious person that he was, and that certain witnesses would be produced, discredited, and others called to corroborate my account.

In other words, Susan wanted a defense based solely on the claim of self-defense, one that would make Felix the crazed aggressor, and further, one that would assert that the authorities had fooled around with the evidence for the purpose of convicting her, whether she was guilty or not.

She was particularly upset that the husband of Judge Brady's clerk was one of the officers in the jail who had refused to take a statement from Susan when she claimed a deputy had used excessive force on her in 2003, and that Brady had refused to permit the defense to inspect that officer's personnel records. Of course, the issue wasn't relevant to the charge against Susan, except for the fact that, to Susan, the denial of access to the records proved that Brady was prejudiced against her, and was trying to protect the clerk's husband. After she'd raised this claim to Brady, Horowitz and Golde had urged her to apologize to the clerk and the court—it had nothing to do with the murder charge, and had every potential to poison the courtroom climate against Susan. Susan should back off, the attorneys told her.

That, Susan would never do—if she wouldn't apologize to Kolin in Eli's case, she certainly wasn't going to apologize to Brady and her clerk. In Susan's mind, it wasn't Susan who was wrong, it was Brady.

In a hearing in early January of 2006, Susan once again asked that Brady recuse herself from the case, and grant Susan the right of self-representation. Brady by this point seemed fatigued by all the back-and-forth from Susan. She told her that she simply didn't have the time at that point to consider Susan's two demands. She postponed any decision for a week, doubtless hoping that somehow Horowitz and Golde could steer Susan back on track, and the case could proceed in ordinary fashion. This was wishful thinking on Brady's part.

After being returned to jail, Susan called television reporters. She told them she suspected that Horowitz may have orchestrated the murder of Pamela Vitale. And, she added, she

thought Scott Dyleski had been "framed." She said she would
testify for Dyleski at his trial if he called her as a witness—
she would say that Horowitz had told her that he'd see to it
that Dyleski was "framed" even tighter than she had been.

This ignited Horowitz; and as Golde later perceived it, it
was Susan's master stroke in trying to get rid of them, so she
could represent herself. How in the world could Horowitz in
good conscience represent a client who had publicly accused
him of the murder of his own wife, and framing the person
who'd actually been arrested? Wouldn't Horowitz have to admit that she was delusional? It was ludicrous, and had put
Horowitz into an impossible position. Either he agreed with
his client and implicated himself, or he had to say she was off
her rocker.

On January 9, Susan met with Horowitz. The meeting did
not go well.

Susan recorded her version of the encounters in a letter to
Horowitz dated the following day:

> *I met with you, Dan, last night, and was dismayed again by
> your behavior. On Sunday, January 8, you raised your voice at
> me on the phone . . . last night, you claimed that I had "ranted
> and raved" at you on Sunday. I couldn't get a word in edgewise.
> You also hung up on me before I could respond.*

The truth was, Horowitz had finally lost his patience with
Susan, as Golde admitted later. When Susan chided Horowitz
over the telephone for failing to get a firm court date for her
request to dismiss him, he'd told her, according to Susan, "I
don't care about your court date. I am not withdrawing. You
don't make any sense. Get your own court date. You are a
baby. You are spoiled rotten," and then hung up on her. Valerie
Harris was also on the line, and later confirmed this conversation.

The following night, according to Susan, Horowitz had
told her that he was thinking of preempting her request to rep-

resent herself by asking that the court proceedings be suspended and that Susan be referred for mental examination and a competency hearing, exactly as Judge Flinn had started to do the year before. She considered this a threat by Horowitz, Susan said, to shove her aside. This meant a trip to the mental ward—Horowitz could get control of her case, and thereby make himself look good on national television at her expense, and this she would never allow.

On January 20, Judge Brady, apparently thinking that if the defendant persisted in this insistence to represent herself, it would be on Susan's own head, and perhaps growing weary of the whole issue, granted her the right to be her own lawyer. Like Pontius Pilate, Brady was in a way washing her hands of Susan—she could help her toward the exit, but if Susan chose not to go there, Brady could not in good conscience intervene. She agreed to the dismissal of Horowitz and Golde.

This made them the fifth and sixth criminal defense lawyers to have quit or been fired by Susan, never mind all the lawyers who had come and gone in the divorce case, the probate case, the wrongful death case, and all of Eli's troubles. It was patently obvious: when it came to lawyers, Susan had no trust and no faith in any of them.

In allowing Susan to be her own lawyer, Brady was caught between two standards: on one hand, the *Faretta* decision seemed to compel the judge to allow Susan to defend herself, at least if she appeared to be competent to understand what was going on, and ostensibly knew what she had to do to defend the case—which her previous written filings seemed to indicate that she did.

But at the same time, the very fact that Susan had fired so many lawyers also evinced an inability to assist her counsel in preparing her defense.

What Brady perhaps should have done, some lawyers and forensic psychiatrists suggested later, was reject Susan's demand to represent herself unless Susan first agreed to be evaluated by a forensic psychiatrist. If the psychiatrist then found

that Susan was unable to assist a lawyer in her own defense, it
would be logical to infer that it would be even harder for her
to conduct that defense herself. At that point, Brady could
have declared her "doubt," as Flinn did, and referred Susan to
the mental health treatment that all except Susan, and Eli,
seemed to agree that she needed.

This would have tracked the Polk case into the mental
health system for disposition, probably an outcome far kinder
to Susan and her children than what was now to come.

Because when Susan Polk won the right to defend herself,
she was essentially condemning herself to conviction, and
probably the rest of her life in prison.

30. READY OR NOT

The second trial of Susan Polk began on February 27, 2006. By this time, the case had become a national topic of water-cooler conversation, fed by tabloid television, extensive local news coverage, and even two articles in *The New York Times*. Susan had helped to whip up this interest herself by giving an interview to Geraldo Rivera, in which he called her "at times erratic," and then allowed her—actually, incited her—to suggest that Horowitz had somehow been involved in his wife's murder. Rivera called Horowitz for comment, but Horowitz cut the conversation short, and apparently hung up on him.

In another unusual move, Susan attempted to file a blanket affidavit of prejudice against the entire Contra Costa County bench: not just Brady, but the O'Malleys, Judge Flinn, Presiding Judge Thomas Maddock, in fact, every judge—lock, stock and gavel. A judge in Santa Barbara County denied the claims, so Susan was stuck with Brady. Susan also asked for permission to keep all the boxes of her case file in her cell; the jail said it was against fire regulations. Brady offered to let Susan store them in the court's evidence locker, but Susan did not want to do this—for one thing, she didn't trust that someone wouldn't prowl through them after hours, while she was in her cell, and for another, she wouldn't be able to have access to them to prepare for the following day in court.

Ever since Susan had once slipped her handcuffs on a trip to court, the jailers had been transporting her with leg shackles, a belly chain, and handcuffs behind her back. How was she supposed to carry so many boxes of files to court? The guards refused to carry them for her.

Another thing: since Susan was incarcerated in a county jail facility in the city of Richmond, some miles away, the guards had to get her up every morning at four A.M. to prepare her for transport to the court in Martinez, the county seat. Then, after court was concluded each night, they shipped her back to Richmond. Arriving around seven P.M., it left no time for Susan to prepare for trial the following day—not if she was going to get any sleep before the next day's four A.M. wake-up call.

So, besides her inherent wariness, her lack of legal training, her sense that she was being unfairly victimized, defending herself was exhausting. To Susan, it was only more evidence that "they" were out to get her.

Nevertheless, Susan's plight attracted a number of sympathizers. Not least among them was Valerie Harris. Susan sought and received approval from the courts to continue the employment of Harris as a sort of case manager/legal runner/investigator. Over the next four months, Harris loyally stood by Susan, tried to suggest ways of presenting her case, dug up bits of information, and kept track of witnesses. She frequently visited Susan in jail, and brought her clothes to wear in court. At first the guards simply shoved this apparel into paper sacks, ruining their folds, wrinkling them; but Harris soon sweet-talked them, and they relented, reasoning that even if they didn't like their difficult prisoner, there was no reason to take it out on Harris.

Harris also rounded up two lawyers to help Susan navigate the shoals of the courtroom, both of whom strategized with Susan, and gave her pointers on the proper procedures for making objections, and establishing a foundation for the proper introduction of evidence. Susan's greatest asset was her acute sense of what was fair—unfortunately, what's fair isn't always what's legal. The Evidence Code is jammed with pitfalls for the unwary amateur litigator.

In short, Susan got a fast-track legal education, on the fly. And some of this seemed to sink in, especially when it came to written motions—with her writing skill, Susan's briefs were models of logic and order, and well illustrated by legal precedents that she retrieved from the jail's law library. In a sense, the briefs were Susan's riposte to the notion that she was "crazy," or "delusional." Even written with the stubby little pencils, they showed that she was perfectly capable of advanced reasoning, no matter her peculiar notions about the Mossad, Felix, being psychic, or predicting 9/11.

Back in October, both sides thought the first trial would take a month to complete. But this second effort would take almost four months. In almost every conceivable way, it was the disaster that Golde had foreseen. By the time it was over, Susan had made no fewer than 102 motions for mistrial on the grounds of prosecutorial and/or judicial misconduct—possibly a record for an American trial court. She also made five separate motions for outright dismissal. All were denied by Judge Brady. Susan was formally admonished by the judge for violating the rules of court on seven separate occasions, and the judge frequently recessed the proceedings to let tempers cool off. Unfolding as it did in a national media spotlight, the court's gallery was packed with rubberneckers, whom the judge frequently admonished for laughing or talking while the proceedings were going on, or loudly voicing opinions in the hallway in the presence of jurors.

Part of the problem stemmed from Susan's unfamiliarity with legal procedure, especially the rules of evidence, despite her coaching. She didn't seem to fully grasp when a question was leading, and soon became flustered and frustrated by the prosecutor's obstructive objections. Although Brady frequently advised her on how to lay a proper foundation to obtain admission of evidence, it didn't seem to sink in. She often interrupted the judge or the prosecutor, arguing her points as they were talking, confusing the court reporter with the babble of dispute. She habitually attacked the court reporter, contending that she fabricated the record at Brady's direction, although how she knew this wasn't clear, since the reporter wasn't preparing daily transcripts. Brady steadfastly refused to order any verbatim records prepared, at least at the expense of the court, and repeatedly denied Susan's request that the proceedings be audiotaped. Both these decisions reinforced Susan's belief that the judge was prejudiced against her.

A second major problem was the very multiplicity of Susan's objectives in defending herself, which would soon take the trial into areas far removed from the self-defense theme. Some of these themes advanced by Susan worked at cross-purposes, and actually undercut her defense.

As she had advised Horowitz the previous December, Susan wanted to prove to the jury that she had been defending herself against an attack by Felix when he was killed; she also wanted to "expose" Felix as a monster and the incompetence of the police authorities. But by the time the second trial began, Susan's list of objectives had multiplied threefold.

Beside proving these original points, Susan also wanted to prove to the world that she was not "crazy," or "delusional." She wanted to expose the conspiracy she believed existed against her by John Polk, Budd MacKenzie and the Briners. She wanted to establish that she was in fact psychic. She wanted to prove to everyone that she'd been a good mother to the boys. And she wanted to reach out to the principal witness against her, Gabriel, to assure him that she still loved him, no matter what he'd said about her, while establishing that he'd been "brainwashed" by the conspiracy she claimed was against her. In short, she wanted to use the trial to validate herself, not just establish the case for self-defense. This multiplicity was disastrous for her defense of herself—trying to do everything, in the end, Susan would achieve nothing.

Intent on addressing all these issues, she seemed oblivious to her effect on the jury.

By this point, Deputy District Attorney Tom O'Connor had resigned from the Contra Costa County District Attorney's Office. He'd decided to take a job in private enterprise. Later, he would expose the CEO of this business in an alleged accounting fraud—a strange twist of fate for someone who'd abandoned public life for private lucre—perhaps showing that one could take the man out of the public, but not the public out of the man. O'Connor had resigned just four days before the trial started. Some thought that Susan had simply worn him out over the years. He was replaced by another veteran prosecutor, Deputy District Attorney Paul Sequeira, who knew almost nothing about the case when it had been dropped into his lap on O'Connor's departure.

But in some ways, that was an advantage—Sequeira could view the case without being influenced by all the uproar that had gone before. "Fresh eyes," as the phrase would have it much later, and in different circumstances, in the same year.

POLK, AS OWN ATTORNEY, QUESTIONS JURY POOL, the *Contra Costa Times* headlined on March 1.

"Wearing a red sweater and black skirt, Polk looked more like an attorney than a county jail prisoner," the *Times'* Bruce Gerstman reported. "Polk appeared confident and, in contrast to earlier appearances, did not interrupt or argue with the judge."

Susan wanted to find out the prospective jury's position on a defendant who chose to act as her own lawyer.

"Does anybody have a bias against somebody who thinks they can do a job themselves?" she asked.

Sequeira, for his part, wanted to know whether the prospective jurors might feel prejudiced *for* Susan, just because she was the underdog.

It took the better part of a week to pick the jury and four alternates. The final group was evenly split between men and women.

Sequeira opened the case of *People* vs. *Polk* on March 7, 2006, with an overview of the events leading up to Felix's death. Susan, Sequeira told the jurors, was "paranoid . . . delusional." He characterized her as a woman who made trouble with almost everyone, and accepted none of the responsibility for it. The paranoia, he said, had begun years earlier, and had continued to build. She had started "making things up," including "graphic" descriptions of having been raped by her father. She believed that her parents had murdered a police officer with a hammer, and buried his body under their house. She even believed Felix controlled the schools, Sequeira said.

Jurors, he said, were "about to embark on a journey through a dysfunctional relationship . . . .

"Slowly, all the anger and delusions were directed toward her husband, Felix Polk," Sequeira said. Eventually Susan came to believe that Felix was in the CIA, the FBI and the Mossad. She told this to the boys.

As Sequeira was threading these assertions together, Susan broke in with repeated objections, at one point weeping in frustration when Brady denied them, and at another throwing her pen down in anger. Sequeira continued, despite the insistent interruptions.

As the troubles between Felix and Susan deepened, Sequeira continued, she had taken more and more of the power in the relationship—controlling the money, belittling Felix, even criticizing the size of his penis—in front of the boys. Susan and her delusions had come to dominate the Polk family, he said. Felix had told friends that he was afraid of Susan.

All this had led up to the fateful night of October 13, 2002, when Susan had stabbed Felix in a premeditated attempt to do away with him, to get final control over the boys and the money. And then, after allowing Gabriel to discover the bloody body of his dead father, Susan had tried to cover things up by hiding his car and denying everything. Eventually Susan realized she couldn't get away with it—the evidence against her was too strong.

"There were lies, and there was a cover-up and destruction of evidence. But because of forensic evidence, 'I didn't do it' has turned into 'self-defense,'" Sequeira told the jury. "Is this the picture of an abused woman, dominated by fear and her abusive husband, or is this the picture of someone who does [just] what she wants to do?"

Sequeira displayed gruesome photographs of Felix on the autopsy table, and indicated the various stab wounds on his body. The evidence would show, he said, that Susan had been the aggressor in the fight, not a victim of spousal abuse.

"Her paranoid delusions and accusations festered into bitterness and anger, until she made a decision to kill the victim," he said. "She made good on her repeated threats. Dr. Polk, the abuser? Or Dr. Polk, the victim of the ultimate act of domestic violence, murder?"

That was what the jury would have to decide, he indicated.

Sequeira's opening statement lasted just fifty minutes, despite the repeated outbursts from Susan. After her tenth objection, Brady lost patience with her.

"This is not the time to argue differences of opinion," Brady told her. The opening statements were not facts, just the interpretation of facts, she indicated, and as such wouldn't be considered as evidence by the jury. Still Susan persisted in objecting to Sequeira's remarks. Brady got exasperated.

If she made one more objection, Brady told her, "I'm going to remove you from the courtroom."

The second trial of Susan Polk was off to a bumpy start,

and it didn't take a psychic to realize that it was soon to get even further off the track of ordinary jurisprudence.

Once Sequeira was done, the judge dismissed the jury for the day. Susan had decided to reserve her own opening statement until after the prosecution rested its case. The wisdom of this tactic is debatable—usually it's best to counter the prosecution case with the defendant's claims to reasonable doubt right in the beginning, so the jury will weigh the forthcoming prosecution witnesses with more skepticism as they testify. By giving the jurors an alternative with which to measure their credibility, the strength of the prosecution case can be tested by jurors even as it's being presented.

But according to Valerie Harris, Susan had decided to reserve her opening statement because she wasn't ready. The sheer logistics of moving her from jail to court and back again every morning and evening had severely limited her ability to prepare—another cost of the decision to defend herself.

In retrospect, despite the inadvisability of this decision to defer her opening, it was probably just as well. Sequeira's opening was crafted in part to ignite Susan's anger and emotional volatility—to precipitate her unruly behavior for the jurors to see. Susan's eruption of objections, the admonishment by Brady, the threat to have her removed from the courtroom, painted a picture worth more than the sum of Sequeira's words. If she had simply sat calmly, saying nothing, as Sequeira made these seemingly outlandish statements, the jury would have had reason to doubt their validity. When she erupted, Sequeira had Exhibit A of his case.

Once the jury had left, Susan demanded a mistrial on the basis of prosecutorial misconduct. Sequeira, she said, had told the jury tales about her that simply weren't so, that had never been reflected in any of the statements given to the police by the boys, or any other witness, at least based on the documents provided to her in discovery. Worse, he had relied on Felix's description of her as "delusional" and "paranoid," without mentioning that it had been Felix who'd been diagnosed as schizophrenic, not her.

Brady denied Susan's motion for a mistrial. Susan was carted back to jail, where she immediately got out her stubby pencils and composed a clear and cogent motion for why the court should declare a mistrial on the basis of prosecutorial misconduct:

> In his opening statement . . . prosecutor Paul Sequeira made inflammatory, prejudicial comments which had no basis in reality, and in some instances contradicted his own witnesses and the former prosecutor, Mr. O'Connor . . . .

There was no established, factual basis for Sequeira to tell the jury that she was paranoid and delusional, Susan said. Any such characterization came only from Felix . . . there was no specific, reliable finding by any expert opinion that such was the case, she said.

> To tell the jury that I am paranoid and delusional, as the prosecution did, is to undermine my defense totally. The jury was effectively told to completely disregard my defense [of self-defense to an attack]. The failure of the judge to halt these remarks could give credence to them. It was particularly onerous that I was admonished to refrain from objecting.

Susan now cited a leading California case, *People vs. Kirkes*, a 1952 murder case, in which a prosecutor told the jury in his closing argument that he personally believed the defendant to be guilty. A prosecutor's statement of personal opinion about guilt or innocence was prejudicial, a higher court had found, and so had thrown out the conviction.

Besides being effectively a personal opinion as to her guilt, Susan said, Sequeira's characterization of her as "delusional"

nd "paranoid," was an appeal to the jury's "passion and prej-
dice." So was his claim that "I had belittled my husband's
manhood and ridiculed the size of his penis to his own sons."

Any claim that these statements weren't "evidence" because they were only in an opening statement—because the
judge had warned the jury that remarks in an opening statement could not be considered "evidence" for the purpose of
deliberation—was insufficient to counteract the damage done
to her right to a fair trial, Susan contended.

> Sneaking in otherwise inadmissible statements through an
> opening statement should not be permitted as it may prejudice
> a jury. In this case, it most certainly will, as I am charged with
> murder and have stated that I responded to my husband in
> self-defense. At issue in self-defense is the "reasonableness"
> of the defendant. If the jury finds a "reasonable" person in the
> same set of circumstances would have acted in the same way,
> then the jury must acquit.

By describing her—"labeling" her, in Susan's words—as
"delusional" and "paranoid," Susan said, Sequeira had led the
jury to doubt her "reasonableness," which inherently eviscer-
ated her self-defense claim.

And with this, Susan arrived directly at the heart of the
case: the only really salient issue in *People* vs. *Polk* was the
question: who had attacked whom in the pool house that fateful night? Delusional or paranoid or not, that was the only real
question, and all the assertions about Susan's odd behavior,
real or only alleged, were simply window dressing used by the
prosecution as circumstantial evidence, and hearsay at that, to
make Susan seem unattractive to jurors, if not evil.

Because—what difference did it make if Susan was delusional or not, if in fact Felix had attacked her, as Susan insisted? Even people who are delusional have a right to defend
themselves.

31. BRAINWASHED?

Susan filed her motion for the mistrial based on prosecutoria[l] misconduct on the following morning, March 8. Brady tol[d] her she would hold a hearing on the matter late that afternoo[n.] This did not satisfy Susan—she wanted the court to declare [a] mistrial before any witnesses were called. Brady admonishe[d] Susan—she'd set the matter for a hearing, and that was that. [If] Susan couldn't play by the rules, Brady said, she could alway[s] revoke her right to act as her own lawyer and appoint someon[e] who would adhere to the proper procedures.

Just after 10 A.M., Sequeira called his first witness—Gab[e] Polk.

Sequeira asked Gabe why he had moved away from Orinda[.]

"Four years ago my mother murdered my father," Gabe an[-]swered. "I was left without a home."

Susan objected to Gabe's answer—it hadn't been estab[-]lished yet that any "murder" had occurred. A homicide in self[-]defense, of course, is not a "murder."

Very early in his testimony, Sequeira elicited Gabe's opin[-]ion that his mother was "delusional." Susan objected to thi[s] on the grounds that Gabe was hardly qualified to render suc[h] an opinion. Brady agreed with Susan, and told Sequeira t[o] confine his questions only to what Gabe had seen or heard.

Sequeira now took Gabe through the events in the War Between the Polks. Gabe told the jurors of the almost constant
confrontations that had occurred over the years at the house
of dreams, and even before. For most of his life, Gabe said,
he'd believed that his father was the cause of all the family's
problems.

"For most of my life, she was telling me what an awful person he was," Gabe said.

"Do you think anyone tried to brainwash you?" Sequeira
asked.

"Yes. My mother."

Depending on the preceding testimony, this could well
have been a leading question—after all, using the word
"brainwash" to predicate the question could be assuming a
fact not in evidence: that Gabe even understood the meaning
of the word, assuming that it had a meaning anyone could
agree on, or that any realistic evidence could be rendered as to
who had done it, if it had been done. In short, unless properly
posed, it could be an improper, even prejudicial question.

Susan apparently did not object—another cost of defending oneself, perhaps. But Sequeira was paid to win cases, not
look out for the interest of his opponent, and if Susan didn't
have a grip on the rules of evidence, it wasn't Sequeira's job
to be a lawyer for both sides.

Sequeira had Gabe describe the events of early October
2002, when Susan had returned from Montana to confront Felix, and how upset she had been that the court had given custody of the house and Gabe to Felix.

"She told me, quote-unquote, 'I'm going to sit your father
in a chair and tell him to wire twenty million dollars into an
account or I'm going to shoot him,'" Gabe said.

On the night she'd come back from Montana and confronted Felix over the unhappy court decision in the divorce,
Gabe said, "She leaned over and said under her breath to my
father, 'I'm going to kill you.'"

After this, the direct examination of Gabe was consistent

with what he'd told the police the night of the death, and wha
he'd later told the grand jury. Gabe was asked to identify four
teen photographs of the house, ending with a shot of th
kitchen door of the pool house, the door Gabe had used on th
night of October 14, when he'd gone in to find his father dea
"lying on his back, with blood all over him."

When Sequeira asked Gabe why he'd assumed that hi
mother had shot his father on the night of October 14, Gab
said, "She talked about killing him every day to me."

For whatever reason, Sequeira did not introduce the vide
tape of Gabe's interview by Detectives Moule and Hebel i
the early morning hours of October 15, 2002. Possibly, thi
was because it contained several untrue statements made b
the then-15-year-old Gabe. It would be up to Susan, cross
examining her own son, to flesh out these discrepancies an
damage his credibility. Was there a worse position for a mothe
to be in—to save herself by branding her son a liar?

Susan got her first chance to talk to Gabe in over three year
shortly after 2 that same afternoon. Unfortunately, it was un
der the circumstances of having to cross-examine him as
hostile witness. It was very clear that Gabe had been we
prepared for his testimony—he'd been calm and direct whe
under questioning by Sequeira, and maintained the same de
meanor when confronted by his mother.

The word that Susan was going to cross-examine her ow
son had jammed the courtroom with spectators—so large
crowd that many couldn't get in. They spilled out into th
hallway.

"It was an extremely powerful moment," Valerie Harris re
called later. "An electric atmosphere." The confrontation be
tween a mother and her child was the sort of utterly dramati
moment no tabloid, print or broadcast, could resist.

"It was so hard for her," Harris recalled. "After all, sh

dn't been able to talk to him for the past three years. Not
ice the night it happened. She loved Gabe beyond belief. He
as her baby."

Susan badly wanted something from Gabe far beyond any-
ing the jury could provide—any sign that he still loved her.
most as much, Susan wanted her youngest son to tell the
ry that she'd been a good mother. But these were Susan's
notional needs—and they interfered with her legal need to
ipeach his credibility. In short, her love for her son trumped
r ability to cast him as a potential fabricator.

"Did you have birthday parties every year?" she asked.
Vho took you to school every day? Did I generally think you
:re brilliant?"

Susan tried to engage Gabe with reminiscences of the good
nes the Family Polk had enjoyed, trying to recapture the life
ey had once had together. For supporters of Susan, watching
is unfold was painful. Susan was so intent on recapturing
r relationship with her child that she lost sight of what she
eded to do legally, which was to bring his testimony into the
alm of doubt.

Referring to Gabe as "Mr. Polk," until Brady told her she
uld address her youngest child by his first name, she asked
abe about stories that Felix had intimate relationships out-
le their marriage, primarily in connection with his teaching
sitions, a reference to Felix's supposed reputation for drugs
d group sex while at the university he'd helped organize.

She wanted to introduce into evidence the February 1988
diotape of Felix's Satanic child abuse rant, and thought the
ace to do it was with Gabe. To Susan, this was proof positive
at Felix was the one who was mentally ill, not her. But
rady ruled that she hadn't established a proper foundation
th Gabe to admit the tape as evidence. A mid-afternoon
eak was taken, and Harris encountered Golde out in the
llway. They discussed the best way for Susan to get the
mning tape into evidence for the jury to consider. Golde,

now off the case, but observing—he was consulting for Cou
TV—told Harris how Susan might use Gabe's testimony
get the tape in. Harris went back into the courtroom, but a
cording to her, Susan had already figured out what to do. S
asked Gabe whether he knew of the tape, and Gabe told h
yes, that Adam had told him about it, and apparently ha
played it for him. That was foundation enough for Brady; s
ruled the tape admissible as evidence.

Having gotten the Satanist tape judged admissible, Sus
tried to get Gabe to admit that she wasn't "crazy"—Felix wa

"Why did your father tell you I was delusional?" she aske

"Because you were acting that way," Gabe said. "I didr
need his evidence. I saw your delusions myself."

Well, said Susan, wasn't it true that both Adam and Gal
had been molested as small children? That Gabe had told h
this?

Gabe said no—in his mind, it was Susan who had ma
this up. She had told *him*, he said. And, he said, Adam hadr
told her this, either—Adam had told him that all this stu
about Satanism was in Susan's mind; she had made it all up

Of course, that wasn't supported by the facts—after all,
had been Felix who had told the Ritual Child Abuse Symp
sium that Adam had been molested, not Susan; it had been F
lix who claimed to have made a nonexistent complaint to tl
Berkeley Police Department, who had claimed to have colla
orated with the FBI for almost a year, who claimed that Ada
had witnessed infanticide, that he had identified "people .
fairly eminent in the community" as wearing triangular re
masks and beating babies to death with hammers inside pla
tic bags, and eating their remains. This was Felix, not Susa
It was Felix, not Susan, who had sued Hugh Clegg, accusir
him of ritual sexual child abuse.

To drive this point home, Susan now played the tape of F
lix's Satanist presentation—the one in which Felix, not Susa
had told the world that Adam had been molested by Satanist
and that Adam had witnessed multiple acts of ritual murder.

"My rage is omnipresent," came the voice of Felix from the tape machine. "I wake up with it every morning. *Every morning. . . .* "

Throwing this all off onto Susan's "delusions," absolving Felix, should have been a major hit to Gabe's credibility as a witness. But Susan loved her son, and she couldn't quite pull the trigger.

There were several other flaws in Gabe's story that Susan could have exploited to render his testimony suspect, particularly as to the truthfulness of what she had supposedly said about "shotguns," or "aren't you glad he's gone?"

For one, the police on the night of his interview had asked Gabe if he'd ever been in trouble with the law. Gabe had said no. That wasn't true. Susan had obtained the records of the Piedmont police, who had arrested Gabe in a juvenile assault case, when he'd used a metal object to attack someone he thought was going to attack him. This incident had taken place after Gabe had called the other student "a fag." Likewise, there was a record of Gabe having been involved in a juvenile burglary, not to mention the trashing of Felix's car just a few months before he was killed. At one point, even after he'd gone to live with the Briners, Eli claimed to have found brass knuckles in the vehicle Gabe was driving.

The police in that early-morning videotaped interview had asked Gabe why he was going to the continuation school. He'd told them that Susan had withdrawn him from high school because she was "crazy," that she didn't like the school. But in fact Gabe had been suspended for misbehavior. It wasn't Susan's decision.

And there was one extremely significant variation between what Gabe had told the police on October 15, 2002, and what he later testified to before the grand jury and at this trial. Gabe had testified that he'd heard Susan whisper to Felix that "I'm going to kill you" on the night she'd returned from Montana. But he'd told the police on the night of the killing that he hadn't actually heard those words spoken by Susan, only that

she'd whispered something he didn't actually hear. Felix ha
told Gabe that Susan had said she intended to kill Felix, an
that if she threatened him, he would call the police. When F
lix dialed 911 that night, Gabe admitted to the police, he'
only assumed that Susan had said the magic words—becaus
of Felix's move to the telephone to call 911. Yet here wa
Gabe testifying under oath that he'd actually heard the word
his mother had supposedly said—not true, if his statement t
the police was accurate. Also, there was the tag end of th
conversation between Adam and Gabe in the early mornin
hours of October 15, after the police had finished their inte
view with him, in which Gabe and Adam had talked abou
money—the income from the Arch Street apartments.

So there were discrepancies in Gabe's testimony. A dispa
sionate lawyer could have used these to cast doubt on h
credibility. Susan brushed over these lightly, but failed t
hammer them home, doubtless out of a desire to spare her so

Finally, there was the fact that both Gabe and Adam ha
sued their mother for their father's wrongful death. That gav
each a financial incentive to testify against her. After all, if
jury decided that Susan had not acted in self-defense, a ve
dict of murder or even manslaughter would give them a co
trol of the estate. Eli had already refused to participate in th
suit. The lawsuit undercut Adam and Gabe's credibility a
witnesses against their mother—made it seem that they had f
nancial reasons to say bad things about her.

Thus, Susan's desire for a reconciliation with Gabe worke
at cross-purposes with her need to diminish his credibility as
witness against her—yet more proof that one should nev
hire oneself as a lawyer.

The following day, Thursday, March 9, Judge Brady informe
both sides that she'd received a letter from Paul Good, th
psychologist who had been assigned by Judge Flinn the prev
ous year to assess Susan's competence, after Flinn had e

essed his "doubt." Brady said she considered the new letter
om Good an "ex-parte communication," meaning that it had
o standing in the trial. She said she would not respond to the
tter, but gave copies to both Sequeira and Susan. After read-
g her copy, Susan asked that it be sealed, and Brady agreed.

Good later declined to say what he'd reported to Flinn, and
nce the letter to Brady was sealed, its contents are not pub-
c, either. But based on what Susan said about Good's previ-
us findings, chances are that Good advised Brady that he
elieved Susan to be suffering from delusional disorder, and
as thus not competent to act as her own lawyer. Susan's per-
rmance on the opening day of the trial, with the repeated in-
rruptions of Sequeira, might have been cited as proof by
ood of the incompetence. But Brady could hardly interrupt
e trial on the basis of an "ex-parte communication" from a
bitzer, however qualified. She'd have to find other, in-court
rounds, to declare her own "doubt," and this she seemed, so
ir, unwilling to do.

The previous afternoon's cross-examination of Gabe had
ken a lot out of Susan, Valerie Harris thought. When she
ame to court the following day, Susan was sick.

"She was under a tremendous amount of stress," Harris re-
lled. "And she caught a bug."

At Susan's request, Brady adjourned the trial until the fol-
wing week, and sent the jury home for the weekend.

That same evening, Eli was arrested again—at least his
fth pinch in the previous five years, including the disaster
om the confrontation at the Jack in the Box.

32. MANO A MANO

Later, this arrest of Eli, while he was living at the drea[m]
house, was cited by Susan as yet more evidence of the con[-]
spiracy against her, and now Eli. The details are a bit murk[y]
but it appears that Eli, after getting out of jail the previou[s]
year, had obtained a job as a fitness instructor at a health clu[b.]
One of his supervisors was a young woman about ten yea[rs]
older than Eli. Eli was a very good-looking young man; on[e]
thing led to another, and soon he and his boss were involve[d.]
The peculiar thing about the relationship was that the woma[n]
happened to be the daughter of an associate of Budd MacKen[-]
zie, or so Susan later claimed.

As already noted, Eli was of a very volatile temperamen[t.]
In October 2005—the day of the funeral for Pamela Vitale, [in]
fact—there had been a domestic uproar between Eli and t[he]
girlfriend/supervisor. Eli tended to lose it when under stres[s]
and, after having initially been considered a suspect in Pame[la]
Vitale's murder, was on hair trigger. The girlfriend/boss calle[d]
911. Eli was arrested and charged with domestic violenc[e]
and violating his parole from the fight at the Jack in the Bo[x.]
Harris and Golde had then bailed him out of jail. The gir[l]
friend/boss obtained a restraining order against Eli. Susan, b[e]
lieving that the girlfriend was a "plant" inserted by John Po[-]

and Budd MacKenzie—tasked with finding a way to take Eli off the playing field—had advised Eli to stay away from her. Nevertheless, the older girlfriend/boss was at the dream house on Thursday night, March 9, 2006, visiting Eli, and two other people. Something happened that triggered Eli's anger, and the next thing anyone knew, the police had arrested him for misdemeanor battery against his now-former girlfriend. The two witnesses, friends of Eli's, told police that the woman had been the aggressor, and that Eli had not touched her. It did no good, and Eli was hustled off to the slammer by the Orinda police. Photographs showed it was Eli with the bruises, not the girlfriend, or so Susan later claimed.

Eli posted bail the next afternoon, but was re-arrested the following week, after Susan's trial resumed, for a new count of domestic violence, and again for violating his probation. Since Susan planned to call Eli as a defense witness—someone to back up her claims that Felix had been violent toward her and the boys—putting Eli in irons had the effect of diminishing the value of his future testimony for Susan. That was certainly how Susan saw things—it was all part of the plot. To her, Eli had been set up, and for the purpose of convicting her.

When Gabe returned to the witness stand for more of Susan's cross-examination on Monday, March 13, she once again tried to induce him to recall the good times mother and son had had together in the past. She introduced numerous photographs of the Polk family in calmer moments. Gabe remained unmoved. Susan ramped up her questioning by asking Gabe about his suspension from junior high school after the "fag" fight, and whether he had joined with Adam in the wrongful death suit. Again, Susan ran into difficulties with foundational questions—part of the problem was that she wanted Gabe to talk about things Sequeira hadn't asked about. This was "going beyond the scope" of direct examination, but it was a concept Susan had trouble with. She wanted to get the whole story from Gabe, and didn't understand why the judge kept sustaining Sequeira's objections to her questions. To her, it was Brady's attempt to subvert the truth.

"Do you remember telling Eli that he was your best friend?" Susan asked Gabe. And it was true—before Felix had been killed, Eli and Gabe were extremely close. But over the previous three years they had become bitter toward each other, with Eli accusing Gabe of being used by the Briners in the plot against Susan, and Gabe accusing Eli of having "Mom's crazy gene."

"Yes," Gabe said, he remembered telling Eli that.

"Do you miss him?"

"Yes."

"Are you still on good terms with Eli?"

"I still have affection for my brothers," Gabe said. "I still have affection for you, but there's bad with the good."

Susan wanted to retrieve the old Gabe—the little boy she remembered from before Felix's death. She hoped that he would show the jury that she had never been delusional—if she wasn't delusional, then she could claim reasonableness and therefore self-defense.

Wasn't it true that it was only Felix who said she was delusional? Susan asked.

No, Gabe said. He'd seen it for himself.

"Some days you just stayed in your room all day, and you never left. . . . I don't think it was the flu. You were depressed. Delusional."

Susan asked Gabe other questions designed to show that she was normal and that it was Felix who was disturbed. To many of these questions, Gabe responded that he could not recall. Sometimes Susan filled in the answers for him, leading Brady to warn her repeatedly about "testifying from the podium."

As the day wore on, Brady suggested that many of Susan's questions seemed designed to reestablish her relationship with Gabe, rather than to bring out facts relevant to the charge.

"Some of the dialogue is almost like you're having a conversation you've wanted to have for three years," Brady told Susan,

Well, that was right, Susan said. She hadn't seen Gabe since the night Felix died, and she had no idea of what poisons had been implanted in his mind by the opposition, the Briners, Budd MacKenzie, John Polk, and Adam. And since Sequeira had made a point of characterizing her as delusional, Susan said, she had to cover ground with Gabe to show that wasn't so—to bring out the truth of their life before October 14, 2002. But Gabe wasn't cooperating.

"At this point I'm kind of shocked," Susan told Brady. "He's not remembering what I'm remembering. I'm like, 'What's happening?' I don't know what he's going to blurt out next."

"I think perhaps you're going to lose the attention of this jury if we continue to spend time on issues that are obviously very important to you," Brady told her. "I'm not telling you how to try your case. I'm just making an observation."

Near the close of the day, Susan asked Gabe what he thought of her, under the strange circumstances they now found themselves in.

"Do you think I love you any less, now?" Susan asked, meaning after Gabe had testified against her.

"I hope not," Gabe said.

Susan was again sick the following day, and Brady postponed the trial until Friday. At that point, Sequeira asked Brady for permission to interrupt Gabe's testimony for another witness—Adam. Adam had been waiting to testify after Gabe, but Susan's cross-examination was taking so long that Adam was now pressed for time. He had final exams scheduled for the following week. He'd also planned a vacation trip to South Africa.

Earlier in the week, the homeowners' insurance company that held a policy on the dream house agreed to settle the wrongful death claims made by Gabe and Adam against Susan and Eli. The policy on the dream house paid the two boys and their lawyers a total of $300,000. Susan and Eli agreed to the settlement, even though Horowitz had, months earlier, vehemently advised against it—a settlement could be used as evidence against Susan. But Susan clearly wanted Adam and Gabriel to have access to some money—evidence, perhaps, that she was willing to sacrifice her own interest for their benefit. Or maybe this was Susan's way of trying to reclaim their loyalty. You could see it either way.

In any event, the settlement meant Adam would soon have access to a pot of cash. He wanted to celebrate the end of the school term by going to South Africa with his girlfriend, a citizen of that country.

Susan objected to Sequeira's request to take Adam out of order so he could get out of town.

"His mother's murder trial is a big enough event, one might think, for him to cancel his vacation plans," Susan told Brady.

Brady told Sequeira it wasn't necessary to call Adam out of order—it didn't make any difference, because, based on the pace Susan was on in her cross-examination of Gabe, Adam wouldn't be able to leave when he wanted to anyway. "If the court allowed Adam to testify today, I can't imagine that his cross-examination would be done in time for his finals," Brady said.

Susan contended that Sequeira had been "coaching" Gabe on how to respond to her questions. That was improper, she said. Brady now admonished her for making allegations of improper conduct against the prosecutor without having any proof to back them up.

The very idea that he'd done anything improper, anything that would warrant a mistrial, was crazy, Sequeira said. He couldn't imagine having to start over.

"I'd rather have needles shoved in my eyes than have a mistrial," he said.

In all, Gabe was on the witness stand for four days—not in sequence, but four different days over more than a week, wha with all the delays for illness and wrangles over admissibility of evidence. And Susan's frequent motions for a mistrial. And Brady's admonishments of Susan for her demeanor. And Sequeira's continuing complaints over the same.

"Are you aware that the district attorney is engaging in a discriminatory and malicious prosecution of Eli because he is a witness in my case?" Susan asked Gabe one day the following week.

This question exercised Brady, who immediately packed the jury off to lunch, then lambasted Susan for an improper, argumentative question.

"I'm extremely close to revoking your pro per status," Brady growled, meaning she might rescind Susan's right to act as her own lawyer. Besides, said Brady, Susan was dragging out the questioning of Gabe far longer than was necessary.

"You are not only losing the attention of this jury," Brady said, "you are extremely close to—"

"You're aligning yourself with the prosecution," Susan shot back.

"I think Ms. Polk's conduct is becoming so pervasive that she is not only losing the jury," Sequeira said, "but she is completely making this trial a farce. She is in filibuster mode. We have gone far beyond the pale of what is reasonable."

But Brady demurred on pulling Susan's permission to represent herself under the *Faretta* case—having gone this far, she had to be concerned that revoking the self-representation permission could set up a mistrial. And a mistrial might result in a finding of double jeopardy, which could require dismissal of the entire case. Brady was in a bind—having declined to declare her "doubt" at the outset, she had little choice but to see the disaster through to the end.

Susan finally wrapped up her questioning of Gabe on the afternoon of March 21, 2006. She played a redacted version of the videotape of Gabe's interview by Detectives Moule and Hebel. Brady had ordered her to remove the portion where Gabe and Adam had talked about money.

"Isn't it true that on the night you were arrested, you were afraid of being blamed?" Susan asked. Of course, Gabe hadn't actually been "arrested"—only "detained." But Susan's point was that the way the police had treated Gabe had influenced his statements to the police about his mother. This was why, she implied, Gabe had told the detectives that she was "delusional"—not because she actually was, but in order to focus their suspicion on her.

"I had no fear whatsoever," Gabe said. "I discovered his body. There was no thought that I'd ever be accused of it."

Gabe denied that he'd ever seen Felix punch Susan, or drag her by the hair to her room.

When Susan again asked Gabe about his assertions that she was "delusional," Gabe said that as far as he could see, Susan sometimes lost touch with reality. He said he recalled Susan's penchant for scouring the newspaper for "secret codes."

"Did I ever say your father was a card-carrying member of the CIA?" she asked.

"You said a lot more than that," Gabe said.

Afterward, Sequeira lauded Gabe for his courage in testifying against his mother.

"How'd you like to be cross-examined by your mom for four days, and [taken] over every detail of your life, and air your family's dirty laundry, and every emotional thing that's ever happened to you?" he asked news reporters afterward. "It's the most gut-wrenching thing I've ever seen."

Once Gabe's testimony was finished—Susan said she intended to call him as her own witness later in the defense case— Sequeira got down to the nuts and bolts of his evidence.

Over the next month he called a series of witnesses to establish his case, among them friends and associates of Felix, to demonstrate that in the days before he was killed, Felix had expressed fear for his life. He played a series of telephone tapes of 911 calls made by Felix in the second week of October

2002, in which he'd told police that he believed that Susan had a shotgun, and intended to kill him.

Sequeira called Sergeant Hansen and Officer Kelly, then Detective Costa, and introduced the videotape of Susan's interrogation, in which she'd denied killing Felix, and Costa had pleaded with her to say what had really happened. Susan objected to the tape, saying that Costa's questioning of her had violated her Miranda rights. Brady allowed the tape in anyway.

Throughout all this, Susan continued to make objections and motions for a mistrial. Worse, in her cross-examination of Sequeira's witnesses, she habitually referred to facts not in evidence by imbedding unproved assertions into her questions. To Sequeira, it was as if Susan was trying to influence the jury by testifying through her cross-examination. Sequeira soon lost his temper. He claimed Susan knew better, was doing this deliberately, and asked Brady to make Susan stop relying on improper questions.

"I really don't know what else to do," he told Brady. "I'm at my wits' end. At this point, it's becoming absurd."

Susan objected to Sequeira's bashing of her legal skills, but Brady cut her off. Susan objected to this, too. It wasn't appropriate, she said, for the judge to refuse to hear her side. It was only more proof that the judge was conspiring with the prosecutor in order to ensure her conviction.

"You've done a lot of speaking, Ms. Polk, at appropriate times and inappropriate times," Brady told her. "It is not in your best interest to continuously interrupt the judge or argue with her legal rulings."

On her cross-examination of Costa, Susan was able to establish that he did not investigate the possibility that Felix had previously been violent toward Susan—a telling point in her favor. She questioned Costa about the diary entry of October 2, 2002, the one in which she'd claimed to have predicted the 9/11 attacks. She asked Costa if he believed the Mossad existed. Costa said yes, he believed the Mossad existed.

"Is it your understanding," Susan continued, "that Mossad agents operate in the U.S. with impunity?"

Costa said he had no knowledge about that.

By the third week of April of 2006, Sequeira had managed to produce evidence from Song Wicks, the criminalist, and Dr. Bruce Peterson, the contract pathologist. This was really the heart of his case—scientific evidence that Felix had been assaulted, and had died as a result of the attack in the pool house.

Susan, meanwhile, had contended that the police investigators had "tainted" the crime scene by moving furniture, using water to spread the blood around to make the scene look worse, and planting the mysterious shoeprints. She said she'd been barefoot on the night of the fight, so the shoeprints couldn't be hers.

Wicks testified that the blood had run to the overturned ottoman, and then had stopped, showing that the ottoman had been turned over before the blood was shed. Moreover, Wicks said, the blood spatter all around the room showed that someone had used a knife in a frenetic fashion. Susan said she doubted that this is what had happened—she was there, she said, and she didn't recall that such a large amount of spatter had occurred. It was the police, she suggested, trying to make the fight look worse than it was, "to create a more dramatic photo opportunity."

Wicks denied this.

"When you frame someone for murder, you don't think you're going to have to come up with an explanation, do you?" Susan said.

"I don't know," Wicks said. "I've never framed anyone for murder."

Sequeira soon moved to foreclose this notion.

"Who had the most time to spend at the crime scene—the detectives, the criminalists, or the defendant?"

"The defendant," Wicks said.

"Would your job have been made easier, to tell where people were, who was on top of whom, who was on their back, if you had the bloody clothing of the defendant?"

"It could have allowed me to draw conclusions, if I had the defendant's clothing."

"Did you find any bloody clothing anywhere?"

"No."

Susan demanded a mistrial again, contending that Sequeira was attempting to prejudice the jury against her. Brady wearily denied it.

In his testimony, Peterson said that the cause of Felix's death was the combination of the knife wounds and the blow to the head.

"It was the entire complex of injuries that caused death," he said. "The most serious wound he had was the one that penetrated his chest and punctured his lung."

Having sustained a collapsed lung would have caused Felix to be very short of breath, and less able to resist an attack, Peterson said. Many of the remaining wounds were defensive in nature—this suggested that Felix was on his back during at least part of the attack.

"There might be times when you want to get your feet between you and the blade," he said. That suggested Felix had been on his back, probably kicking at Susan as she wielded the knife. "Otherwise it's pretty hard to get your feet between you and the blade."

What about the head wound? Sequeira asked. Was it more likely to have occurred in a fall, or as a result of being hit by some object?

"I believe it was more consistent with being hit by something," Peterson said.

Susan tried to suggest that Peterson had exaggerated the number of wounds by calling some small cuts "stab" wounds, when some of them were actually minor nicks. In this, she was following the line that had months earlier been put forward by Horowitz and Golde, who had all along suggested that

Peterson's count of "twenty-seven stab wounds" was wildly inflated, that there were only five serious wounds.

What about Felix's heart—could he have died of a heart attack?

No, Peterson said, although the hardening of his arteries could have contributed to his inability to successfully thwart the attack.

"Heart disease was not necessary for his death. It might have made him an easier victim, so to speak."

Susan suggested that Peterson, being paid by the county sheriff coroner's department, was biased in favor of the authorities.

"That's absolutely ridiculous," he said. "Everybody's paid by somebody. Never have I been approached [by an official], asking me to skew or misappropriate [sic]."

All of this was attended by continual bickering between Susan and Sequeira, and between Susan and the judge. Frequently Brady would declare an unscheduled recess, or send the jury to lunch early—usually when Susan began interrupting people and refusing to follow the court's orders. Some thought it only showed what happened when defendants tried to represent themselves.

"Mrs. Polk is proving that a little knowledge is very, very dangerous," Michael Cardoza, a criminal defense attorney, told the *San Francisco Chronicle*'s Henry K. Lee, who was covering the trial for that newspaper. "She seems to have grasped some of the objections, but doesn't know quite when to use them properly. She objects to insignificant questions and lets the big ones go by when she really should be objecting."

But others thought they saw method in Susan's madness— they thought she was deliberately bollixing things up in order to force Brady to revoke her pro per status over her objections, and appoint a lawyer to represent her. That might well require declaring a mistrial, and starting over with a new jury.

That would raise an interesting legal point—if Brady insisted on appointing a lawyer for Susan over her objections, and Susan refused to agree to the mistrial, would it be double jeopardy? And would a higher court later vacate a conviction on those grounds?

Some thought that was what was in Brady's mind, as she gritted her teeth through Susan's diatribes. Faced with two bad choices—allowing Susan to represent herself, or having to start all over and face a possible reversal—Brady had chosen the lesser of the two.

More than a month into the trial, *Chronicle* columnist C. W. Nevius dropped in to see what was going on. In a column published the following day, Nevius wondered whether it was a case of "a smart, quirky murder suspect hijacking the process for her own purposes. . . .

"It's all become a somewhat loopy version of 'Boston Legal,'" Nevius wrote, "offbeat legal entertainment that would be a hoot to watch, if only her husband hadn't been hit in the head and stabbed repeatedly in their pool house."

Some of those watching, Nevius continued, were wondering if Susan was getting off on being the center of attention. Or perhaps the long, tedious, repetitive, improper quality of her cross-examination was aimed at the jury—an effort to drag the trial out for so long that some jurors would be forced to drop out by the imminence of other long-planned commitments. If the jury dropped below twelve, that would make for another mistrial.

Sequeira, interviewed by Nevius, suggested that the snail's pace of the trial was simply the result of Susan's personality.

"One of the things she really likes," he noted, "whether we like it or not, is, in the courtroom she has a certain amount of control. And that control is something that she craves."

By April 18, Sequeira was close to finishing his case. For his final witness, he called Adam Polk. Originally, he'd intended to open his case with Gabe, then call Adam next, but when he wasn't allowed to put Adam on the stand out of order early on, he'd realized it worked just as well, maybe even better, to call him as the last witness, in effect "bookending" the case.

While Susan could be obstreperous with other witnesses, particularly officials, and where she'd tried to cajole Gabe into recanting his version of the events, with Adam it was different. In her mind, Adam had become a junior Felix, aping his tone, his mannerisms and even his words. There was bound to be an explosive confrontation between Susan and her firstborn.

Sequeira had Adam describe the Polk family's home life. Adam said that his mother frequently had problems with people, that she had "a pattern" of initially being warm with strangers, then later turning on them. His mother and his father argued all the time, and much of the dissension was caused by his mother's stubbornness.

"My mother always had a problem," he told Sequeira. "There was never a moment in my childhood where there wasn't drama. . . . My mother had a conflict every single day. There came a point when I realized a lot of these conflicts weren't really justified."

His father had never abused his mother, Adam said. He had never "bumped" her around the room to intimidate her. Susan had made this up.

Susan had told him, Adam said, that Felix was in the CIA or the FBI, and that he was a double agent for the Mossad.

As he described the various crises of the family over the years, Susan frequently objected. He recalled his mother's growing hatred for his father, and said that at one point Susan had told him, "I should just kill him."

What did you say to that? Sequeira asked.

"I told her that's a very bad idea."

When it was her turn, Susan asked Adam if he really thought she was the one who was controlling, rather than Felix. When

Adam said she was, Susan objected, saying he wasn't qualified
to use that term, because he wasn't a psychologist. Adam said
he'd been his father's confidant—he knew what Felix had been
thinking. In fact, he was so close to his father, Adam said, that
Susan had once told him, " 'You're not my son.' "

Crying, she asked if Felix had ever told Adam that she was
delusional.

"No," Adam said, "I told *him* you were delusional. I knew
he wasn't in the FBI and that I wasn't Satanically abused. So I
knew you weren't properly grounded in reality."

"Adam, when did you learn to lie so well?" Susan asked,
still weeping.

"Objection," Sequeira thundered.

"Sustained," Brady said.

As the session broke for lunch, Sequeira spoke quietly to
Adam.

Susan objected, saying that Sequeira was "coaching" Adam
on how to testify.

Sequeira lost his temper again.

"You're unable to be a human being," he told Susan. He
was tired of her "pathological lies," he said. He'd only been
telling Adam when to be back in court after lunch. He said he
wanted to make sure that Adam didn't have "a complete melt-
down" because Susan was "treating her son like crap."

"That's unprofessional," Susan said. Sequeira was "tampering" with the witness.

"You're a liar," Sequeira said.

"Stop! Stop! Both of you, just stop," Brady called out.

The circus broke for lunch.

That afternoon, things got out of hand again, and this time
Brady called an unscheduled thirty-minute recess, and had
Susan confined to the holding pen.

The battle between mother and son consumed most of the
next two days, with Susan trying to impeach Adam's testimony.

"Are you unable to remember anything?" Susan asked.

"I can't believe you would call my integrity into question," Adam said. "How can you call yourself a mother? This is why we have no relationship, and never will."

Adam continued to insist that he'd never been "Satanically abused," and that this had been a figment of Susan's imagination. He suggested that Felix's rant had come only as a result of Susan's convincing him of the truth of the allegations, despite Felix's admission on the tape that "we even become 'the bad people,' sometimes" reminiscent of the McMartin approach to discovering child abuse.

He smiled at one of Susan's questions on this subject.

"You think this is funny?" Susan demanded.

Yes, Adam said, there were elements of the absurd involved.

Susan began to cry again.

"You think my defending myself in a murder trial is absurd?"

"Yes, that's absurd."

"So you remember threatening to kill me, Adam?"

"No," he said, "you are fabricating that. I don't know if you go to sleep and have dreams and think they're real. You're twisting the facts." Susan was not "grounded in this world," he said. "You are somewhere else."

Susan wanted to show Adam her diary, when she'd noted, in September 2001, that Adam had threatened to kill her. But Brady wouldn't allow it—as hearsay, it had nothing to do with Adam as a witness. After all, he had no way of knowing what Susan had written.

His mother, Adam told the jury, was either "extremely disturbed or evil . . . trapped in a chaotic whirlwind of conspiracy and drama."

When Susan tried to get Adam to confirm that the Briners, Budd MacKenzie and John Polk were bent on looting Felix's estate, Adam lashed out at her for impugning the Briners' integrity.

"Shame on you! Where's your gratitude? This is the woman

who took care of your son. You're bonkers! You're cuckoo for Cocoa Puffs!"

Brady had to hide her smile behind her hand, on hearing this riposte from Adam, according to the *Chronicle*'s Henry Lee.

Wasn't it true, Susan asked, that Adam had once told Eli that he believed that Susan had acted in self-defense? And that he wanted to become a lawyer so he could defend her?

"I never said any of that," Adam said. "You may have had a dream about that.

"What you told me is that, 'I'm just going to plead guilty.' You said, 'Things just got out of control.' Word for word. I fall asleep remembering that every night."

Susan asked Adam if he really believed that she could have intentionally killed his father without it being an act of self-defense. Didn't he understand that the authorities were trying to frame her for a murder she did not commit?

"I don't think the whole county would conspire to convict a housewife. . . . Whatever conspiracy theories you develop, they're just going to be as baseless as this defense." Susan's stories about the CIA and the Mossad were just as loopy as her version of the abuse by Felix, he said.

Wasn't it true that Adam had threatened to testify against her if she didn't agree to give up fighting for the estate? Susan asked. Adam denied it.

"You're just a cruel-hearted person," he said. "You should never have had children."

Susan began weeping again, and Brady told her to wrap up her cross-examination.

"This is not a therapy session between you and your children," Brady said.

Susan played a portion of the tape of Felix's Satanic child abuse presentation.

"Do you think I put those ideas into your father's head?"

"I don't think it's such a huge leap that it's outside the realm of possibility," Adam responded.

By the end of the day, April 20, Susan still hadn't finished her cross-examination, but Adam had to get back to UCLA to finish his finals. Brady ordered him to return to court on May 5 so that Susan could finish.

On the following Monday morning, Sequeira rested his case. Susan now gave her own opening statement.

33. THE OTHER SIDE
OF THE STORY

The case of the death of Felix Polk was not what it seemed, Susan told the jury when she began. She had been charged on the basis of lies—lies told to ensnare her in a crime that she did not commit, lies told to remove her from society because she was different. Throughout history, society had punished people like her, because it was frightened of them. People like Galileo, Patrick Henry, Ingrid Bergman and Henry David Thoreau were often ridiculed or despised in their time, but that didn't mean they were wrong.

She was like a woman back in medieval times, Susan continued, when they had been immersed in water to see if they were witches—if they drowned, they were innocent. If they didn't drown, they were guilty and were executed.

"Did I have to die to be found innocent?" Susan asked, meaning that if she had succumbed to Felix's onslaught, would she have ever been charged with murder?

Don't assume you've heard the truth about what happened in the pool house, she went on. There were such things as surprise endings, when it turned out that the conventional wisdom was completely wrong.

"You may think you know all there is to know, but it's my

turn now. . . . I did not stab my husband twenty-seven times, nor did I hit him. He fell. I'm not crazy."

It *was* true, though, that she was psychic. She had predicted the 9/11 attacks.

"I served my country," Susan said. "For over twenty-five years I provided information in trances to help thwart terrorist attacks here and abroad." Felix was a secret agent for the Mossad while he had only pretended to work for U.S. intelligence, Susan insisted. In short, he was a "mole," who did not report the pending attacks to the U.S. authorities from his fear it would expose him as a secret Mossad double agent. There really were spies, Susan said—it wasn't just in fiction. Felix had used her psychic abilities as an intelligence asset, which was one reason he refused to let her go: she knew too much.

"If you doubt psychics exist, examine your own experience," Susan suggested. How was it that fish and birds travel together in flocks and schools? They had extrasensory perception. It wasn't impossible that human beings could have it too. Had the jurors ever heard of Edgar Cayce?

"I don't believe in little green men from Mars, but I do still believe in fairies," she said. Just because science hadn't documented something didn't mean it didn't exist.

Susan read from portions of her timeline and her diary, sketching in the two decades of events that led up to October 13–14, 2006.

"The D.A. would have you believe that I was demanding, that I was a Lolita," she said. But the truth was far different: Felix had seduced her "under the guise of therapy" when she was still a teenager, had "drugged, hypnotized, raped and mentally enslaved me," and from then on had controlled her life, and that of their three sons. He'd tried to brainwash the boys, and, using hypnosis, treated them "as if they were lab rats."

The entire family "lived in terror of what he would do next," she said. Felix had once told her, " 'I am your Jewish

God,' " Susan claimed. "Felix demanded subservience like a God-man. We walked on eggshells around him . . . .

"What happened to me could happen to any family," Susan said. Felix had threatened to kill her at the very beginning of their relationship, should she ever try to leave him, she said. He'd poisoned two of their dogs and had twice tried to poison her, she said.

"On the last night of his life, when I went to the cottage to talk to him, I still believed that reason could prevail." But the reason had given way to angry words, and Felix had charged at her with the ottoman, shoving her back against the west wall of the pool house. He'd knocked her down, grabbed her hair and begun stabbing at her with a knife. She'd had only a split second to decide whether to die or fight back.

"I chose to live," she said.

The evidence would show, she continued, that the authorities had later altered the crime scene to make it seem like a murder had occurred, wiping out indications that what had actually happened was a plain case of self-defense. She would call witnesses to demonstrate that, including a pathologist and a crime-scene expert who would both testify that Felix had attacked her, and that he'd died, not as a result of his wounds, but from a heart attack.

"I will speak to your reason and sense of justice . . . you will see that the scene was staged by those who would make self-defense look like murder . . . truth is often stranger than fiction." The real story of the death of Felix might sound like some sort of "nail-biting" Hollywood mystery-suspense story, she said, but it was nevertheless true.

But, she said, the story didn't have an ending yet. That would be up to the jury.

"The pen will be handed to you. It will be up to you to write the ending."

With that, Susan called her first witness—her mother, Helen Bolling.

Helen was 72, and in frail health. But after the intensity of the exchanges between Susan and her sons, she seemed refreshingly light, almost "whimsical," as one reporter described her.

Under questioning from Susan, Helen told how Susan had first been sent to Felix as his patient as a teenager. Helen hadn't understood what was going on at the time, she said. It was only when the teenaged Susan told her about a new boyfriend, and then later said it was Felix, at the time married to Sharon, and the father of two, that Helen had first had her doubts about him.

She'd confronted Felix, Helen said, telling him, "You're not exactly what I had in mind as a son-in-law." She'd told him to break off the relationship, and he had told her he would. But Helen admitted that she hadn't persisted, although she wished she had.

"He promised me he would. Felix had that ability to take you in, and make you believe him . . . .

"I'm not going to bad-mouth Felix," she said, "but he was a flawed man."

Susan asked how her mother had gotten along with her and the boys over the years, and Helen admitted that they'd often been estranged. She believed that the estrangement was mostly Felix's doing.

Felix, she said, could put on a good front, "but hidden under that is all this shit."

She apologized to the court for her language, but that was how she felt.

"I certainly made a serious mistake with Felix," she said. "And I'm afraid God will punish me when it's my time."

Sequeira decided to use Helen to undercut Susan's credibility. He asked whether Helen was aware that Susan had claimed to her sons that her father had molested her. Susan vociferously and repeatedly objected to this.

It was Felix who had told her this tale, Susan argued, and it was unfair to ask her mother to accuse her father in court.

"It's torture of my mom on the stand," Susan said, "and it's not right."

Sequeira, again over Susan's objection, played a portion of the videotape of Susan's interrogation by Detective Costa, in which Susan had said her father was a "pervert."

"She made that up, correct?" Sequeira asked.

"I can tell you it's not true," Helen responded. If Susan had said that, it was because Felix had made her believe it, Helen said.

On redirect, Susan asked her mother if she believed Susan was capable of murder.

"Absolutely not," Helen said. Susan might have a vivid imagination, but she was no murderer. She believed that Susan had been defending herself from imminent death.

"When you're under threat of death . . . 'How do I save myself, what do I do?' . . . that's what yells at you. You'd better make the right decision or you're dead."

Late the same afternoon, Eli was brought to the courtroom by the authorities, wearing his jail jumpsuit and in chains. Harris had brought civilian clothes for Eli to wear while testifying for his mother, but someone at the jail had slipped up, and Eli appeared in the garb of a prisoner. The contrast between Adam and Gabe, in civilian clothes, and Eli, clearly a jailbird, was as obvious as it was prejudicial to the credibility of his testimony for his mother. To Susan, this was just one more example of how the system was out to get her.

Susan played an audiotape of the interview Eli had given to detectives after the killing. He had insisted that his mother could not have killed Felix, that she was "a mellow person."

"What did you see when you were growing up?" Susan asked Eli.

"I don't know where to start to explain how overcontrolling my father was," Eli said. "We had to figure out ways to avoid confrontation."

Susan asked how Felix had tried to intimidate him.

"He would charge at me, raising his fists," Eli said. "He would get right up in my face."

"Did he hit you?"

"Yes."

Susan asked Eli about the time he himself had hit her in the mouth.

Eli admitted it, suggesting that he'd done it to get the approval of his father.

"That night my father took me to my favorite restaurant and told me it wasn't my fault, but my mother's," he said.

Was Felix really a spy?

Oh yes, Eli said. He'd even heard Felix tell Susan he'd have friends in "the Jewish mafia" kill Susan if she left him.

"Did you love your dad?" Susan asked.

"Yes," Eli said. "He was just a damaged person."

Susan called two other witnesses on the first day of her defense. One was the psychiatrist at the hospital near Yosemite where Susan had been taken after her suicide attempt in early 2001. Susan had overdosed on aspirin, Vicodin and Scotch, the doctor said, and as far as he could tell, Susan was suffering from post-traumatic stress disorder. She showed no sign of being delusional while discussing her marriage, the doctor said, and seemed quite capable of distinguishing fantasy from reality.

The other witness was a forensic computer technician who had been retained by Harris for the first trial. He testified that someone had gotten access to Susan's computer before the search warrant was approved, and failed to follow proper procedures. Data had been lost, he said. There was no evidence that Susan had altered any of the diary entries after Felix's death to boost her self-defense claim, or her claim that Felix had often abused her. In other words, the diary entries were largely contemporaneous with the supposed events—always assuming Susan hadn't imagined them—but someone had, after Susan's arrest, damaged some entries and erased others.

Some thought Susan had made a good beginning—her questions were crisper, and her witnesses bolstered her story. But Eli hadn't yet been cross-examined by Sequeira, and if past performance was any guide, once Sequeira began to grill him, Susan was sure to ignite. She and Eli had a mutual defense pact—an attack on one was an attack on the other.

The day after Susan began presenting her case, she produced something of a surprise witness: a former resident of the Elmwood neighborhood, Elizabeth Drozdowska. As Valerie Harris later described it, this was a "*Perry Mason* moment." Seventy-eight years old, in a wheelchair, Susan's old neighbor came forward to testify that Susan had been a marvelous mother, and neighbor.

What was happening to Susan, she said, was terrible. She'd seen a reporter on television, Drozdowska said, "and she was demonizing Susan in such a way that I was shocked." The reporter was slandering Susan, Drozdowska told the jury. "So I decided my voice needed to be heard."

The fact was, the Susan she knew wasn't at all like she was being portrayed in the media.

"In my lifetime, I never met a more diligent housewife, mother and assistant to her husband," she said. "I know so many women who are so mean to their husbands, and you—you worked so hard. It breaks my heart. You deserve better."

As for Felix—Drozdowska was less impressed. She'd once seen him hit one of the boys in punishment. "The beating was cruel."

Drozdowska's testimony had a strong impact on the jurors, with at least one of them wiping her eyes of tears.

There was almost no way for Sequeira to impeach this elderly, wheelchair-bound woman, so he declined to ask any questions.

"Bye-bye, honey," she said to Susan, as she wheeled her way out of court. "God bless you."

After Drozdowska left, Eli resumed the witness stand. He testified that his father had regularly hypnotized the boys—"twice a week"—as they were growing up. Felix had given them "tea," and after the sessions, he couldn't remember what had happened. Given that Gabe and Adam had denied being hypnotized by Felix, and the fact that Eli's testimony on this subject so closely resembled Susan's own assertions, the credibility of this version of events was undercut. Adam, Eli said, was often aggressive, and picked fights with him; he recalled that Adam had cursed Susan as a "crazy bitch" at breakfast in an Oakland café. It was true, he said, that he'd also called Susan crazy at times, but that was how the boys got their father's approval.

It was true he'd cut off his ankle bracelet and broken probation in the summer of 2001, Eli admitted, but it was only because he couldn't stand living in the Berkeley cottage with his father. He said he and Gabe and Susan had spent much of the summer camping and traveling out of state.

"It was the best summer we ever had, as a family, without Dad," he said. He wept.

Susan wanted Eli to testify to some hearsay about Adam and Felix, but Brady forbade it. Susan objected, and Brady abruptly terminated her direct examination. Susan objected to that too, and when Susan persisted in talking over the judge, the judge lost her temper.

"Stop, stop, stop, stop, stop, stop," Brady told her. "What part of the word 'stop' do you not understand?"

"You're shaming me in front of the jury," Susan shot back. She made yet another motion for a mistrial on the basis of judicial misconduct.

Brady decided to recess the trial early for the day to let tempers cool off.

34. NOT FROM BEHIND

When Sequeira began his cross-examination of Eli the following day, Susan objected to nearly every question put by the prosecutor. Not only was Susan bent on preventing Eli's impeachment by Sequeira, she was shielding her son from what she saw as an unwarranted personal attack, intended to insult him. Of course, Sequeira knew she'd react this way—that's why he chose to go after Eli so vigorously. It only unmasked the emotional volatility of both Eli and Susan, and thereby undercut their credibility with jurors. It also served as yet another example of why defendants shouldn't represent themselves, especially when their own children are under attack on the witness stand. But this was exactly the sort of situation that had made Susan determined to act as her own lawyer. A defense attorney would never have made so many objections, a reluctance which would have agitated Susan beyond endurance.

"Objection," Susan interjected to one of Sequeira's questions. "He's yelling at my son and he better stop it."

Because the brunt of Eli's testimony was that Felix had been assaultive and manipulative of everyone in the family, it was Sequeira's purpose to cast him as a liar. This he did by forcing Eli to admit to his various transgressions—his school

suspensions, his arrest in the Jack in the Box fight, his violation of probation, his numerous other arrests for marijuana,
burglary—the whole dog's breakfast of Eli's repeated clashes
with authority. Susan tried to protect him with her repeated
objections, accusing Sequeira of being "tricky, nefarious and
devious" with his questions. The court should protect Eli from
Sequeira out of a sense of "compassion for a young man who
lost his father and whose mother might go to prison," she said.

Sequeira suggested that Eli was Susan's tool in the divorce
fight, and suggested that she had "brainwashed" him, and otherwise induced him to make statements that weren't true.

"That's ridiculous," Eli said.

Wasn't it true that his mother was more argumentative than
most people?

"My mom is awesome," Eli replied, which could have been
taken as either agreement or disagreement.

Eli returned to the stand the following week for his mother's
redirect examination. She attempted to show that Eli's arrest
on the domestic violence charge the previous March was a
setup.

Susan showed photographs of Eli's bruises from the fight
with his older girlfriend/boss to the jury, and suggested that
she was a predator aligned with the conspiracy against her.

Had the police only arrested him "to make you look bad for
this trial?"

"Yes," Eli said.

Susan now wanted to interrupt the redirect examination of
Eli to call a new witness, who was from another state. This
was Dr. John Cooper, her forensic pathologist. The two had
been in correspondence, and Susan believed that his evidence
would demolish the prosecution's claim that murder had occurred. Cooper, from Texas, was pressed to get his testimony
over with because of other commitments.

Sequeira objected to interrupting Eli's testimony for a new

witness, saying he'd "bent over backward" to be accommodating to Susan up to then.

"The man needs a spanking," Susan said of Sequeira, a reference to his "bending over."

Brady denied Susan's motion to interrupt Eli's redirect testimony, contending that it would be too confusing to the jury. Susan again objected, and when the jury was led out of the room for another break, fireworks erupted, with Eli, still on the witness stand, challenging Sequeira to "just knock it off."

Sequeira told Eli that he had no right to address him—that he was in custody. Susan jumped in, berating Sequeira. The courtroom bailiff jumped in, pounding his fists on Susan's counsel table, telling her to stop talking. Eli pounded his fists on the railing of the witness dock. Susan pounded her fists on the counsel table. Eli was handcuffed and removed from the courtroom, muttering "Jesus Christ" as he left. Susan was consigned to the holding pen for another cooling-off period.

Cooper eventually made it to the witness stand the same afternoon.

After establishing Cooper's credentials as a pathologist and expert witness, Susan asked Cooper the four-million-dollar question:

"In your opinion, was my husband killed?"

"No," Cooper said.

Well, what caused Felix's death?

"I came to the conclusion that the manner of death should be categorized as 'natural.' The severity of injuries was not that great."

The most likely explanation for Felix's death, Cooper said, was advanced heart disease. Pointing to Dr. Peterson's own findings that major heart vessels were up to 75 percent blocked, the most logical explanation for Felix's demise was a heart attack that had occurred during the fight. Felix's heart condition, Cooper told the jury, was "a time bomb."

What about the head wound?

"He hit his head on the tile floor after he fell back from his cardiac arrest," Cooper said. The fact that there was no bleeding from the head wound showed that it had occurred after Felix's heart had stopped, not before. That proved that the prosecution's theory—that the fight had begun with an unprovoked blow to Felix's head from behind—was hogwash.

In fact, Cooper said, it appeared to him that someone had flipped Felix's body over after death, and that in so doing, had contaminated the crime scene.

This reflected an earlier assessment of former defense lawyers Horowitz and Golde, who were perplexed by the mysterious bloody shoe prints on the tile floor. They had come to believe that the first responder to the pool house, Sergeant Hansen, had been less than forthcoming in his testimony at the grand jury—that, in fact, it had been Hansen who'd flipped the body over when he'd first entered the pool house to see if Felix was really dead. Then, realizing he'd disturbed the crime scene, he'd kept quiet about it later.

In retrospect, this was a good try at muddying the waters, but little more. For one thing, the bloody shoe prints were made by an athletic type shoe, and while Hansen's shoes were never examined for comparison to the prints, he hadn't been wearing soft-top athletic shoes as a patrol supervisor. For another, the print size was much smaller than Hansen's. There is, however, another explanation for the flipping of the body and the post-mortem blow to the head that neither side would bring out at Susan's trial, as we shall see—in part because it did not fit with the prosecution's "hit from behind" theory of the crime, and also because it did not make Susan look very good.

Cooper's evidence about the head wound was quite powerful, and it provided Susan with an opening to ask Cooper what he thought of Peterson's autopsy. Cooper was dismissive of Peterson's work, contending it was "excessively dramatic . . . inflammatory" in recounting "twenty-seven stab wounds,"

hen in fact there were only five wounds that were deeply
enetrating, and which even Peterson had testified were not
atal in themselves.

Even though Felix had died in the course of the fight,
Cooper said, it wasn't murder or even manslaughter. It was
nalogous to a would-be killer dying of a heart attack just as
e was about to pull the trigger, he said. But Cooper admitted
aat it all depended on who had the weapon to begin with, and
ae original intent—if it had been Susan with the knife and in-
ent, Felix's death by heart attack could still be murder or
aanslaughter. Cooper tried to say that, to him, the evidence
uggested that it had been Felix who had attacked Susan, not
ae other way around.

Sequeira objected to this, contending that the issue of self-
efense or murder was up to the jury to decide, and beyond
ae expertise of a forensic pathologist. Brady agreed, and the
ary was instructed to ignore Cooper's opinion about self-
efense.

At one point, during Sequeira's objections to Cooper's tes-
mony, Helen Bolling, sitting in the audience, began making
emarks about Sequeira's objections and Brady's rulings. She
vas ejected from the courtroom by the bailiff.

"I warned you three times," the bailiff told Helen as he led
er away.

"It's a phony trial," she afterward told the *Chronicle*'s
Ienry Lee. "I'm sorry to say that."

Sequeira began his cross-examination of Cooper late the
ame afternoon. He wanted to know whether Cooper had any
otes from his assessment of the case—Cooper had claimed
e'd spent almost fifty hours studying the autopsy and written
ommunications from Susan.

Cooper said he did not have any notes with him.

"I don't consider it appropriate for you to know exactly
vhat I'm going to testify to," Cooper told Sequeira.

This was at the core of a long-running dispute between
equeira and Susan—for months, Sequeira had demanded that

Susan turn over any notes or reports from Cooper, as the state's reciprocal discovery rules required. Susan kept claiming she had none, and she probably didn't, if Cooper hadn't sent any to her. But the rules required the disclosure of Cooper's notes—otherwise, the testimony could be stricken from the record. Given that Cooper's testimony was the most powerful evidence for Susan's story, that would be catastrophic for Susan.

Brady ordered Cooper to return to court the following day—with his notes.

But when court resumed on Friday, May 5, Cooper still did not have any notes with him. They were lost, he said. Perhaps he'd mistakenly left them on the airplane from Texas. Or maybe someone had gone into his hotel room and taken them. He didn't know where they were.

Brady and Sequeira were both nonplussed. Nothing like this had ever happened to them before—an expert witness who did not have the supporting documents for his opinion. These included, it appeared, a number of "long-winded" letters and diagrams from Susan which purported to explain just what had happened in the pool house that night.

Sequeira told Brady he was convinced that someone was up to something—that the missing-documents claim was merely a ploy to prevent him from adequately cross-examining Cooper. Soon he and Susan were in another of their cross-talking arguments. Losing her patience, Brady dismissed the jury for the weekend and told Cooper to return with copies of his documents for cross-examination on the following Monday. She also asked Valerie Harris to look for copies of any letters sent by Susan to Cooper that had helped him form his opinion of what had happened in the pool house.

But on the following Monday, Dr. Cooper was a no-show in court.

35. "SUSAN POLK IS TELLING THE TRUTH"

Having gone back to Texas for the weekend, Cooper thought things over. He'd decided that the prosecution had no right to review his notes and other documents—that it would be "circumventing fairness in these proceedings," as he put it in an email to Judge Brady. He was "withdrawing from the case," Cooper told Brady; he was "resigning."

"Mr. Sequeira's machinations are improper and underhanded, and it causes me great concern to see that they have been tolerated to such an extent by the court," Cooper advised Brady, sounding almost exactly like Susan. Peterson's "deceitful presentation of evidence," Cooper continued, made him "nothing less than a public menace."

Brady was flummoxed by Cooper's non-appearance.

"In all my years as a litigator, a prosecutor and a judge," he said, "I have never heard of anything like this before, or anything close to it. I've never had an expert take on the role of being an advocate and then indicate that he's chosen not to come back. For him to do this to you [Susan] in the middle of testimony—I'm trying to think of an appropriate word—is bizarre and somewhat inexcusable, because it puts the defense in an untenable position in some respects."

This appeared, at least to Sequeira, to be yet another attempt

on Susan's part to force a mistrial, one seemingly abetted by
Cooper. If Cooper refused to return, Brady had only one
alternative—order Cooper's testimony stricken, and instruct the
jury to disregard it entirely as unreliable. This might give Susan
more grounds for reversal on appeal, especially if she could
prove that Sequeira had erred by demanding that Cooper produce the documents sent to him by Susan.

Predictably, Susan now asked Brady to declare a mistrial.
Sequeira had no right to examine the "long-winded" letters
she'd sent to Cooper, Susan insisted. It was "work-product,"
she maintained, communications between Susan as her own
lawyer and her expert witness. Brady rejected that argument.

"This is B.S.," Susan said. "You want a murder conviction
and you've been determined to get one." She made yet another
motion for a mistrial, and Brady denied this one, too.

But Brady didn't want to strike all of Cooper's
testimony—not unless she had to. She wanted to make sure
that all other options were exhausted first. She persisted in
asking Susan what she wanted her to do—throw out Cooper's
testimony, or order Cooper back to court? Susan finally asked
Brady to order Cooper to come back, and Brady said she'd try
to induce Cooper to return, this time with the documents.
Then, said Brady, she'd study the documents to see if they
were "work-product," or relevant out-of-court declarations by
the defendant, and therefore admissible. After a recess, Brady
announced that she'd been able to reach Cooper by telephone,
and that he'd agreed to return for cross-examination the following week.

Over the ensuing week, Susan called more witnesses, including a former member of her therapy group from the years before the marriage. Susan, said Kathy Lucia, had always felt
uncomfortable in her relationship with Felix—she'd expressed
the belief even then that he was too controlling.

"It was hard for you," Lucia told Susan, whom she hadn't

seen in almost three decades. "You didn't want to hurt him. Plus, I also think you were dependent on him." Which was true, if first wife Sharon had been correct in asserting that Felix had been paying Susan's living expenses while still married to Sharon.

But Felix was controlling over all his patients, Lucia said. She recounted one incident when she hadn't felt like attending a group session, and Felix incited all the other members of the group to go to her apartment and "kidnap" her to force her to participate.

After Lucia, Susan called Marjorie Briner, apparently with the intent of demonstrating that the Briners had "conspired" with Budd MacKenzie and John Polk to see that she was convicted of murder. Susan suggested in her questions that the Briners had influenced Gabe to testify against her, and that they had a pecuniary interest in maintaining control over him.

"That's ludicrous," Marjorie Briner said. The fact was, the Briners had spent over $30,000 of their own money supporting Gabe, Marjorie said.

Soon Briner and Susan were talking over each other, anger clearly flashing between the mother and the woman who was her replacement.

"Hold it. Hold it," Brady told them. "I understand the dynamic here." But proper procedure called for a question and an answer, not two people incessantly interrupting each other. The court reporter was simply unable to keep up with the rapidity of the testy exchanges. Susan made another motion for a mistrial based on judicial misconduct, which Brady again denied.

Susan continued questioning Marjorie for the next two days as a hostile witness, trying to develop the theme of the Briners' supposed untoward influence on Gabe and Adam. Briner responded that Susan had been abusive toward her over the telephone. Susan tried to rebut that by introducing a series of polite letters she'd sent to the Briners, and asking Marjorie to point out exactly where she'd been abusive.

But that didn't mean anything, Marjorie responded—
Susan was always polite and logical in her writing. It was only
when you knew her in person—face-to-face—that the abusive
side came out.

"There was an incredible pattern," Marjorie said. "[First]
you were incredibly nice, [then] you were undermining, and
then you blew up."

After a break, Susan asked to bring in another witness out of
order. This was Karen Saeger, a Ph.D. psychologist who had
worked with Felix from 1978 to 1986 at the California Graduate School of Psychology, the school in part founded by Felix,
which later became part of Argosy University. Before Saeger
could testify, however, Sequeira asked for a hearing out of the
presence of the jury. He wanted Brady to limit what Saeger
could testify to—he wanted to prevent any testimony as to Felix's purported cocaine use, his propensity to mix his personal
life with his professional responsibilities, and any reputation
for violence. Any of this would be hearsay, he maintained,
and anyway, it wasn't relevant to the issue at trial. Brady decided to allow the jury to hear about "dual relationships," as
the court clerk put it, and "reputation of violence . . . the defendant cannot ask about cocaine use."

Under questioning from Susan, Saeger told the jury that
she believed "there were two Felixes. One was tightly coiled,
like he would spring at you." But the other Felix could just as
easily be "charming and charismatic."

"I had mixed respect for Felix Polk," Saeger said. "I re-
spected him in some ways, and I found his behavior in other
ways very disturbing and unprofessional." In the unprofessional category, Saeger said, was his tendency to merge his
personal life with his professional responsibilities—an echo
of the rumors that Felix occasionally had sex with his patients
as part of the "therapeutic" process.

Susan asked how Felix comported himself in the teaching

environment, and Saeger responded that he appeared to collect young female psychology students as acolytes and admirers, while being more reticent around older women. Susan asked whether people at the graduate school knew that Felix had married his former patient—Susan. Saeger said that a lot of people had talked about it at the school. It was, she suggested, an example of how a therapist could jump the lines of professional boundaries. With this, Susan hoped to demonstrate to the jury that Felix had been a man who considered himself above the law.

But Saeger admitted that she'd never seen Felix physically attack anyone; only that at times he could become visibly angry and verbally abusive—just like Susan, in a way.

After Saeger was excused, Marjorie Briner was returned to the witness stand for more of Susan's questioning, which took up the rest of this day and half of the next. By this time, Brady had apparently had enough. To her, Susan wasn't getting anywhere with her questions—all she was doing was torturing poor Marjorie Briner. Just before noon on Thursday, May 11, Brady cut Susan off—she could ask no more questions of Marjorie Briner.

Susan responded with a new flurry of motions for mistrial—two before the judge halted the inquisition, then three more after court resumed in the afternoon. Sequeira said he had no questions for Marjorie—clearly wanting to get her off the stand to prevent Susan from inflicting still more abuse on the woman she'd come to hate. Soon Susan made two more motions for mistrial.

Brady denied them all.

The following Monday, May 15, saw the return of Dr. Cooper for his cross-examination by Sequeira, cut short when Cooper had been unable to produce his notes.

He had by now found copies of the letters sent to him by Susan, including her sketches of the crime scene and the events. He turned these over to Brady. But it still wasn't necessary for the prosecutor to have them to complete his cross-examination, he insisted—he'd based his findings on the crime-scene photographs and Peterson's autopsy report to reach the conclusion that Felix had died of a heart attack. The only value Susan's letters and sketches had for him, Cooper said, was that they helped convince him she was being truthful about what had happened in the pool house. They were only for his determination of that issue, and weren't germane to his factual testimony.

Sequeira attempted to discredit Cooper as a "for hire" pathologist who would say whatever the defendant wanted him to, and pointed out that Cooper usually testified for defendants. Cooper said it wasn't so, he routinely consulted with prosecutors, too.

Well, said Sequeira, what about a case in 2002, in Maine, when you testified that a 5-year-old girl had succumbed from a "seizure disorder," despite evidence that she'd been tied to a chair with duct tape—forty-two feet of duct tape? The duct tape was irrelevant to the medical cause of the death, Cooper insisted—in other words, in his opinion, the little girl would have died anyway, even without the duct tape.

Why had he refused to come back to court for his cross-examination when first ordered to do so by the judge? He'd had other commitments, Cooper said. He hadn't actually refused to come back—it was just that he had schedule conflicts.

But wasn't it true that he'd told the judge in his email that he wouldn't be back? Sequeira persisted.

"Evidently not, because I'm here," Cooper said.

Did Cooper think that the prosecution would just accept his testimony without question? That he, Sequeira, would just tell the jury, "You know what, folks? I was wrong," about murder having been committed?

"You figured I'd turn tail and run after your testimony?" Sequeira asked, sounding incredulous.

"I thought you had that option," Cooper said.

By this point, Brady had read the letters Susan had sent to Cooper, and after redacting portions of them, provided copies to both sides to facilitate the questioning of Dr. Cooper. Sequeira's goal was to get Cooper to explain how, based on Susan's descriptions of the events, he'd reached his conclusions as to Susan's innocence. The main point made by Susan in these various descriptions was that she'd gotten control of the knife held by Felix after incapacitating him by a kick to the groin.

While these different recitations of the fatal events were generally consistent with one another, and with Susan's story almost from the outset—apart from her disastrous initial encounters with Detectives Costa and Moule, in which she'd denied any violence at all—there were some significant discrepancies between her versions of the events to Cooper, and the physical evidence found at the scene and on Felix's body.

In short, Susan's descriptions to Cooper suggested that they had been concocted after the fact, much as a screenwriter might refine a fight scene—calculated to make her the heroine of a battle to the death, leaving out some parts while exaggerating others, much as a film editor varies camera angles to create a particular impression.

Could, for instance, Susan have generated sufficient leverage with a kick to the groin, while lying on her back, to incapacitate Felix to such a degree that he would drop the knife? Based on her sketch, it wasn't very likely—there would have been little room for enough momentum to deal an incapacitating blow, and Felix's testes would have been too far forward for a debilitating hit.

Or Susan's description of Felix biting her hand while he was being repeatedly stabbed—in such a situation, it would have been almost impossible that Felix's bite would not have drawn Susan's blood, and have left prominent tooth marks on her hand. Yet Susan's hands, when inspected by the police afterward, showed no such death bites. There was evidence of a nip, but hardly the tooth marks of a man who was dying. Only someone who had never before been in mortal combat could have made such a mistake in her scenario.

Another example of a discrepancy was Susan's assertion to Cooper that the ottoman had been on the floor near the front door. Yet it had actually been found across the room, on the other side of the "stage," upside down. The blood flowing from Felix's body had stopped at the upside-down edge of the ottoman, which showed that it had been there while Felix was still bleeding.

But the sketch of the room provided to Cooper by Susan had an arrow drawn from where she remembered the ottoman had been to where it was found by police. Susan had contended that the ottoman had been moved by the police in their attempt to "frame" her. But the interrupted blood flow showed that wasn't true, at least insofar as the movement of the ottoman. The ottoman had to have been where the police later found it at a time when Felix was still bleeding for the blood to have stopped at its edge. So Susan's sketch could not have been accurate.

Yet another example was one of the deeper knife wounds, this one to Felix's back. This wound, one of the five "major" stabbings, entered his body just to the left of his spine, midway down his back, penetrated three inches, including one inch into his diaphragm. It was a jagged wound, as if it had torn the flesh on entrance or exit. Below this larger wound were two smaller cuts.

How, if Felix had been kneeling over Susan, with her back to the floor, had Susan's right arm been able to reach so far around his back? And—three times? This was unlikely, to say the least. If Felix had really been kneeling over Susan when these back wounds occurred, Susan's arm would have had to have been much longer than it really was, at least for the force apparently employed.

But Sequeira, having been stung by Cooper's analysis of the non-bleeding head wound, which drove a stake through the heart of his attack-from-behind theory of premeditation, seemed wary of engaging Cooper in these pertinent details. It appeared instead that he wanted to cast Cooper as a consciously paid dupe, a charlatan, or at best a naïve true believer in Susan's innocence. How could he know what had really happened in the pool house? Sequeira demanded. Wasn't he only relying on Susan's version of the events?

Cooper said he believed that Susan was a reliable witness to what had happened.

"She's a reliable eyewitness?" Sequeira asked. "Are you aware that she says she predicted nine/eleven?"

"My understanding is that she has considerable psychic abilities."

"You believe she has psychic abilities?"

"I have no reason not to," Cooper said. By inducing him to seem to claim he believed in psychics, Sequeira hoped the jury would see Cooper as a flake.

Once Sequeira was done with Cooper, Susan began her redirect examination.

Drawing stick figures on an easel, Susan went through the phases of the fight, drawing out Cooper's opinion that it was in fact possible for a much smaller woman to incapacitate and defeat a larger man, even from a supine position.

"Don't men have a particularly more vulnerable area of their bodies that women don't have?" she asked.

"So stipulated," Sequeira broke in.

Susan got down on the floor of the courtroom to demonstrate how she'd kicked Felix in the groin in order to halt his assault. Could such a kick have caused Felix to loosen his grip on the knife?

"That's not hard to understand at all," Cooper said. "There was evidence showing that he was in a dominant position relative to you. In other words, he had the upper hand." The autopsy photographs showed that there had been no intent to kill on Susan's part, he said.

"Why are there no knife thrusts aimed at the heart or vessels of the neck?" he asked. It was obvious that Susan had not been intent on murder—if she had been, why wouldn't she have delivered a fatal wound?

Susan went to the bottom line: was she telling the truth?

"Susan Polk is telling the truth," Cooper told the jury.

"And Dr. Peterson isn't, correct?" Sequeira asked when it was his turn again.

It wasn't that Dr. Peterson was inaccurate, Cooper said, only that his understanding of what had happened was off.

"So, why did you agree to testify on my behalf?" Susan asked.

"I felt that if I didn't," Cooper said, "you might not get justice."

36. "HURRY UP!"

The following day, Wednesday, May 17, 2006, Susan took the stand as her own witness. By agreement with the court, Susan was permitted to testify in a narrative form, rather than go through the rather silly process of asking herself a question, then answering it.

"This is not *carte blanche*," Brady told Susan. "This is not the opportunity for a speech. This is a privilege, not a right. You may not like it, but the reality is now that the defendant—you—do[es] not dictate how we proceed in this courtroom."

In all, Susan would be her own witness for six days—six days in which she held the jury as a literally captive audience. There was no place for them to run, no place to hide, as she went over her entire life, from childhood up to the events of October 13–14, 2002, often relying upon her timeline and her diary. It was a little like being trapped in an elevator for days with someone who won't stop talking. Actually, it was worse—unlike in an elevator, the jurors couldn't talk back.

Well, Susan had wanted to run her case her way, and now she was doing it. Some later thought that her notoriety had, in Susan's mind, metamorphosed into a sort of celebrity. At last, after almost a half-century of living, she, not Felix, was the star of the show.

But it was tedious—so tedious. Off-putting, even. Did the jurors really need to hear all about the family's dogs, Mitzi, Tuffy and Ruffy? Or about the Polks' vacations, about their accomplishments, their continuous squabbles, their numerous petty resentments? The stream of material spewed forth, washing over the silent twelve and their alternates, day after day, as Susan in essence attempted to justify her entire existence. It was almost like a scene out of the Albert Brooks/Meryl Streep movie *Defending Your Life*. Soon there were so many trees the jury was in real danger of getting lost in the forest.

"Hurry up!" someone whispered loudly from the gallery. But Susan wanted to make sure that the jury had the complete picture.

To illustrate the story, Harris projected photographs onto a screen—Susan as a schoolgirl, her parents' wedding pictures, the boys, the dogs, and her own wedding with Felix.

She told the jurors that she'd been sent to Felix as a troubled young girl, and said that Felix had hypnotized her, given her drugs, and soon seduced her. She didn't want to marry Felix, she said, but went through with the wedding only because she'd promised him.

"I didn't believe it was right, that I married my therapist," she said. "I was ashamed of it."

The marriage had turned violent almost from the start, she said. She'd kept quiet about the abuse because she was afraid that telling anyone would cause Felix to have her killed, and also because she thought she could make things better. Like many women, she believed that she had the power to transform, even if the object of the transformation was more than two decades older than she was.

But Felix wasn't interested in changing, Susan said. What he really wanted was "someone he could control and dominate . . . he wanted a doll. No resistance was tolerable for him. No individuality. There was nothing left for me . . . it was like having my life hijacked."

It was not until her 40th birthday, Susan said, that she remembered all of what had happened to her when she'd been Felix's captive, teenaged patient.

"I knew I wanted a divorce," she said. "Turning forty was like a landmark. I'm thinking, 'My God, what am I doing?' I didn't think it was right that I had married my therapist, who was a married man. I wouldn't have wanted any of my sons to do that."

Felix, she said, controlled all aspects of their lives, including their friends—all of them either Felix's patients or his colleagues. She had no friends of her own—no one who had come into her life who hadn't been screened by Felix for Felix's needs. Felix disapproved of the Cub Scouts, she said, because he thought they were too "feminine"; he refused to let her volunteer as a den mother, because he'd told her that the family couldn't spare her. He became jealous of her hairdresser, refused to let her go places by herself, and warned her repeatedly that if she left him, he would have her killed. He repeatedly warned her to "think of the consequences."

"It was like walking on eggshells," she said. "It was like living with a very abusive, dominating parent."

Susan recounted the fight of October 2001, in which Felix had blocked her from going to the beach, and Eli had punched her. Felix had a way of using the boys against each other, and against her, she said—it was all part of his method of control, to pit one family member against another, so he could rush in as the expert arbiter.

Susan told of an encounter with Sharon Mann Polk in Felix's office.

"She told me I was playing with fire, and I didn't know what the heck she meant," Susan said. "She said, 'You have no idea of what you're getting into.'" Sharon had told her that Felix was schizophrenic—even while he was there in the room.

"He was so embarrassed," Susan said. "It was like, *I can't even take it in, because it conflicts with the illusion I was given."*

Sharon had asked her whether she thought she really loved Felix, Susan recounted.

"I'm like, 'Yeah.'" Susan recalled.

At that point, Sharon had told her, "Okay, you can have him."

After this, Felix dominated her and the boys with physical violence or threats of violence, Susan claimed. That was especially the case when it came to their sex life.

"His attitude toward sex was that rape is the way things are done between men and women," Susan said.

On the afternoon of her first day of this narrative testimony, Susan talked a bit about her supposed psychic abilities. As a child, she said, she'd participated in an ESP experiment in school, and discovered that she could see things that were hidden. Not long after this, she said, the school had sent her to see Felix. Felix began trying to enhance her psychic abilities with hallucinogenic tea and hypnosis. This practice continued throughout much of the marriage, she said, although she did not realize it until years later. She gradually became aware that there were huge blocks of her memory that were simply blank. Felix was using her psychic abilities for intelligence work, she said.

"I wouldn't wish that on anybody," she said. "It's the cruelest, cruelest thing to do."

Over the years, she said, she'd predicted the 1978 assassination of Mayor George Moscone of San Francisco, the attempt to kill Pope John Paul II in 1982, and the 1993 bombing of the World Trade Center, as well as the 9/11 attacks. She'd had a vision of Armageddon, the end of the world, in which Colin Powell had appeared as the Antichrist. The trances and visions were troubling to her, but there was no escape—she didn't want to be a medium, but Felix insisted.

"He said, 'I put twenty years of my life into this project. 'm not going to just shuffle away,'" Susan told the jurors.

Part of the way into her six days of being her own witness, Susan was allowed to interrupt her examination of herself to call another witness out of order: Adam Polk. Susan's plan was to show how Adam's attitude toward her had changed over the years—this would set up her own return to the stand so she could explain what had happened between her and her eldest son.

Susan asked Adam if he thought she was crazy.

"I've testified that I don't know if you're crazy, or you just contrive these fantasies to somehow rationalize and justify what you're doing, and what you've done in your mind," Adam told her. "I'm not a psychologist, but I'd definitely say you're sick."

When Adam referred to Felix's death as "murder," Susan erupted with a barrage of objections. Adam had no way of making that judgment, she said. In fact, she asked, hadn't he once told her that he believed she'd acted in self-defense?

Adam said that Susan had twisted his words.

"You say anything and everything to harm innocent people," Adam told her. And at another point he said, "Honestly, you're just making things up right now. You're living in a fantasy world."

As for Susan's characterization of Felix as violent, homophobic and racist, Adam was particularly upset: "You will say anything you feel like to drag him and our name through the mud to serve your cause," he told his mother.

Susan handed Adam a Mother's Day card he'd once sent to her, and asked him to read it.

"'Mom, I know we've all had our share of troubled times, but I'll always love you,'" Adam read. "'Thanks for being here. I love you. Adam.'"

"So, did you mean that?" Susan asked.

"Yes, I do love you, and I will always be there, but you need to get some help."

And after one difficult exchange between mother and son, Adam seemed to lose his temper.

"You're a sick, sick person who's in dire need of a very controlled environment for a very long time," he said, doubtless reminding Susan of the way she claimed Felix had repeatedly threatened her with institutionalization. "If that doesn't happen, I won't feel safe, and I'm sure a lot of other people won't feel safe."

Susan objected to this as both inflammatory and nonresponsive, and was sustained. But the effect on the jury had to have been devastating—Adam Polk was asking them to lock up his own mother for a "very long time." Even more than devastating, it was incredibly sad.

37. NOTHING FUNNY ABOUT IT

When she resumed her own testimony, Susan tried to explain to the jury that things hadn't always been so strained with her eldest child.

Adam, she said, had "two sides," one "foulmouthed," and the other "very loving."

There had been a time when mother and son shared everything. After the death of Felix, Susan said, Adam had asked her, "How could you have stabbed Dad twenty-seven times?"

"I said, 'I didn't do it. I didn't stab him twenty-seven times.'"

It was only five or six times, she'd told Adam.

"I told him, 'They might as well take me out and shoot me. I'm being framed.'"

When she'd told Adam that she'd only stabbed Felix five or six times, and only in the course of a fight started by Felix, Susan said, Adam had told her, "'Mom, that's not murder, that's self-defense.'" That was when Adam had sworn to become a lawyer—"'so I can get you out if you're convicted,'" she quoted him as saying.

"That gave me courage," Susan told the jury. "I hung on to those words for a very long time."

What Adam hadn't told them, Susan said, was that he'd offered to testify for her at the first trial, the one that had ended in a mistrial when Pamela Vitale had been murdered. But all that changed when John Polk and Budd MacKenzie got control of the estate, she said. Adam was made to believe that if he testified for her, he'd be cut off from the money. He and Gabriel had sued her and Eli for possession of the dream house.

After she'd been arrested, Susan went on, she'd been advised by one lawyer to "play crazy"—something Adam had suggested, too, at first. Another lawyer told her she would try to negotiate a plea for involuntary manslaughter that could have resulted in a 3-year sentence. If she'd agreed to that, she might now be nearly free—she'd already spent more than 2 years in custody. But she'd turned down the proposal, she said, because she wasn't guilty.

It wasn't true that she'd accused Felix of being a Mossad agent, Susan said. Or at least she hadn't, until she'd predicted the 9/11 attacks, and Felix had failed to warn anyone.

At that point she'd decided that Felix had to be working for "foreign intelligence." Why else wouldn't he have told anyone about her prediction? So she had become even more frightened of Felix and what he might do to her . . . she knew too much.

After she had tried to kill herself with the overdose at Yosemite, Susan said, Felix had regretted calling the emergency people to save her life. He'd told her, she said, " 'I should have let you die. You should just kill yourself.' "

Susan apologized to the jury for taking so long in her testimony.

She knew that it was tedious, she said, but it was important that the jury know the whole story. "It doesn't make sense that I should hurry up at the end, here," she said. "I have to take the time to refute what's been said that's not so. I'm sorry."

The next day Susan finally reached the events of October 13–14. By now, of course, the jury had already heard most of these details, in part from the portions of the letters she had sent to Dr. Cooper. But this would be a chance for Susan to explain herself once more in her own words, and just as important, a chance for the jury to see her demeanor as she described the events.

Occasionally weeping, Susan told the jury that despite what Gabe had said, she'd "never, ever threatened to kill my husband, ever. I just didn't do that." The supposed threat to use a shotgun to force Felix to transfer $20 million from the putative secret bank account was just a joke, she said. "Those kinds of jokes were not unusual in our family," she said.

She'd gone down to the pool house to talk with Felix about the status of the divorce case, and to work out some agreement on what to do about their debts, she said. The discussion became an argument, and then Felix had rushed at her with the ottoman. It was Felix who first produced the knife, she said.

As she lay on the floor, she said, she thought she was going to die.

"I had this small, tiny, fleeting thought that I could just die there, then it would be over and I wouldn't be stuck in the situation I was in." But then she decided to live, and kicked Felix in the groin. She stabbed him first in the side and then the back. She had no idea how Felix had come to have so many wounds, except that she believed the wounds had been exaggerated by police using a photo-editing program, or possibly adding wounds later to make her look more guilty. She could only recall stabbing Felix a few times before he stood up, said he was dying, and then toppled over backward.

Afterward, she sat on the steps leading to the bedroom of the pool house and tried to think of what to do. She was afraid to call the police; she thought no one would believe her that she had killed her larger, stronger husband in self-defense. She returned to the main house and took several showers, trying to clean up. She was sure that she would soon be arrested—"railroaded," as she put it. The authorities would be out to get her because of her previous conflicts with the courts and police over Eli and the divorce.

For the next twenty hours or so, Susan said, she kept trying to "hold on to some semblance of a normal life."

"It was like living in two worlds," she said. "My husband was dead in the cottage, and I was acting and pretending that he didn't die."

Gabe had it slightly wrong when he'd testified that she'd asked him if he was "happy" that Felix was "gone." What she'd really said was, " 'He's gone. You aren't happy, are you?' "

Then the police arrived, and she decided to deny any involvement in the death. She was worried about what would happen to Gabe, and who would feed Tuffy and Ruffy if she went to jail. So she just decided to deny everything as the best chance of staying out of jail, and maintaining a normal life.

"I didn't murder him," Susan said, "but I didn't want the stigma of being suspected of murder, and the stigma of stabbing him."

So she'd lied—it was that simple.

Sequeira began his cross-examination of Susan just before noon on Thursday, May 25, 2006.

"All set?" he asked Susan, as she took her place in the witness box.

"Well, I wouldn't call it 'set,' " she said. "I said I wasn't scared, but I'm getting a little scared now." The packed gallery erupted in laughter. Susan tried to smile.

Sequeira began by projecting a gruesome photograph of a bloody Felix lying, arms akimbo, dead on the tile floor. He kept the photograph up while he questioned Susan.

"Isn't it a fact, Ms. Polk," Sequeira asked, "that you let your fifteen-year-old son find his father's body in the pool house?"

"No, that's not a fact at all," she said.

Wasn't it cruel of her to suggest to Gabe that he call the California Highway Patrol to see if Felix had been in an accident, when all along she knew that Felix was dead?

Susan said she didn't remember saying that to Gabe.

Well, said Sequeira, was she saying that Gabe had lied?

"It puts me in an awkward position, to suggest that my son is a liar . . . it's not an either/or situation."

"You didn't do anything to prevent him from finding his father's body, did you?"

"That's a tricky question," Susan said. She did lock the front door to the pool house, she said; she hoped that Gabe would simply decide that Felix wasn't going to come home, and that he would go to bed. She only wanted things to be normal again, she repeated—she kept trying to pretend to herself that nothing had happened, so she could enjoy whatever time she had left before the inevitable arrest.

The photo of Felix's bloody corpse loomed over the courtroom. Susan asked Brady to order Sequeira to remove it. It was prejudicial, she said. Brady denied her request. Susan renewed her objection—this wasn't a movie, she said, it was real life. Once more Brady denied her.

Sequeira's objective in cross-examining Susan was, first, to puncture her claim that she had no intent to kill Felix, and second, to show that Susan was lying about the way the fight had unfolded. For the first objective, Sequeira had to show that Susan had a motive for wanting Felix dead—the money, the dream house, and Gabe. For the second, he had to show that the physical evidence proved that Susan had attacked Felix, not the other way around.

For most of the afternoon, Sequeira took Susan over her story of the events leading up to the fatal night. She dodged the point of many of his questions, often fencing with her words, disagreeing with Sequeira's definitions. When faced with an incontrovertible fact, Susan simply dismissed it as something fabricated by "liars." Soon Sequeira had put up a running list of people who were "liars," including police, criminalists, the pathologist Dr. Peterson, Felix's colleagues, his lawyer friend, even two of her three sons.

All of these people were liars? Sequeira asked, gesturing at the long list.

"That title should be changed to 'deceptive persons,'" Susan said.

It was, as *Chronicle* reporter Henry Lee described it, a battle of wills, and if there was anything that Susan had a surplus of, it was will.

After a five-day break for the Memorial Day weekend, Susan resumed the witness stand on Wednesday, May 31.

Projecting crime-scene photographs, Sequeira asked Susan to explain once more exactly what had happened in the fight. Susan said she couldn't recall every detail. In fact, she said, she might have blacked out during part of the fight. Sequeira asked her to explain minor differences between her statements to the news media and her testimony. Why had she talked to the media, anyway? Sequeira asked.

"Perhaps it was a good idea to set the record straight," she said. "Because the district attorney was controlling the media spin and there was no one speaking for the defense."

They continued squabbling over the meanings of words, and even proper grammar. Susan complained that Sequeira was "testifying" through his facial expressions, usually a countenance showing his disbelief.

Susan's story kept evolving, Sequeira said. Was that because she kept thinking of new ways to avoid appearing guilty?

No, Susan said—she didn't make things up as she went along.

Was it really self-defense when she had "plunged" the knife into her husband's back, his chest, his side, his stomach? When one thrust had in fact collapsed his lung?

Susan objected to the word "plunged."

"Just little pokes?" Sequeira asked.

"You weren't there," Susan told him. "You're trying to make it look like something it wasn't."

Sequeira asked what was going through her mind as she stabbed Felix, but Susan insisted that she could only remember thinking that she was going to die unless she did something to save herself. She'd been given the gift of survival, although she was unhappy that the gift came with the cost of being tried for murder.

"I was either the luckiest person in the world or the most unlucky," she said.

"It's a gift your husband wasn't given, was he?"

"Would it be a gift [to him] to have killed me to live?"

And so it went, almost every question being answered by Susan's own unresponsive question.

Sequeira tried to tear down Susan's claim to self-defense by demonstrating that she was conscious of her guilt. Why had she washed her clothes, taken repeated showers, gotten rid of the knife, sewn up a hole in her pants, moved Felix's car?

"I was in a state of shock," Susan said. "I took a shower because it was grisly to be covered in blood."

As Sequeira persisted, Susan often lapsed into long, rambling answers that avoided the questions. Brady warned her that she was getting "offtrack."

Since she was being "railroaded," Susan said, it was good to be "offtrack."

"We're not having a contest for pithy comments today," Brady growled.

"Pithy, that's a good word," Susan said.

Sequeira referred to portions of Susan's diary, trying to show that Susan had a hard time getting along with people, even her mother.

Wasn't it true that she was just an extremely argumentative person?

No, Susan said, although she admitted that she was outspoken. That was a good thing, she added—all too often people failed to stand up for what was right, because it was easier to say nothing. That was why Hitler and Stalin had prospered, she said.

"Are you done?" Sequeira asked, when she'd finished a long speech on injustice in the world.

"I would say more," Susan said, "but I don't want to take up the jury's time."

Watching this battle of words unfold had set *Chronicle* columnist C. W. Nevius thinking. A month before, he'd had some fun with the circus-like aspect of the trial. But listening to her bandy words around as if they were some sort of shield had soured him on Susan:

> As this week began, there was really only one question: Fourteen weeks into this, could Sequeira focus the trial into a coherent legal proceeding . . . ? The simple answer is no. Polk is as elusive, maddening and as uncontrolled as ever . . ."

Susan's claim of self-defense just didn't add up, Nevius said. The idea that she could have kicked Felix in the groin and grabbed the knife away without sustaining any cuts herself seemed impossible.

"Even Polk admitted, 'I think there was something miraculous about that,'" Nevius noted. "No kidding."

There was a "guilty pleasure" in "watching Polk take this civics lesson into outer space," Nevius said.

> However, we are coming upon crunch time. . . . If Polk manages through delays, stalls and amateur lawyering, to get off, howls of indignation will be heard from sea to shining sea. . . . Having worn them down with months of self-indulgent foolishness, she's hoping jurors will ignore the mound of evidence and let her off.
> If that happens, there will be nothing funny about it.

38. CRAZY OR NOT

After reading extensively from her timeline and diary entries, Susan concluded her testimony on Friday, June 2. In so doing, she related some of her dreams to the jury—dreams that she believed had been prophetic, and which proved she was psychic. This led Sequeira to ask her on his recross-examination if it wasn't true that she was enjoying being in the spotlight. Who would she like to play her, he asked, if they decided to make the case into a movie?

"Winona Ryder," Susan laughed. And Anthony Hopkins should play Felix, she said, adding that Felix had been worse than Hannibal Lecter.

"This is funny?" Sequeira asked.

"This part is," Susan shot back. "Is it a crime to be able to find some humor in my situation? I don't think so. I don't think that's wrong. My husband tried to kill me. He raped me when I was fourteen years old. He took advantage of me, he killed the dogs, he threatened to kill the children, he was absolutely brutal on the night he died. He attacked me."

Over the next week, Susan called several other witnesses for her defense. One, Laura Castro-Shelley, holder of a black belt in martial arts, told the jury that it was quite possible that Susan could have disabled Felix with a kick to the groin while on her back, and that it was possible for her to have avoided getting any cuts, if she'd been quick enough to grab Felix's hand as he loosened his grip on the knife.

Susan next called a former Los Angeles County sheriff's deputy, Roger Clark, who told the jury that he'd examined the crime scene as well as all the photographs. It was clear to him, Clark said, that the evidence supported Susan's contention that she'd been fighting for her life.

"I think that's consistent with the entire sequence of events," Clark said. The small size of the room, and the number and type of wounds sustained by Felix indicated clearly that there had been mutual combat—the notion of a sneak attack by Susan was ludicrous. Even the wounds showed that a struggle was under way at the time of their administration, he said—the random, haphazard nature of their location showed that they had been sustained in a struggle, rather than planned out. If they had been intended as fatal blows, Clark said, why weren't they in vital areas of the body, such as the heart or neck?

The most important thing about the scene, Clark told jurors, was the relative lack of blood. That, and the fact that the head wound had no bleeding, was clear evidence that Felix had actually died of a heart attack. He certainly had not bled to death.

"When you don't have a continual flow of blood, that means the heart stopped," Clark said. "The volume is not there, in my opinion."

After Clark, Susan called Dr. Linda Barnard, the expert on post-traumatic stress and battered-spouse syndrome.

It wasn't unusual that Susan stayed in the marriage for as long as she did, Barnard testified; the pattern of abuse in domestic violence cases can become almost a habit. Sometimes the victim would rather endure the abuse than break up the relationship—the devil you know is better than no devil at all.

Having Barnard on the stand gave Susan an opportunity to elicit an expert opinion about Felix's mental health. Susan asked Barnard whether she'd reviewed Felix's mental health records from the Navy, which showed that he had been diagnosed as schizophrenic in the 1950s, that he had spent more than a year in mental hospitals, and that he was, at least for a time, "out of touch with reality." Susan provided other records for Barnard: the Satanist rant of 1988 was disturbing, Barnard said, as was Felix's referring to himself in the third person in "Thoughts of Chairman Felix." So too was Felix's concept of psychotherapy, in which his cult of personality had, at least in his mind, become a therapeutic tool. Like others before her, Barnard thought that Felix had gone grievously wrong as a professional when he'd mixed up his own needs with those of his patients.

Felix's behavior with Susan and the boys was all too typical of an abusive spouse, Barnard said. First came the "training" phase, in which Susan was conditioned to obey Felix; then later, when Susan began to rebel against the control, Felix reinforced his obedience "training" with threats to Susan, the boys, the dogs. At the same time, Felix would have played on Susan's guilt—if things went wrong, it would always be Susan's fault.

The guilt-induction was extremely exacerbated by the fact that Felix had been Susan's therapist, Barnard said.

"That would be equal to sort of a double whammy," she said. Felix could have used information obtained from Susan's therapy sessions to set her up. Because it was often vital for a patient to maintain the approval of her therapist, it would have given Felix the whip hand over Susan.

"The ability to distort reality is at least tenfold what we would expect in a traditional abusive relationship," she said. The fact that Felix continually told Susan she was "delusional," and threatened to have her "institutionalized" was quite typical among professional therapists who were also spousal abusers, Barnard said. The mere fact that the professional therapist is seen by the public—or the authorities, including the police—a an "expert" gives credibility to the claim, whether true or not. was just one more technique to control the spouse, she said.

Susan asked Barnard how much time she'd spent inter viewing her. At least thirty hours, Barnard said. In all tha time, Susan asked, did Barnard ever form the opinion that she Susan, was delusional?

"I never recognized any delusions," Barnard said. "I woul expect that delusions would be present at some point in those thirty hours."

"Did I seem out of touch with reality to you?"

"No, you did not."

"Wasn't it reasonable for me to think my husband was ou to get me, because he was?"

"Yes."

But Sequeira moved to head this off when it was his turn t cross-examine Barnard.

He opened a copy of the *Diagnostic and Statistical Manua of Mental Disorders*, a reference book which catalogued var ous types of mental illness. He turned to the section on Delu sional Disorder. He read a portion of the definition. A perso with the persecutory subtype of Delusional Disorder, Sequei read, has the belief that " 'he or she is being conspired agains cheated, spied on, followed, poisoned or drugged, maliciousl maligned, harassed or obstructed in the pursuit of long-ter goals.' "

Didn't that sound like Susan? Sequeira asked. And wasn it true that Delusional Disorder often wasn't apparent whe the sufferer wasn't being queried directly about her particula delusion?

She'd seen no sign that Susan was delusional, Barnard saic But even if Susan had a hidden delusion, that had nothing t do with what had happened to Felix. Felix was dead becaus he had attacked Susan, not because of any delusions she migl have. One thing was very clear to her, Barnard said, and tha was that Susan was a victim of post-traumatic stress syndrom

rom years of living with an abusive husband. And it wasn't
lways physical abuse, but mental abuse, made much worse
ecause of Felix's occupation as a psychologist.

At 11:03 A.M. on June 8, Brady finally heard the blessed
words she had so longed for:

"The defense rests," Susan said.

"The prosecution rests," Sequeira said.

After sixty-five days of trial, one crazy circumstance after
nother, the thing was finally over. Or almost: There still were
nstructions to be given to the jury, and then closing arguments.

After that, the whole mess would be turned over to the ju-
ors, who would finally get their own say—the last and the
nly words that would really count: guilty or not guilty.

39. ALL OR NOTHING

In the week prior to resting their cases, both sides had bee[n] arguing over the specific instructions to be given to the jur[y]. Jury instructions, while often the driest part of a crimin[al] case, are sometimes the most crucial: the instructions giv[en] can channel the jury's scope of deliberations. For her part, S[u]san wanted Brady to instruct the jury that they should not co[n]sider any "lesser included offenses" in determining her gu[ilt] or innocence.

Susan thought it should be all or nothing. The jury, s[he] said, should decide solely whether a murder had occurred—[if] they decided there had been no murder, they should be i[n]structed to find her not guilty. Manslaughter should not b[e] considered.

"I'm terrified about being convicted of murder," Susan to[ld] Brady. "I'm terrified about being convicted of manslaughte[r] also . . . it doesn't fit the facts."

By this point, Susan felt fairly confident that she ha[d] demonstrated that Felix had died of a heart attack, not the sta[b]bing. Hence, in her mind, there had been no murder. She ha[d] potent testimony from Dr. Cooper and former detective Rog[er] Clark that suggested that Felix had died during mutual co[m]bat; and she had testimony from Linda Barnard that suggeste[d]

hat Felix was likely to have attacked Susan, along with the
martial arts expert's opinion that it was possible that Susan
could have defended herself in the way she claimed. That
should be sufficient, she thought, for the jury to have reasonable doubt that any murder had taken place, let alone one that
was premeditated, as the prosecution had contended. By getting manslaughter out of the mix, Susan believed, she might
foreclose a jury decision to affix some remnant of blame if
only because Felix was dead.

Most legal experts kibitzing at the trial were aghast at Susan's maneuver, with one calling it a "riverboat gamble"—not
a good idea. With manslaughter off the table, the jury might
decide for murder anyway, and for the same reason—after all,
Felix *was* dead.

Yet as Susan had pointed out to the jury, she'd already rejected a proposed plea bargain for manslaughter—one that
might have yielded a sentence of less than 4 years.

So why did Susan want the manslaughter option off the
table? It might have been the money—as Budd MacKenzie
had pointed out early on, a conviction assigning her the criminal onus of Felix's death would have the effect of deeming her
"predeceased" to Felix, and preventing her from having control over the estate. But more likely, the real reason that Susan
did not want to be convicted of manslaughter, even though it
might result in minimal additional incarceration time, was that
she didn't want "the stigma" of such a conviction—especially
when she did not believe she'd done anything wrong.

It wasn't a matter of Susan trying to fool people—to her,
the story was simple: Felix had attacked her, she'd defended
herself, Felix had died of a heart attack, and that was all there
was to it. The jury should be made to see the facts for what
they were, and vindicate Susan.

Brady said she wasn't sure that she could do that—not give
the "lesser included offense" instruction. She thought she was
obligated under the law to tell the jury it could consider lesser
included offenses, such as manslaughter.

Now Sequeira piped up: if Susan wanted to go all or noth
ing, he had no objection. He was confident that he had prove
that murder had occurred. He told Brady he thought that cas
law permitted the judge to give the all-or-nothing instructio
Brady said she still had her doubts. She asked Sequeira to re
search that, and reserved her ruling on the issue until Sequei
found the cases that would permit her to grant Susan's re
quest. In the end, however, Brady ruled that the jury was ent
tled to consider manslaughter as well as murder in either th
first or second degree, the difference being in whether the jur
believed that Susan had planned to kill Felix, or if it had ju
occurred on the spur of the moment.

Brady had allotted three hours to each side for the closin
arguments—Sequeira had to split his three hours between hi
initial closing and his rebuttal. Six hours of arguing meant tw
days of talk, divided equally between Sequeira and Susan.

For Sequeira, convincing the jury that Susan was guilty c
murder required reiterating the salient facts of his case, an
caustically dismissing the claims if not the credibility of Su
san's defense witnesses.

The evidence showed that Susan had attacked Felix, no
the other way around, Sequeira said. It had been Susan wh
had the motive to see Felix dead—the money, the house an
Gabe. It had been Susan who repeatedly threatened to ki
him. It had been Susan who had come back from Montan
Susan who had sought Felix out at a time when he was tire
from the day's driving and likely most vulnerable to an attack
maybe even asleep. Susan was the volitional agent in all th
events: nothing would have happened if Susan had stayed i
the main house.

It wasn't Felix who ignited the confrontation, but Susan. I
was Susan who brought the knife to the encounter, not Felix
No one could believe that Susan could have taken the knif

away from Felix without sustaining injuries to her hands in the process. It simply defied reasoning. It wasn't Susan who was fighting for her life, he said, but Felix—Felix, who had told numerous people in the week before the fatal fight that his wife intended to kill him. And he'd been right—that was exactly what happened.

The jury, he said, had been flooded with irrelevant information by Susan—"background noise," Sequeira called it. The issue wasn't whether Susan had been a good mother, or if she was a psychic. "It's still going to come down to what you think happened in that pool house," Sequeira said. Everything else was a diversion.

He ridiculed Dr. Cooper. "The great Dr. Cooper, he was a piece of work," he said, and then told the jury that Cooper's medical license had expired. "He can't prescribe any of you folks cough syrup."

As she had in Sequeira's opening statement, three months before, Susan repeatedly interrupted him with motions for mistrial—sixteen in all. All were denied by Brady, and Sequeira plowed on.

Even if it was true that Felix had died of a heart attack, it was Susan who had caused it, he said. "If you put the heart attack in motion, you're still guilty of murder."

Susan was a liar, pure and simple, he said. Her story kept changing to fit new information. First she'd denied killing Felix, then said that she was defending herself, then concocted a tale that had her grabbing the knife out of his hand.

"You pick a story. None of them fit. She's lied to you, folks. She's lied all along."

But Susan said she wasn't lying—she was being persecuted.

"This trial has become a witch trial," she said. "Make no mistake about it. Charged with murder, I'm now being tried for heresy and delusions."

Calling Felix a "schizophrenic, psychotic psychologist," Susan claimed she was being martyred, as gifted women had been martyred in earlier times. Drawing on literary and his torical allusions, Susan tried to convince the jury that she was the victim, not the perpetrator.

It was Felix who had drugged and "raped" her when she was still a teenager, Susan said. "What kind of man would do that?"

She'd been called delusional by two of her sons, she said, while a third son said she was not delusional. A psychologist who'd spent thirty hours with her had testified she was not delusional. But even if jurors believed she was delusional, it had no bearing on the question of self-defense.

"Even if you think I'm crazy as a bedbug . . . I would not have been precluded from defending myself when my husband attacked me."

It was true that she'd lied to the detectives at the outset, Susan admitted. But that was because she was worried about Gabe and the dogs. Once she'd been able to make arrangements for their care, she would probably have told the whole story to police, she said.

"If they had let me go to sleep and come back in the morning, I very likely would have told what happened," she said.

The next morning, June 13, Susan finished her closing argument. She asked the jurors to rely on their common sense—there was no way she would have attacked Felix, since he outweighed her by fifty pounds. Of course there were variances in her story—it would have been odd if there weren't, given the trauma of the events, and the way the mind works.

"Felix's actions caused the heart attack," she said, not her. "It was the result of his own rage. There was no provocation on my part."

Then it was Sequeira's turn for rebuttal.

All the jury had to know was that it was Susan who had brought the knife to the pool house.

"She took it down there. If she took it down there, ladies

and gentlemen, that's evidence of premeditation and deliberation," he said.

Sequeira fished out his copy of the *Diagnostic and Statistical Manual of Mental Disorders* and reread the section on the persecutory subtype of delusional disorder:

" 'Small slights may be exaggerated and become the focus of a delusional system,' " he read. " 'The focus of the delusion is often on some injustice that must be remedied by legal action . . . and the affected person may engage in repeated attempts to obtain satisfaction by appeal to the courts and other government agencies. Individuals with persecutory delusions are often resentful and angry and may resort to violence against those they believe are hurting them.' "

Susan had tried to make herself into the victim, Sequeira said—so much so that it might be easy to forget who the real victim was: Felix Polk.

"Felix Polk certainly wasn't the monster that the defendant made him out to be," Sequeira said. Susan's disparagements of her husband's character had done enormous damage to his reputation, all while he was unable to respond—because, after all was said and done, the fact remained: Felix Polk was dead.

"Justice for Dr. Polk and his children is now in your hands," he concluded.

At 11:10 A.M., the jury began its deliberations. Within a few hours, they asked to see all the crime-scene photos, the autopsy photos, the videotape of Susan's initial interrogation by Detectives Costa and Moule, and the Peterson autopsy report.

While the jury was deliberating, Adam and Gabe gave an interview to the *Contra Costa Times'* Bruce Gerstman. The way their mother had characterized their father during the trial was completely untrue, they said.

"The one thing that may have had some basis in fact is that he met her when she was his patient and that at some point after that, they got married and had kids," Adam told Gerstman. "That's the only thing that had basis in fact. The idea that she's been this battered and abused woman, there's really no foundation for that."

"There's never been any abuse in the house," Gabe said. "He was a pretty laid-back guy . . . a connoisseur of art and antiques and food. And his only crime was being too lazy on Sunday afternoons and falling asleep in the sun."

Adam said he thought that the case had revealed "major weaknesses" in the criminal justice system. "The qualifications for being able to defend yourself are way too low."

Gabe added that he hoped that his mother would get the mental health treatment he believed she needed.

"It's either out in the streets, or jail," Gabe said, meaning the decision was up to the jury. "Between that, jail, for I think, a long time."

40. A VERDICT

The jury deliberated the rest of Tuesday afternoon, June 13, and all day Wednesday. On Thursday morning, one juror asked to speak to Judge Brady.

He'd warned the court back in March that he had to be in Los Angeles for a new job on Monday, June 19, the juror said. Back then, no one had thought this would be a problem. Surely the trial would be over long before then. But it had dragged on and on, and now the deadline was approaching. The juror asked if the first alternate juror could join the deliberations, in case no verdict could be reached before he had to leave for Los Angeles.

No, said Brady—that would be inappropriate. Just do the best you can to reach a verdict.

Susan ignited. Brady's refusal to excuse the juror and replace him with the alternate had the effect of putting pressure on the juror to rush to a verdict, she insisted. It was wrong; it was unfair; it was just one more example of how Brady had stacked the deck against her.

Brady had finally run out of patience with Susan. When she tried to explain why she couldn't replace the juror with the alternate, Susan interrupted her. With that, Brady ordered Susan taken to the holding area once again.

A few minutes later, after the unhappy and worried juror

returned to the jury room, Brady ordered Susan back into the courtroom.

"Don't interrupt me again," she told Susan. "That was grossly inappropriate to do in front of a juror."

Valerie Harris, sitting next to Susan at the counsel table, reached the entirely reasonable conclusion that Brady, in fact all of Contra Costa County, had had enough of Susan.

"She's going to drive this case to verdict," Harris recalled thinking. Replacing the juror with the alternate would mean that the jury would have to restart their deliberations from the beginning—that would mean the case would go on into the following week, and maybe longer. It was, to Brady, an unendurable thought, Harris realized. She wondered what Brady would do if no verdict was reached by Monday, and the juror simply failed to show up. Would she order the juror's arrest in Los Angeles? It was an absurd situation, but then, the whole trial had been filled with absurdities from the very beginning. But Harris also thought Susan was right—Brady's refusal to replace the juror in effect encouraged him to rush to judgment in order for him to be in Los Angeles the following Monday.

Susan made a new motion for a mistrial on the basis of judicial misconduct; Brady denied it.

That afternoon, Susan drafted another motion to disqualify Brady as the judge in the case. The following morning, she gave it to Harris to serve on the judge's clerk.

Later, Harris remembered entering the courtroom and giving the motion to the clerk. The clerk said something, but Harris, preoccupied, didn't quite catch it.

"I don't think you heard me," the clerk told her. "I said, we have a verdict."

The jury had one last lunch together, then returned to the jury room at 1:30 P.M. By then they'd had their picture taken with the bailiff, a fact which some thought was highly inappropriate.

As Susan Polk and Valerie Harris sat at the counsel table,

Adam, Gabe and the Briners came into the courtroom, finding seats in the first row, directly behind Sequeira. Susan could only stare at them as tears began forming in her eyes. Harris was acutely aware that Susan believed that her sons had only come to witness her demise. The emotionality of the moment was almost overwhelming.

"It was very tense," Harris recalled. The courtroom rapidly filled with spectators, many of whom were whispering to each other.

Brady finally entered the courtroom, and then the jury came in.

Scanning the jurors' faces as they entered, Harris realized it was bad news for Susan. One juror was weeping, another gazed distantly through a window.

"I knew it wasn't good," Harris said.

"I understand we have a verdict," Brady told the jury. The foreman confirmed that it was so. She passed the written verdict form to the clerk, who passed it to the judge. Brady read the form and passed it back to the clerk, who gave it back to the foreman.

"On the charge of murder in the first degree, how does the jury find?"

"Not guilty, Your Honor."

Susan stopped breathing. She looked at Harris. Harris looked at her. Was it possible?

"On the charge of murder in the second degree, how does the jury find?"

"Guilty, Your Honor."

The blood rushed out of Susan's face.

"Oh my God, my life is over," she told Harris.

While Harris attempted to console Susan, telling her that it was only the first round, that there were still appeals to come, eight of the jurors gathered in a room in the courthouse for a press conference.

The critical testimony, most agreed, was that of Gabe Polk. He was believable, and Susan was not, most of the jurors said.

Much of the debate during the deliberations concerned a division of opinion between first-degree and second-degree murder. In the end, the jury had voted for second-degree murder because the evidence supporting premeditation was weak. In other words, Susan hadn't planned to kill Felix, but she'd formed the definite intent to take his life at the moment she'd begun her attack.

This suggested that jurors simply didn't believe Susan's story that Felix had attacked first, and most especially, they didn't believe that she had wrested the knife away from him.

And if Susan were lying about that, then it followed that she had lied about Felix's abuse of her.

"We didn't think Susan was credible," said jury foreman Lisa Cristwell. The fact that she had minimal injuries and Felix had numerous wounds indicated that Susan's reenactment of what had happened in the pool house was fake. While they didn't believe that she'd hit Felix in the head from behind, the stab wounds in the back convinced them Susan had to be lying—her arm simply wasn't long enough to reach around to the small of Felix's back if he'd been kneeling over her. And even if Felix had died of a heart attack, it would still be murder, if he'd had the coronary while Susan was stabbing him.

The jurors seemed mixed in their impression of Felix, with some indicating that they did not believe Susan when she'd claimed Felix had abused her for years. Others wouldn't go that far—but still agreed that even if Felix hadn't been a model husband, there was no reason for Susan to have killed him.

"He was an imperfect person," Cristwell said, "but he didn't deserve to die."

EPILOGUE

The words *paranoia* and *delusion* have expanded their meanings over the past fifty years. Once used with some degree of precision in psychological terms, they have seeped into popular culture and are now often used with reckless abandon. Thus, U.S. Senator Carl Levin could in early 2007 describe Vice President Richard Cheney as "delusional," and no one really believed that the second-ranking person in the government was actually psychotic, no matter how much one might disagree with him. At the same time, the word "paranoia" is flung around in ordinary conversation so casually as to almost lose its definition.

Because the tragedy of Felix and Susan Polk was marked by allegations of delusion and paranoia, it might be useful to be more precise about the original meaning of the terms. According to the American Psychiatric Association's *Diagnostic and Statistical Manual of Mental Disorders (DSM)*, a delusion is:

> A false belief based on incorrect inference about external reality that is firmly sustained despite what almost everyone else believes and despite what constitutes incontrovertible and obvious proof or evidence to the contrary. The belief is not one ordinarily accepted by other

members of the person's culture or subculture (e.g., it is not an article of religious faith).

When a false belief involves a value judgment, it is regarded as a delusion only when the judgment is so extreme as to defy credibility. Delusional conviction occurs on a continuum and can sometimes be inferred from an individual's behavior. It is often difficult to distinguish between a delusion and an overvalued idea (in which case the individual has an unreasonable belief or idea but does not hold it as firmly as is the case with a delusion).

According to the *DSM*, delusions can occur in a variety of mental illnesses, most obviously as a symptom of schizophrenia. But not everyone who has a delusion is schizophrenic. Those who hold fast to a delusion but are not schizophrenic are said by the *DSM* to be suffering from "Delusional Disorder," which, in earlier times, was characterized as nonschizophrenic paranoia, and is a far milder form of mental illness, albeit one that is potentially deadly.

The current edition of the *DSM* distinguishes "Delusional Disorder" from schizophrenia based on the nature of the delusion. Delusions are said to be either "bizarre"—a belief, say, that man-eating daffodils are conspiring to take over the universe—or "non-bizarre," something that might be possible, but is implausible, such as the belief that the FBI is watching someone around the clock.

The *DSM* recognizes seven "subtypes" of Delusional Disorder:

the erotomaniac, in which the sufferer becomes obsessed with another person, often to the point of stalking;

the grandiose type, in which the sufferer is convinced that they have some special talent not recognized by the rest of the world;

the jealous type, in which the sufferer is convinced that his spouse or lover is cheating, despite a lack of evidence;

the somatic type, in which the sufferer has a delusion that something unpleasant has happened to his body, when things are perfectly normal;

the persecutory subtype, in which the sufferer has the persistent delusion that someone is conspiring against him;

the mixed type, which might combine, say, grandiosity with beliefs of persecution;

and *the unspecified type*, in which a predominant delusion can't be clearly determined.

In reading from the *DSM*'s description of Delusional Disorder during the trial of Susan Polk, Assistant District Attorney Paul Sequeira was suggesting that Susan had a delusion, and that it was of the persecutory subtype. A similar suggestion was made by Dr. Paul Good in his arm's-length evaluation of Susan in June of 2005.

Was Susan Polk delusional, as Sequeira and Good suggested, and as Felix and two of their three sons insisted? On the surface, it might seem so: the belief that she was psychic in her dreams and had predicted world-changing events before they happened might be seen as a classic delusion of the grandiose subtype. The same might be said for Susan's belief, or at least suspicion, that Felix was a secret Mossad agent who covertly controlled the courts and the police, while using her as some sort of intelligence tool.

By the *DSM*'s broad definition, these beliefs would be delusions, because their reality would not be accepted by most people, and because there is no evidence, other than Susan's insistence, to prove their validity. In short, these assertions by Susan about herself and her husband defy credibility.

The interesting thing about these beliefs of Susan's, however, is that they did not become prominent in her presentation until after Felix was dead. Yet Felix had been calling Susan "delusional" for four years before the events of October 9–14, 2002. Why?

When Susan accused Felix of having drugged and raped her when she was his teenaged patient in the 1970s, Felix told

her that she was suffering from a delusion—that it had nev
happened, that she had formed the delusion to suppress h
supposed memories of sexual abuse within her birth family

But Susan refused to believe this: she thought that this
agnosis by Felix was only his attempt to cover up his ov
wrongdoing by manipulating her into believing somethi
that wasn't so. This was the main reason she steadfastly
fused to be evaluated by any psychologist or psychiatrist—
her, they were all, or at least most, liars and manipulators,
tent on getting her to believe things that weren't true, if not
cast her into a mental institution. In some ways, this fits t
definition of the persecutory subtype, as Sequeira and Go
suggested.

One leading expert on Delusional Disorder, Dr. Alist
Munro, a psychiatrist and emeritus professor at Dalhou
University in Halifax, Nova Scotia, has made some interesti
observations about Delusional Disorder. In *Delusional Dis*
der: Paranoia and Related Illnesses (Cambridge Univers
Press, 1999), Dr. Munro summarized the course of a numb
of Delusional Disorder cases of the various subtypes. Mur
noted that Delusional Disorder is often misdiagnosed, even
competent psychiatrists, as schizophrenia. But in sharp co
trast to true schizophrenia, Munro concluded that Delusio
Disorder was eminently treatable with the drug pimozi
usually prescribed to mitigate the effects of Tourette's Sy
drome. Of 209 cases of diagnosed Delusional Disorder treat
with a small dose of pimozide (sometimes as low as two m
ligrams), Munro found that more than 80 percent respond
favorably, with the delusion completely disappearing in mo
than half of the cases. To Munro, this suggested that the u
derlying cause of Delusional Disorder was organic—the
sult of illness or injury to the brain. In this regard, it might
useful to recall Susan Polk's 106-degree fever after havi
given birth to Adam Polk in 1983—such a fever could in fa
have caused brain injury, according to neuropsychiatrists.

In his study of patients with Delusional Disorder, Mur

served a number of commonalities: for one, the person with
elusional Disorder tended to hold to the "reality" of the
lusion as the very centerpiece of his or her life:

> The individual clings to the delusion with fanatical inten-
> sity and nearly always spurns any suggestion that he is
> ill . . . It is almost pathognomonic [distinctly characteris-
> tic] of the disorder that the individual refuses to see a
> psychiatrist.
>
> Any illness associated with delusions may lead to
> criminal acts if the patient is sufficiently lacking in judg-
> ment and in normal levels of inhibition, but there are cer-
> tain unique features in Delusional Disorder which make
> it especially dangerous. First, it is chronic and this allows
> the individual enormous time to brood on his beliefs. Sec-
> ondly, the individual's intellectual ability, his thought
> form, and his reasoning ability are relatively unimpaired.
> Thirdly, he often remains in society and continues to
> function, which in most people's minds betokens relative
> sanity.

Being in the community allows the sufferer to "inter-
eave" real events with his delusion, which has the effect of
engthening it, and even, to some extent, making it plausible
others.

> If judgment is becoming seriously affected and ordinary
> behavioral inhibitions are weakening, and especially if
> outbursts of anger are becoming more common, violent
> and possibly murderous behavior may erupt . . . After-
> wards, the individual may feel and express regret but
> usually continues to believe that his action was totally
> justified.

As to the persecutory subtype, Munro had some other trench-
t observations:

The persecutory beliefs are often associated with queru-
lousness, irritability and anger, and the individual who
acts out his anger may be assaultive at times, and even
homicidal. In expressing his feelings thus, the motivation
for violence may be predominantly either a belief that he
is defending himself or may be a desire for revenge.

People suffering from persecutory delusional disorder te
to find sinister significance in even the most mundane occ
rences, Munro noted.

The presence of persecutory delusions naturally makes
the patient extremely wary and guarded, and it is not un-
common for people involved in his life to become incor-
porated into his delusional system. This may include his
physicians, or, if he becomes litigious, members of the legal profession.

Munro found that people suffering from the persecuto
subtype tend to be highly sensitive to issues of fairness, p
ticularly when it comes to following proper procedures. In
legal setting, this can be aggravating to nearly everyone—
Judge Brady would likely agree.

Notes Munro:

What we are discussing here are people who have a profound and persistent sense of having been wronged and
who ceaselessly and endlessly seek redress, in some
cases ... through the legal system ... [a] relatively high
functioning individual may be able to conceal the more
psychotic aspects of his beliefs.

This seeming appearance of sanity may convince a co
that a person suffering from Delusional Disorder is compete
to assist in his defense, simply because the person seen

part from the obvious delusion, to be rational. But in almost
very such case, trouble lies ahead.

> These individuals readily fall out with their lawyers, re-
> fuse to pay their fees, and threaten to complain to higher
> authority, which they often do. If thwarted they may take
> to unpleasant harassing tactics. In some cases they dis-
> miss legal advice and conduct their own cases. They be-
> come expert at exploiting loopholes in rules of procedure
> and will pursue cases far beyond the bounds of reason-
> ableness, sometimes losing sight of the original purpose
> of the whole process.

When a person suffering from persecutory delusional dis-
rder is put on trial for a criminal act resulting from the delu-
ion, the persistent belief in justification can have very
dverse effects in a courtroom.

"The law of insanity is particularly hard to apply to cases
vith this illness," Munro noted. Since the accused believes his
ct was justified, he cannot be said to not know the nature and
uality of his act, which is the standard for finding a person
ot guilty by reason of insanity.

> [T]he delusional disorder sufferer is perfectly aware that,
> by societal standards, what he did was legally wrong . . .
> [But] within his delusional system he fully believes that
> what he did was morally right and transcends any legal
> niceties. Not only does this put a judge and jury in a dif-
> ficult decisional quandary, but their attitudes are bound
> to be affected by the accused's arrogance, self-justification
> and lack of regret.
>
> In fact, the individual's ability to acknowledge the
> wrongness of his act in general terms, while refusing to
> accept that it was wrong for him specifically to commit it,
> may be seen as willfulness or hypocrisy.

Thus, the person suffering from delusional disorder has very grim prognosis at the hands of the criminal justice system.

Susan Polk's jury expressed its mystification as to her motive for killing Felix, and this seemed to show that Sequeira's reading of the *DSM* affected them as just so much psychobabble—senseless jargon, perhaps. The most salient fact in Susan's conviction was the fact that the jury simply didn't believe her—they thought she was lying.

But what they saw as Susan's consistent prevarication was actually Susan's way of reordering events in a way that made sense to her, one that justified her feelings of being persecuted—first by Felix, later by the authorities. By the time of her trial, this reordering had become the true facts of the case as Susan perceived them. This wasn't lying in the conventional, moral sense of the word, but what Susan truly believed had happened. It was a direct product of the delusion—to Susan, people were out to get her because the all-powerful Felix had somehow orchestrated it. He would always prevent her happiness—he had, in her words, "hijacked" her whole life.

Removing Felix from her life became a matter of survival to Susan; even if she was the one who started the fatal fight, in Susan's mind it was always about self-defense, whether physical or mental. Later, while under the stress of arrest and prosecution, Susan escaped into her own fantasies of being persecuted for her hidden powers, so much so that people believed she was loopy. It was how she could explain what had happened to her.

And the system's failure to understand the dynamic of Susan's thinking led directly to a collision between two constitutional rights—Susan's right to represent herself, versus her right to a fair trial. In effect, one cancelled out the other, because, in being permitted to act as her own lawyer, Susan did *not* receive a fair trial.

In this, Judge Brady probably should have intervened at the very beginning, declared a "doubt," and compelled Susan to undergo a mental evaluation, and to be represented by adequate counsel. If Susan was incompetent to assist her defense lawyer, as she demonstrated again and again by her firing of them, she was certainly incompetent to represent herself. The fact that the courts have consistently held that the right to represent oneself is more powerful than the right to a fair trial doesn't mean that justice should be blind—after all, the right to a fair trial belongs to the public as much as the defendant. Unfair trials erode confidence in our system of justice; it's up to our judiciary to sort out what's fair to *all* sides, not just what's expedient.

In fact, as the legal pundits consistently opined, before, during and after the trial, Susan's multiple objectives in representing herself—to demonstrate that she'd been a good mother, to prove that she was psychic, to portray Felix as a bad man, to excoriate the Briners, Budd MacKenzie and John Polk, to reestablish her relationship with her youngest son, to attack the honesty of the police—only distracted everyone from the real issue in the case: whether there was evidence to support Susan's claim of self-defense.

Had Susan allowed a competent lawyer to defend her, the case would have been simple: did the evidence in the pool house support the accusation of murder? The fact was, the physical evidence was equivocal at best—the most likely explanation for the struggle is that each thought the other was about to attack. In other words, it was a case of double paranoia.

After the verdict came in, Court TV's Catherine Crier, sitting in a makeshift outdoor studio, interviewed Dr. Keith Ablow, a psychotherapist who was about to inaugurate his own television show on another network. While Ablow hadn't been privy to all the ins and outs of the case of *People* vs. *Polk*, he certainly understood enough of the dynamic to make some credible observations.

Crier: "Looking back at the history of this family, it was a train wreck waiting to happen. Is that fair?"

Ablow: "I think that's absolutely correct."

The "dual relationship" between Felix and Susan was at the core of all the dysfunction, Ablow indicated.

"This is somebody who was highly manipulative," he said, referring to Felix, "going back to when he was treating her as an adolescent. You may have someone here who was being treated for her [entire] life by an in-house psychiatrist. It's always ill-advised to try to do a high-wire act, where you enter the life of your patient and try to play husband, father and therapist."

In the case of Felix and Susan, it was even worse than most therapist/patient relationships. Felix's age had given him tremendous power over Susan in their earlier years—he in effect had substituted for her father, and with the added imprimatur that he was a psychologist, the one who knew best. Felix had taken control of Susan's life—never mind that Susan might have invited him to do so. Felix should have known better. The relationship virtually required her to be subordinate to him, and was inherently dishonest and unstable.

Worse, it was exacerbated by Felix's own underlying psychological weakness, his obvious need to be seen as powerful and important. Rather than treat Susan with tolerance and respect—as most therapists are advised to treat paranoids—he condescended to her, belittled her, disparaged her, until she lashed out in anger.

When she finally reacted, rebelling against the "parent," it gave Felix grounds once more to assert the upper hand, to accuse Susan of being "provocative"—even though Felix himself was, passive-aggressively, doing the first provoking. The inevitable result that Susan deluded herself into believing that Felix was the cause of all problems, whether hers or the boys'.

"I think that whatever rage, whatever feelings this young woman had, when she went to Felix Polk for treatment, never really got addressed because they got lost in romance," Ablow observed.

"And all of that gets submerged in a marriage . . . and when it comes time to separate, all these demons from her past really come out to play. And now they're all focused on one man who's seventy years old. And he's not prepared to deal with them, because he's lost in the drama himself, he's entered the drama. That's why you never cross that clinical boundary."

In the case of Felix and Susan, this crossing by Felix was incredibly destructive, not only of Susan's right to grow and mature as a human being, but also to Felix—in the end, in fact, the spillover actually led eventually to his death at his patient's hands. Likewise, the inherent conflicts spawned by the "dual relationship" created havoc in the lives of the three boys, and prevented Susan from getting any effective mental health treatment in a timely fashion. If Susan is telling the truth, Felix actually prevented her from getting help, at a time when it could have been effective, from Dr. McKay.

The sordid mess was compounded by Susan's Delusional Disorder, and by Felix's seeming inability to understand and cope with the disorder, despite his background as a psychologist. Merely defining the illness is insufficient—it's really no more than labeling, unless accompanied by some sincere attempt to grapple with it. Felix's repetitive talk about putting Susan in an institution could only have been his attempt to intimidate her by asserting his bona fides—convincing her that he was the expert, and that she was the crazy person. Yet the fact remains, Susan's illness was relatively benign, and eminently treatable.

As Munro observed in *Delusional Disorder*:

> If no other conclusion can be reached from the literature to date, the one which must be emphasized again and again is that delusional disorder, properly diagnosed and ade-

quately treated, has an optimistic outlook. Whatever the neuroleptic employed, the overall rate of response, total or partial, is approximately 80 percent, an outcome that compares well with any other in psychiatry . . .

In the weeks following the verdict, Susan reconsidered her position on defending herself. She asked Brady to appoint a lawyer to represent her in a motion for a new trial. Altogether nineteen lawyers turned Susan down—some because they were obligated for other matters—before one was finally found to take the case.

And even then, many thought it wouldn't last: Susan was sure to fire her newest lawyer sooner or later, Sequeira predicted.

Susan, he said, just couldn't help herself—she was too paranoid.

AUTHOR'S NOTE AND
ACKNOWLEDGMENTS

This book was based on approximately 3,600 pages of Contra Costa County court records: the twelve volumes of the criminal file of *People* vs. *Susan Polk*, and additional volumes contained in eight related civil cases in both Contra Costa and Alameda Counties.

Additionally, I relied upon several thousand pages of investigative material generated by the Contra Costa County sheriff's department, and a like number of pages of transcripts, computer reports, diaries, criminalists' findings, crime-scene photographs and drawings, federal government records, and other documentary sources, as well as associated emails exchanged between the principals, later placed into evidence as trial exhibits. Altogether, the documentary basis of this book comprised well over 10,000 pages of documentary materials reviewed and analyzed, along with hundreds of pages of newspaper and television coverage that the Polk case generated, which were also reviewed.

Re-creating a series of events that took place over more than sixty years is inherently a difficult proposition. The past is fragmentary; that which is retained for subsequent disinterment by historians may often be skewed by unseen agendas of those who have saved it. Official records may survive, at least in part. But they usually don't tell the whole story.

For that, one usually needs eyewitnesses—along with skepticism that the eyewitnesses have the whole truth.

In the matter of Felix and Susan Polk, these inherent difficulties are compounded because of the charges of manipulation and delusion the two antagonists leveled against each other and that many have made against them.

Now, of course, Felix is dead, and Susan's claims must be viewed with some skepticism—if only because of her current status as a convicted murderer whose protestations of innocence have been rejected by a jury of her peers.

An additional problem, unavoidably confronted in writing about the Polks' relationship, and Felix's murder, is that the story cannot be told without recounting Susan's—and, through Susan (and others), Felix's—versions of events. But these versions include the many dubious and unproven accusations they have made over the course of tumultuous events, not only against each other, but also against third parties—other family members, friends, neighbors, law enforcement and judicial officials and personnel.

In recounting this story, under these circumstances, I have attempted throughout to make clear that I am merely reporting the Polks' claims, not adopting them. It is worth repeating, to the extent it is difficult in such a convoluted tale to make this clear in all instances, that in so reporting I am by no means asserting the truth of these accusations.

In writing this book, I was very fortunate to have had the assistance of a large number of people—some familiar with Susan Polk's attempt to defend herself against the charge of murder, others equally intent on seeing that she was convicted of the crime.

Because at this writing the case has not yet reached its final judgment—it may linger on in appellate courts for some years—it would be inappropriate to identify many of those who assisted the author, solely in the interest of explicating the truth on either side. I apologize for not giving these many the recognition they deserve, but I know they are grateful that I leave them in anonymity for their valiant efforts to explain.

Nevertheless, I owe enormous gratitude to many: certainly and most obviously to Dr. Alistair Munro, who generously and graciously granted permission to use excerpts from his classic book on "paranoia," *Delusional Disorder: Paranoia and Related Illnesses*, and who very generously consulted repeatedly throughout this book's preparation as to various concepts, and helped educate me as to the phenomenon he had first helped explicate two decades earlier.

Dr. Munro's generosity in sharing his insights about the different manifestations of delusional disorder, and how they might have come into play in various aspects of the Polk case, was invaluable in guiding me toward a conceptual framework. It should nevertheless be understood that any conclusions in this book are mine alone, and not those of Dr. Munro.

I also wish to thank the staffs of the Superior Courts of Alameda and Contra Costa Counties, who laboriously but with good cheer collected so many thousands of pages of old and new records, and copied them for my review.

Very special thanks are due Valerie Harris, who was exceedingly generous with her time in explaining what she thought had happened, and how various events unfolded. Likewise, Linda Barnard was particularly invaluable in her explanation of her interpretation of the peculiar psychological dynamic which unfolded over the years between Susan and Felix Polk.

I also wish to express my appreciation to Yaniv Soha of St. Martin's Press, who exhibited great patience and fortitude as this book labored through to its conclusion, despite delays occasioned by continuing dollops of new information. Most especially I wish to thank Jane Dystel of Dystel & Goderich Literary Management for her continued faith, despite various setbacks.

Finally, once more I wish also to express my love and appreciation to Carol Stuart of San Francisco, a loyal and beautiful friend, whose support over the years has been beyond any price.

Carlton Smith
South Pasadena, California
December 2006